New Frontiers in Social Iı

New Frontiers in Social Innovation Research

Edited by

Alex Nicholls
Professor of Social Entrepreneurship, University of Oxford, UK

Julie Simon
Research Programme Lead, The Young Foundation, UK

and

Madeleine Gabriel
Principal Researcher, Nesta, UK

palgrave
macmillan

First published 2015 by
PALGRAVE MACMILLAN

Palgrave Macmillan in the UK is an imprint of Macmillan Publishers Limited, registered in England, company number 785998, of Houndmills, Basingstoke, Hampshire RG21 6XS.

Palgrave Macmillan in the US is a division of St Martin's Press LLC, 175 Fifth Avenue, New York, NY 10010.

Palgrave Macmillan is the global academic imprint of the above companies and has companies and representatives throughout the world.

Palgrave® and Macmillan® are registered trademarks in the United States, the United Kingdom, Europe and other countries.

Paperback ISBN 978–1–137–54953–2
DOI 10.1007/978-1-137-50680-1
E-PDF ISBN 978–1–137–50680–1

A catalogue record for this book is available from the British Library.

Library of Congress Cataloging-in-Publication Data
New frontiers in social innovation research / [edited by] Alex Nicholls, Julie Simon, Madeleine Gabriel.
pages cm
1. Social entrepreneurship. 2. Social change. 3. Diffusion of innovations—Social aspects. 4. Technological innovations—Social aspects. I. Nicholls, Alex.
HD60.N436   2015
338'.064—dc23   2015014422

Typeset by MPS Limited, Chennai, India.

For Samuel, Harriet and Juliette: the kids are alright (AN)
For Guy, with love (MG)
To NMS, always (JS)

This page intentionally left blank

Contents

List of Figures and Tables

Figures

Tables

Foreword: The Study of Social Innovation – Theory, Practice and Progress

Introduction

How should social innovation be researched? And what should be the relationship between research and action? This piece discusses what can be known about social innovation, how research agendas could evolve and how the study of social innovation fits into the broader picture of research on innovation.

Definitions, boundaries and character

The first challenge for any researcher is to define their boundaries – what is the object of study, and with what disciplines is this object to be understood? Much of the discussion of social innovation is vague, and there are many competing definitions of social innovation that attempt to delineate a field of study (Jenson and Harrison, 2013). Some present it as simply a new term for the study of non-profits; for others it can encompass almost anything from new types of democracy to the design of products for poor consumers. The definition that I have found more useful describes the field as concerned with innovations that are social in both their ends and their means (Young Foundation, 2012). While this leaves some fuzzy edges, it captures the dual interest of the field in, on the one hand, finding better ways to meet human needs and, on the other, its interest in strengthening bonds of commitment and solidarity. It is a definition which also deliberately internalises the unavoidable tensions that are always present in any kind of social change, since all societies argue about what counts as social good or social value.

The next challenge is to be clear what kind of field this is. For now, at least, it is not a discipline, a profession, a functional domain or the preserve of any particular organisational form. Instead social innovation can best be understood as a loose movement founded on ideas: above all the idea that in the right circumstances people can make, shape and design their world, and more specifically, that they can invent and grow new forms of social organisation. That idea is not new and there has been writing on social innovation for nearly two centuries (Mulgan,

2012). But the spread of education and democracy, and new generations of technology, have made it much more feasible for people to take
control of their lives and their world, and have helped turn the deeply
democratic ideal of self-government into a more practical possibility.

The appeal of this idea explains why social innovation has attracted interest and adherents. The last five years have seen the spread of social innovation funds (from Australia and Hong Kong to France), incubators (many
hundreds), offices (from the White House to City Halls), Mayors (such as
the 'Social Innovation Mayor' in Seoul, whose work is explored by Kim
et al. in this volume), global networks (such as SIX, the Social Innovation
Exchange), and prizes (from China to the European Union). Corporate
social innovation is beginning to displace corporate social responsibility
within some large firms such as Danone or BASF and, as a sign of the times,
several of the biggest consultancies have set up social innovation teams.[1]

This evolution of the practice of social innovation has happened ahead
of research and theory, but the same was true of the two great systems of
innovation that modernity has brought to maturity. One is the science
system, which now employs millions of people, and is rich in money, institutions, rules and procedures. It is a system richly funded by governments,
that is truly global in scale, linked by common procedures and values, and
animated by the confidence which comes from a century or more of often
dramatic success. It is also a field with plenty of theory – but nearly all
the theory came after the practice rather than before it.[2] The other great
innovation system can be found in business, which takes new technologies and ideas to market, and which is even richer in money, institutions,
procedures and ideas. That system too has won extraordinary prestige, and
combines some elements of openness with the strict hierarchy of the large
corporation and the worlds of finance. Here, too, theory followed practice
in the form of economic theories of intellectual property, public goods
and rates of return. Both systems share a commitment to exploration and
discovery, measurement of what works and replication of successes.[3]

Social innovation by contrast is far less developed. It happens all the
time, but with only a small fraction of the massive public subsidy that
accrues to science, or the dense web of research, practice and profit that
sustains innovation in business.

Linking research to practice and mission: the epistemologies of social innovation

So how should social innovation be studied? If social innovation rests
on an idea – an idea about possibility – rather than being a field with

clearly defined boundaries, and if its practice inevitably leads theory, then the study of social innovation can never be just a detached, empirical object of analysis within social science.

That social innovation is rooted both in practice and in a mission to tap creative potential makes some things easier and some more difficult. The part that is easier is the connection to practice. The intellectual task of understanding intersects with the work of thousands of people around the world trying to do social innovation, to develop ideas, put them into practice and find out if they are working. How can collective intelligence be harnessed to make the most of tools like crowd sourcing platforms, prizes or accelerators? How can citizens be involved in generating ideas? How can social innovation reconfigure the boundaries between state, market and civil society? How should governments internalise innovation?

To the extent that the research agenda is intertwined with an emerging field of practice, the test of research is whether it is useful, relevant and applicable, and whether the practitioners can, in fact, make use of its insights. All of this is a kind of 'craft' knowledge, grounded in practice, and then fed back into that practice. In terms of epistemology, this connects to the philosophical approaches of pragmatism in its 19th century sense, the pragmatism of John Dewey and William James, which argued that ideas are not things waiting out there to be discovered but rather tools that people devise to cope with the world as they find it (Menand, 1997). Most of those ideas are socially generated – not coming from individuals alone – and, because they are provisional responses to particular situations, their survival depends not on their immutability, but on their adaptability (see Howaldt *et al.* in this volume).

The study of social innovation has drawn on many existing disciplines, from sociology to psychology, regional studies to economics. But the pragmatist approach suggests that it should be thought of as more than a new topic for existing disciplines, or as a new theme for interdisciplinary research. Instead it should be understood as a praxis, a body of knowledge closely tied into evolving practice (Menand, 1997). In this respect its epistemology is perhaps less different from other areas of social science than it first appears. Macroeconomics mainly grew up as a set of craft tools to help governments manage economies before and after the Second World War. Of course there was plenty of theory, and over time the field became ever more theoretical (DeVroey and Malgrange, 2011). But many of its leading thinkers saw it primarily as a way to help practitioners running government economic departments. In the natural sciences, most of the big 20th-century theoretical breakthroughs in physics, chemistry and biology did not arise in a detached ivory tower but as responses to the practical problems of the real world, and much of the theoretical distinction between basic and applied research, which became institutionally embodied in the late 20th century, misread that history – a point eloquently made in Jon Agar's recent book (2013).

Yet to describe the study of social innovation as a craft knowledge is not to imply any less need for research rigour. There is still a need for falsifiable hypotheses – the more clear-cut, or surprising, the better. There is certainly a need for data – time series data on the growth or decay of social organisations, their contribution to GDP, their social make-up, their geography, and so on – and we should hope that over the next decade social innovation can begin to catch up with the rapid progress being made in the statistical study of other fields of innovation. Examples of this include the progress being made in measuring intangibles, the pioneering work on measuring the creative economy (Bakhshi *et al.*, 2012) and the use of web-scraping and other tools to show economic phenomena before they have been captured by official statistics (Bakhshi and Mateos-Garcia, 2012).

That sort of rigour is bound to take research away from the immediate concerns of practitioners, and so a balance needs to be struck. The Italian philosopher and politician Antonio Gramsci (1979) famously commented that we should cultivate pessimism of the intellect and optimism of the will; perhaps what we most need here is to combine enthusiasm of the spirit and scepticism of the intellect.

Striking that balance is a challenge both for the field and for individuals. Many individuals researching social innovation are also practitioners and activists; they are advocates as well as scholars, immersed in the mission as well as the measurement and analysis. This is bound to create tensions. But again, it is not so different from other areas of social science – from late 19th-century sociology to late 20th-century rational choice economics, many of the most apparently detached intellectuals were also in truth advocates for new ways of seeing the world and new ways of acting on it. Joseph Schumpeter, for example, was the finance minister of Austria in 1919 (Backhaus, 2003).

Social innovation and social change

The harder task for social innovation research is to understand the place of social innovation in much bigger processes of social change. From where do ideas come? Why do some flourish and others wither away?

One root of much social innovation is the experience or observation of pain and suffering, and the experience and observation of how people respond with love, care, learning, empathy or cure. Out of that observation grew attempts to replicate these things – the love, care or learning – in institutional form or with technologies. Another root of social innovation is the exploration of evolutions or 'adjacent possibles' (Kauffman, 1995). Once you have a school or a hospital or a micro-credit organisation, then other innovations flow logically from these – extending, adapting or combining them in new ways. A third root is ideas – the idea of a world based on cooperation, rights or ecological sustainability turns something good in everyday experience into a universal.

An interesting avenue for research could be to track important innovations upstream – to map their aetiology. But with any idea it is then important to understand under what conditions it might spread or scale. Previous research has examined the dynamics of scaling: the interaction of 'effective demand' and 'effective supply' and the various organisational options ranging from growth through licensing, franchising, federations to takeovers (Mulgan *et al.*, 2007). But what makes the 'effective demand' possible in the first place? It could be argued that some ideas in particular periods align with the dominant technologies and political systems (Wyatt, 2007). Welfare states and trade union rights seem to fit better with mass, industrialised societies, collaborative consumption with pervasive internet technologies and mobile consumers. Another lens emphasises national or cultural particularities, which may explain why some kinds of micro-credit worked in Bangladesh but not India, why some models of mentoring worked in the United States and not the United Kingdom, or some models of childcare worked in Denmark but not Spain (Ghysels, 2004). Clearly systems create constraints, nested structures of environment, culture and policy that shape what does, and does not, spread.

Yet there is a risk in all of this analysis to see too much order. As Calvino explained in his letters (2013): 'imagining the world as a "system", as a negative, hostile system (a symptom that is typical of schizophrenia) prevents any opposition to it except in an irrational, self-destructive raptus; whereas it is a correct principle of method to deny that what one is fighting can be a system, in order to distinguish its components, contradictions, loopholes, and to defeat it bit by bit'. This is the constant challenge with systems thinking – how to see the interconnections between things without becoming intellectually overwhelmed, and trapped by them into a fatalism which presumes that change is impossible.

This is likely to become more, not less important, in the years ahead. Many social innovators soon come to understand that lasting change depends on changing whole systems, not just individual services. Major advances in primary healthcare, education or jobs depend on how systems are rewired, often with shifts in power from existing incumbents to new players, or to citizens themselves. Some of the most important changes have depended on the interaction of social movements and campaigns, new laws and regulations, new technologies and business models. The movement to large-scale recycling is a good example of this (Murray *et al.*, 2010). Yet traditional disciplines struggle to make sense of these complex processes, and we badly need better theoretical methods – combining quantitative and qualitative analysis – as well as better tools (Mulgan, 2013).

As the field of social innovation grows, and becomes more subtle and complex, there is a need to be patient. It is at least fifty years since the innovation studies field took shape, led by such great figures as Richard Nelson, Christopher Freeman, Carlota Perez and Giovanni Dosi. Yet it is, in some respects, heartening to know that after half a century there are few agreed definitions of innovation; few agreed metrics (and some certainty that the dominant ones, like patents and R&D spend, are misleading); and little confidence about what works when it comes to policy. Indeed one of the conclusions of a major review of global innovation policy evidence was that relatively little is known, and that how policy is implemented matters as much as the policy itself (Rigby and Ramlogan, 2012).

Four arguments that could help advance the field

While we should be patient, we also need better arguments. All disciplines and fields advance faster with the help of passionate, serious and uncomfortable debates than through cosy consensus. Here, four arguments could be particularly productive in sharpening thought.

The first is about investment and social investment. There is now great interest in the application of investment methods from venture capital and private equity to social problems, and many claims that these can deliver better – or, at least, different – social outcomes than traditional grant funding or government action. While these claims are plausible, there is as yet little hard evidence to substantiate them one way or the other. There is limited research on the financial returns of the social sector across major economies, and surprisingly flimsy evidence on the long-term returns of other asset classes. Stock markets do seem to rise several percentage points each year on average. But many are surprised to discover that the average returns to venture capital are barely 3% in the United States and 0% in the United Kingdom; that private equity appears to offer no advantages once tax subsidies are discounted; and that, of course, many banks have achieved negative returns in real terms in recent years (Lerner *et al.*, 2011). So, there is a need for sceptics arguing that social impact investment is all hype and others countering them, but with facts, analysis and evidence rather than just assertion.

A second useful argument would be a variant of the one happening in innovation studies: namely, is innovation slowing down or speeding up? Some writers, including Tyler Cowen (2011) and Peter Thiel (2011), have claimed that innovation has dramatically slowed down compared to twenty or thirty years ago, which is why people travel in 1960s aeroplanes, why we do not have jet packs on our backs, and why the pharmaceutical industry struggles to develop useful new drugs. Others say that the world is in a golden age of perpetual digital invention, benefitting from a flood of new ideas in fields like genomics and new materials. Elements of both arguments seem to be right. But we need an equivalent dialogue on social innovation: are things speeding up or slowing down, and is there a coherent model for understanding under what conditions social innovation might be expected to speed up or slow down?

A third, even more useful, argument would be about which innovations are good and which are bad. This is a glaring gap in innovation studies and, indeed, in most of economics. History shows that most innovations create value for some people and destroy it for others. The car was good for drivers, but not much good for pedestrians who did not own a car. A high proportion of financial innovations in the last twenty years destroyed more value than they created – Paul Volcker, Head of the Federal Reserve, said he could only think of one financial innovation that created any public benefit and that was the ATM (WSJ, 2009). Military technologies destroy value for the people they kill or maim. A similar pattern of value creation and destruction applies to social innovations – and even very benign ones like hospices or kindergartens may put some people out of work. Yet most of the analytic tools for understanding innovation have no way of distinguishing one from another. Book after book and journal after journal on innovation studies explore the strategies of innovation agencies but do not even hint that it matters to know whether value is being destroyed or created. Even the fashionable analyses of disruptive innovation are wholly silent on these issues – assuming that disruption is basically a good thing – even though a moment's reflection shows that many innovations are disruptive in bad ways, destroying more than they create. If mainstream innovation lacks the intellectual resources to think these things through, then it is all the more important that there are passionate, empirical and rigorous arguments about these issues in social innovation: both for the sake of understanding and to ensure that more funding goes to the good innovations than the bad ones.

The fourth argument needs to be about politics. During the 1990s and 2000s some of the leading organisations involved in the fields of social entrepreneurship did their best to push politics and argument out. They also airbrushed out the role of social movements, contention and mobilisation. A generous explanation would be that they were seeking to pull in the broadest possible support. A less generous explanation might point to dominance by club class elites, management consultancies and billionaire funders, who were hardly likely to favour the more radical end of social innovation. Either way what was left behind was often rather bland and unconvincing, sometimes implying that lone social entrepreneurs, philanthropists or businesses, or individual technological advances, could solve the world's social problems singlehandedly. A more plausible view sees social innovation as unavoidably bound up with politics. Grassroots innovators can come up with novel ideas, but they lack the power to generalise them. Conversely, governments and political parties may have the power to legislate new rights but usually lack the means to create and experiment. In practice there is complementarity, and wise innovators work as much to influence the conditions in which their ideas may spread as they work to spread their idea. That complementary interaction of grassroots innovation and top-down policy certainly happened during past periods of social reform. But parties and governments often struggle to hear what is happening on the ground, and those on the ground often struggle to understand how the world looks to a minister or a global agency. That is why we need more research on the alignment and misalignment of social innovation and structural reform, and a more honest debate about the limits of each.

Social innovation and the pursuit of human potential

Finally, if the deep underlying idea of social innovation is an optimistic one about human potential to govern individual lives and design the world, then there is a need to understand how societies can make the most of that potential.

For a long time, a common theme of conservative politics was the claim that it was inherently impossible for more than a tiny elite to rule, create and think. It was argued that attempts to widen participation were bound to be futile. In the modern era, by contrast, the democratic argument has become mainstream: parties of all stripes purport to want to amplify human creativity and potential.

Yet even within social innovation the arguments are not clear-cut. Social entrepreneurship organisation Ashoka has suggested that there is only one serious social entrepreneur per ten million of population (Ashoka, 2012). Acknowledging the role of individual agency is in some respects a healthy counter to the 20th century's love of big organisations and big systems.

But history shows that it is wrong to presume a fixed, and limited, stock of human social ingenuity. Estonia with a population of not much more than a million is bursting with innovative creativity in the economy and technology. Iceland, with not many more than 300,000 people, has been a powerhouse of new ideas. Meanwhile places that were thought to be lacking in creativity have within the space of a generation transformed themselves – Taiwan and South Korea are impressive recent examples which confirm that in the right circumstances there is dramatically more human potential for innovation than might be imagined. Some of the recent innovations in social innovation have aimed to tap this latent potential: crowd-sourcing of ideas, large-scale deliberative processes and inducement prizes draw on the notion that the best ideas may come from anyone, anywhere (see, e.g., Tjornbo in this volume).

The field of social innovation often claims, whether implicitly or explicitly, that better ways of tapping human creative potential are not only good for social health, but also likely to support economic growth. But we lack hard evidence, and, for now, there are no ways of mapping or measuring this innovative potential or the extent to which it is made use of. This could become an important theme for research, and it is not so hard to imagine how it could be done, for example surveying the depth and breadth of public involvement in creating ideas and putting them into effect.

Going in this direction would help the field of social innovation move from being a marginal topic, concerned with the management of NGOs, to a much more central one, concerned with how governments, foundations or businesses could truly maximise the creative potential of their societies.

Geoff Mulgan
Chief Executive of Nesta

Notes

1. http://firestation.pwc.co.uk/centre-for-social-impact.html [Accessed 27 November 2014].
2. See Idhe (2009) for a discussion of this.
3. For a history of scientific ethos, see Thorpe (2007).

References

Agar, J. (2013) *Science in the 20th Century and Beyond*. Cambridge: Polity Press.
Ashoka (2012) 'How in the world are Ashoka fellows chosen?' https://www.youthventure.org/how-world-are-ashoka-fellows-chosen [Accessed 9 December 2014].
Backhaus, J.G. (ed.) (2003) *Joseph Alois Schumpeter: Entrepreneurship, Style and Vision*. Heidelberg: Springer Science & Business Media.
Bakhshi, H. and Mateos-Garcia, J. (2012) *Rise of the Datavores: How UK businesses can benefit from their data*. London: Nesta.
Bakhshi, H., Freeman, A. and Higgs, P. (2012) *A Dynamic Mapping of the UK's Creative Industries*. London: Nesta.
Calvino, I. (2013) *Letters: 1941–1985*. (Trans. Machlaughlin, M.) Princeton, NJ: Princeton University Press.
Cowen, T. (2011) *The Great Stagnation: How America Ate All the Low-Hanging Fruit of Modern History, Got Sick, and Will (Eventually) Feel Better*. Penguin e-Special/Dutton.
De Vroey, M.R. and Malgrange, P. (2011) *The History of Macroeconomics from Keynes's General Theory to the Present*. Discussion Paper 2011028, Institut de Recherches Economiques et Sociales, Université catholique de Louvain.
Ghysels, J. (2004) *Work, Family and Childcare: An Empirical Analysis of European Households*. Cheltenham: Edward Elgar.
Gramsci, A. (1979) *Letters from Prison*. London: Quartet Books.
Ihde, D. (2009) 'Technology and Science', in Olsen, J.K.B., Pederson, S.A. and. Hendricks, V.S. (eds), *A Companion to the Philosophy of Technology*. Oxford: Blackwell, pp. 51–60.
Jenson, J. and Harrison, D. (2013) *Social Innovation Research in the European Union. Approaches, Findings and Future Directions. Policy Review*. Luxembourg: European Union.
Kauffman, S. (1995) *At Home in the Universe*. Oxford: Oxford University Press.
Lerner, J., Pierrakis, Y., Collins, L. and Bravo-Biosca, A. (2011) *Atlantic Drift: Venture Capital Performance in the UK and the US*. London: NESTA.
Menand, L. (1997) 'The Return of Pragmatism', *American Heritage*, 48 (6).
Mulgan, G. (2012) 'The Theoretical Foundation of Social Innovation', in Nicholls, A. and Murdock, A. (eds), *Social Innovation: Blurring Boundaries to Reconfigure Markets*. Basingstoke: Palgrave Macmillan.
Mulgan, G. (2013) *The Locust and the Bee*. Princeton, NJ: Princeton University Press.
Mulgan, G., Ali, R., Halkett, R. and Sanders, B. (2007) *In and Out of Sync: The Challenge of Growing Social Innovations*. London: NESTA.
Murray, R., Caulier-Grice, J. and Mulgan, G. (2010) *The Open Book of Social Innovation*. London: Young Foundation.

PWC (2014) 'PWC Centre for Social Impact' http://firestation.pwc.co.uk/centre-for-social-impact.html. [Accessed 27 November 2014].

Rigby, J. and Ramlogan, R. (2012) *Support Measures for Exploiting Intellectual Property. Compendium of Evidence on the Effectiveness of Innovation Policy Intervention.* Manchester: Manchester Institute of Innovation Research.

Thiel, P. (2011) 'The end of the future?', *National Review*, 3 October 2011. http://www.nationalreview.com/articles/278758/end-future-peter-thiel [Accessed 8 December 2014].

Thorpe, C. (2007) 'Political Theory in Science and Technology Studies', in Hackett, E.J., Amsterdamska, O., Lynch, M. and Wajcman, J. (eds), *The Handbook of Science and Technology Studies* (Third Edition). Cambridge, MA: MIT Press, pp. 63–82.

WSJ (2009) 'Paul Volker: Think More Boldly', *Wall Street Journal*. Available at: http://www.wsj.com/articles/SB10001424052748704825504574586330960597134 [Accessed 8 December 2014].

Wyatt, S. (2007) 'Technological Determinism Is Dead; Long Live Technological Determinism', in Hackett, E.J., Amsterdamska, O., Lynch, M. and Wajcman, J. (eds), *The Handbook of Science and Technology Studies* (Third Edition). Cambridge, MA: MIT Press, pp. 165–80.

Young Foundation (2012) *Social Innovation Overview – Part 1: Defining Social Innovation.* A deliverable of the project: 'The theoretical, empirical and policy foundations for building social innovation in Europe' (TEPSIE). Brussels: European Commission, DG Research.

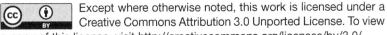

Acknowledgements

We would like to thank and acknowledge all those who helped in the development and production of this collection. First, our thanks to The Rockefeller Foundation and Nesta who jointly funded the production of this book and made it possible to publish it Open Access. We would also like to thank all the staff at The Rockefeller Foundation, Nesta, The Young Foundation, Glasgow Caledonian University and SIX who were instrumental in organising the Social Frontiers Conference in 2013, which provided the starting point for this collection. We would like to thank the Advisory Panel that selected papers to be presented at the conference, including Josef Hochgerner, Agnes Hubert, Karen Miller, Maria Elisa Bernal, Taco Brandsen, Zhou Hongyun, Antonella Noya, Peter Droell, Johanna Mair, Jeremy Millard, Jürgen Howaldt, Alex Nicholls, Geoff Mulgan and Robin Murray. Special thanks goes to Kippy Joseph, Jo Casebourne, Laura Bunt, Anna Davies, Rachel Schon, Katherine Stevenson, Sophie Reynolds and Mark Anderson, without whom this collection would not have been possible. We would also like to thank the editorial and commissioning team at Palgrave Macmillan for their help and support, especially Philippa Grand, Emily Russell and Judith Allan. Finally, our thanks to all those who contributed chapters to this collection for their patience and hard work.

Early versions of chapters 1–10 and the conclusion are available as working papers at http://www.scribd.com/Nesta_uk.

Notes on Contributors

Editors

Madeleine Gabriel is a principal researcher at Nesta, United Kingdom, focusing on social and public innovation. She is the author of *Making It Big: Strategies for Scaling Social Innovations* and co-author of *People Helping People: the Future of Public Services* (both 2014). She is working on the European Commission–funded TRANSITION project, which is testing and developing methods for incubating social innovation. Before joining Nesta, Gabriel was Head of Impact, Research and Evaluation at UnLtd, The Foundation for Social Entrepreneurs, United Kingdom, where she developed new ways of measuring the organisation's impact and led its programme of research on social entrepreneurship. Her background is in evaluation and she has led or participated in several major programme evaluations for public sector organisations in the United Kingdom, including the evaluation of the Social Enterprise Investment Fund for the Department of Health.

Alex Nicholls is the first tenured Professor of Social Entrepreneurship appointed at the University of Oxford, United Kingdom. In 2010, Nicholls edited a special edition of *Entrepreneurship, Theory and Practice* on social entrepreneurship – the first time a top tier management journal had recognised the topic in this way. He is General Editor of the Skoll Working Papers series and Editor of the *Journal of Social Entrepreneurship*. Nicholls is the co-author of the most widely cited book on Fair Trade (with Charlotte Opal, 2005) and the co-editor of the first scholarly collection of papers on social innovation (with Alex Murdock, Palgrave Macmillan, 2012). He is also editor of a collection of key papers on social entrepreneurship (2008) and another on social finance (2015). He has held lectureships at a wide variety of academic institutions including University of Toronto, Leeds Metropolitan University, University of Surrey and Aston Business School.

Julie Simon is Research Programme Lead at The Young Foundation, United Kingdom, specialising in social innovation. She has authored several major reports on social innovation as part of the European Commission–funded project TEPSIE (2011–2014), which explored the theoretical, empirical and policy foundations of social innovation in

Europe. Earlier, Simon worked on the Social Innovator Series which analysed ways of designing, developing and growing social innovations. She co-authored the *Study on Social Innovation* for the Bureau of European Policy Advisors (2010), *The Open Book of Social Innovation* (2010), *Social Venturing* (2009) and *How to Innovate: The Tools for Social Innovation* (2008). Before working at The Young Foundation Simon worked on education policy at the Social Market Foundation, where she co-authored *Fade or Flourish: How Primary Schools Can Build on Children's Early Progress* (2008).

Contributors

Marie J. Bouchard is a professor at Université du Québec à Montréal, Canada, and a regular member of the Centre de Recherche sur les Innovations Sociales (CRISES), Canada. She was a Canada Research Chair on the Social Economy from 2003 to 2013 and codirector of the Community Housing research partnership of the Community University Research Alliance (CURA) on the Social Economy, Canada, from 2000 to 2011. Her recent publications include *Se loger autrement au Québec* (2008), *The Worth of the Social Economy* (2010) and *Innovations in the Social Economy, The Québec Experience* (2013).

Louise Briand is a professor in the Department of Social Sciences at Université du Québec en Outaouais, Canada, and a regular member of the Centre de Recherche sur les Innovations Sociales (CRISES), Canada. Her main research interests concern intra- and inter-organizational control and new organizational forms in private and social economy sectors. Her work focuses on managerial innovations that represent, for the workers, new modes of control and surveillance.

Carla Cipolla has been involved since 2004 in projects on design for social innovation in Europe, Africa and in Brazil where she is now Associate Professor of the Universidade Federal do Rio de Janeiro, UFRJ – Coppe. She coordinates the DESIS Lab at UFRJ – Coppe, which is one of the founding members of the DESIS Network (Design for Social Innovation and Sustainability). In 2004, she started a research and design activity that relates social innovations with the service sector. Social innovations are analysed in terms of new service models (based on interpersonal relations and collaborative qualities) that are able to offer alternatives to a delivery approach to services.

Adalbert Evers is Professor for Comparative Health and Social Policy at the Justus-Liebig-University in Giessen (emeritus since autumn 2013) and is a senior fellow at the Centre for Social Investment (CSI) at the University of Heidelberg, both Germany. His research interests are located in the field of social policy and social services. He has published extensively, spoken at conferences and done policy consultancy for national and international bodies on issues of civil society, the third sector and volunteering as well as democracy and governance issues in relation to social policy and the social services. He can be reached at: adalbert.evers@uni-giessen.de

Benjamin Ewert completed his PhD in social science at Justus-Liebig-University Giessen, Germany. From 2010 to 2014 he was a research fellow with the EU project 'Welfare Innovation at the Local Level in favour of Cohesion' (WILCO). At present, he works for an interdisciplinary project on integrated palliative care at University Hospital Bonn, Germany. Ewert's main research interests are social innovations, comparative welfare studies, health politics and integrated care. He can be reached at: benjamin.ewert@ukb.uni-bonn.de

Sunkyung Han is Co-Founder of C. (Cdot). Before founding C., she coordinated research projects on community issues and urban regeneration as well as social innovation in general while working at the Hope Institute, South Korea. She was also in charge of international projects, creating a platform for Asian Social Innovators, ANIS (Asia NGO Innovation Summit, 2010–2012) and organising several international conferences in terms of social innovation. She is a member of the inaugural committee of GSEA (Global Social Economy Association) and an Asia Region Coordinator.

Jürgen Howaldt is Director of Sozialforschungsstelle Dortmund and Professor at the Faculty of Economics and Social Sciences at TU Dortmund University, Germany. A world-renowned expert in the field of social innovation, he has written numerous books and articles on the issue. He has advised German and European policy makers and presented his ideas worldwide. Howaldt is also Affiliate of Social Innovation and Entrepreneurship Research Centre (SIERC) at Massey University, New Zealand, and Co-founder of the board of the European School of Social Innovation.

Jane Jenson was awarded the Canada Research Chair in Citizenship and Governance at the Université de Montréal, Canada, in 2001, where she is Professor of Political Science. She has also been Senior Fellow of the Successful Societies programme of the Canadian Institute for Advanced Research, Canada, since 2004. Her research focuses on comparative social policy and particularly on the politics of the creation and diffusion of social policy concepts such as 'social cohesion', 'social investment' and 'social innovation'.

Jungwon Kim is Co-Founder of Spread*i*, a UK-based enterprise, founded in 2013, which aims to spread ideas, innovation and inspiration across borders, especially between Europe and Asia. Its main emphasis lies on introducing and exchanging expertise and innovators through digital stories, study trips, research, workshops and seminars. Kim acts as an adviser to Korean and UK professionals in the social innovation sector and has been actively involved in social innovation research projects focusing on cases in Korea, Thailand, Japan, China, India and the United Kingdom.

Juan-Luis Klein is a full professor in the Department of Geography at the Université du Québec à Montréal (UQAM), Canada. Since 2009, he has been the director of the Centre de Recherche sur l'Innovation Sociale (CRISES), Canada. He is also in charge of the series on *Géographie contemporaine* and has authored and co-authored several books, chapters and articles on the topics of economic geography, local development and socio-territorial innovation.

Ralf Kopp is a senior researcher at Sozialforschungsstelle Dortmund, TU Dortmund University, Germany. He is a member of the management board and coordinator of the research field organisation and networks. He works in application-orientated transdisciplinary projects about open innovation and learning networks. Against this background he is engaged in the development of a theory of social innovation.

Benoît Lévesque is Professor Emeritus at Université du Québec à Montréal and Associate Professor at École Nationale d'Administration Publique, Canada. He is Co-founder of the Centre de Recherche sur les Innovations Sociales (CRISES) and of the Community-University Research Alliance (CURA) on the Social Economy, Canada. He was President of CIRIEC-Canada from 1996 to 2002 and President of the Scientific Council of CIRIEC International from 2002 to 2010. He is Co-director of the collection *Social Economy and Public Economy* and has authored numerous books and papers on social economy and social innovations.

David Longtin holds a master's degree in political science from Université du Québec à Montréal, Canada, and is a research assistant at the Centre de Recherche sur les Innovations Sociales (CRISES), Canada. His research interests focus on social imaginaries, citizenship studies, theoretical and empirical perspectives on democratization and collective actions in Latin America. Since 2009, he has contributed to different partnership research projects of CRISES on philanthropy and social innovation in Quebec. Since 2011, he has been part of the research team building the CRISES database on social innovation.

Ezio Manzini has been working in the field of design for sustainability for more than two decades. Recently, he has focussed his interests on social innovation and started, and currently coordinates, DESIS: an international network on design for social innovation and sustainability (http://www.desis-network.org). He has worked at the Politecnico di Milano, Italy, throughout his professional life and is Honorary Guest Professor at the Tongji University, China, at the Jiangnan University, China, and, since 2014, at the University of the Arts London, United Kingdom.

Katharine McGowan is a post-doctoral fellow at the Waterloo Institute for Social Innovation and Resilience, Canada, attached to a project that partners the University of Waterloo with representatives from the community, business and government of the Regional Municipality of Wood Buffalo, Alberta, Canada. McGowan brings her interest in social innovation and resilience to this initiative, researching how social change partnerships work.

Patricia Melo is an industrial engineer with a master's degree in Management and Innovation from the Universidade do Rio de Janeiro, UFRJ – COPPE, Brazil. She is a member of the DESIS Lab at UFRJ – Coppe and has developed research on corporate social responsibility and social innovation.

Geoff Mulgan has been Chief Executive of Nesta, the United Kingdom's innovation foundation, since 2011. Previously he was Chief Executive of The Young Foundation, United Kingdom, which became a leading centre for social innovation. Between 1997 and 2004 Mulgan had various roles in the UK government, including Director of the Government's Strategy Unit and Head of Policy in the Prime Minister's office. His most recent book, *The Locust and the Bee*, was published in 2013.

Ahyoung Park is Co-Founder of C. (Cdot) based in Seoul, South Korea. C. promotes social innovation by connecting knowledge and experience among people pursuing social change in Asia and other countries. It provides services to encourage international exchange and build relationships that facilitate collaboration and cooperation, including running international conferences and study tours, providing training, and coordinating and advising organisations in terms of building international networks. Park was previously a researcher at the Center for Social Economy of the Hope Institute, a civic think and do tank in Seoul, Korea. Park has conducted various projects in terms of community regeneration, community business, social enterprise incubation and consulting in partnership with local governments and social organisations.

Mathieu Pelletier is a postdoctoral researcher at Université du Québec à Montréal, Canada. As Banting Fellow, he has co-founded and is the coordinator of the Observatory on urban and peri-urban conflicts. His work concerns urban studies, decision-making processes and geographical information science. His recent publications focus on urban conflicts and citizen participation (Géocarrefour, 2014) and the location of urban conflicts regarding the social and environmental characteristics of territories (Applied Spatial Analysis and Policy, 2010; Canadian Journal of Regional Science, 2013).

Sojung Rim is Co-Founder of Spread*i*. She also works at Social Innovation Exchange (SIX), United Kingdom, where she coordinates SIX's annual flagship event, SIX Summer Schools. She has previously worked at The Young Foundation, United Kingdom, on a global study geared at surfacing and spreading social innovation methods, with deeper regional studies in Africa and Asia. Rim has also worked at the Hope Institute, a social innovation centre in South Korea.

Michael Schwarz is a sociologist. From 2005 to 2012 he worked as senior researcher and project manager at Sozialforschungstelle Dortmund, TU Dortmund University, Germany, in the fields of organisations, networks, innovation and climate change with special interests in pathways to sustainable development. During this time he made an important contribution to the development of social innovations as a research subject and analytic category, on which he has written numerous books and articles. Since 2012 he has worked freelance, focusing mainly on the social-theoretical foundation of social innovation as a driving force of transformative social change.

Lina Sonne heads Okapi's Mumbai office and leads research on inclusive innovation and entrepreneurship across South Asia. She previously managed research at Intellecap, India, on urban poverty and social entrepreneurship and was editor of Searchlight South Asia, a monthly newsletter on urban poverty. Before that, Sonne was assistant professor, Inclusive Innovation and Entrepreneurship, at the newly started Azim Premji University, India, where she helped set up MA in Development Studies.

Eva Sørensen is Professor of Public Administration and Democracy at Department of Society and Globalization, Roskilde University, Denmark and Professor II at the University of Nordland in Bodø, Norway. She is Vice-director of the Centre for Democratic Network Governance and Director of the 'CLIPS' research project on collaborative innovation in the public sector. Her main research interests are new forms of public governance and their impact on role perceptions among citizens, public administrators, public employees and politicians. She is studying the role of politicians in policy and service innovation.

Ola Tjornbo is McConnell Post-Doctoral Fellow at the Waterloo Institute for Social Innovation and Resilience, Canada. His work focuses on the transformation of complex social-ecological systems and social media. Tjornbo's work combines governance theory and complexity theory to help us understand how we can better manage challenges such as climate change and sustainability. He also uses social innovation theory to explore how our governance systems can change and adapt to a changing external environment and what role social media might play in such transformations.

Jacob Torfing is Professor of Politics and Institutions in the Department of Society and Globalization, Roskilde University, Denmark, and Professor II at the University of Nordland in Bodø, Norway. He is Director of the Centre for Democratic Network Governance and Vice-Director of the large-scale strategic research project on Collaborative Innovation in the Public Sector (CLIPS). His research interests include networks, public innovation, governance reform and local democracy.

Catherine Trudelle is a professor in the Department of Geography at Université du Québec à Montréal, Canada, and a regular member of the Centre de Recherche sur les Innovations Sociales (CRISES), Canada. She is Canada Research Chair in Socioterritorial Conflict and Local Governance. She co-founded the Observatory on urban and peri-urban conflicts (www.observatoireconflits.org/). She is also Fulbright Fellow. Her work focuses on urban conflicts, social mobilisation, urban democracy and humanisation of cities. In the recent years she has published papers on urban conflicts and local governance.

Roberto Mangabeira Unger is a philosopher, a social and legal theorist, and a politician. Among his books are: *Passion: An Essay on Personality*, *False Necessity*, *What Should Legal Analysis Become*, *Democracy Realized*, *The Left Alternative*, *The Self Awakened* and *The Religion of the Future*. He served as Minister of Strategic Affairs in the administration of President Lula in Brazil.

Frances Westley is the JW McConnell Chair in Social Innovation at the University of Waterloo, Canada, and leads the Waterloo Institute for Social Innovation and Resilience. In this capacity, she is one of the principal leads in a Canada-wide initiative in social innovation, Social Innovation Generation (SiG).

This page intentionally left blank

OPEN

Introduction: Dimensions of Social Innovation

Alex Nicholls, Julie Simon and Madeleine Gabriel

Introduction

Social innovation is not new, but it appears to be entering a new phase – a phase in which it is increasingly seen as offering solutions not just to localised problems but to more systemic and structural issues. Nevertheless, the growing set of examples and attendant discourses and logics of social innovation have yet to coalesce around a single, common definition, a set of standards or performance measures or an agreed policy agenda. Partly, this is the consequence of the 'liability of newness' experienced by all new fields of action: namely, they lack the legitimacy needed to support significant investment or research. It may also be because the range and variety of action that constitutes social innovation today defies simple categorisation. Indeed, this fluidity and diversity may be seen as one of the field's great strengths in terms of addressing complex social problems and challenges. So, as yet, there is no established paradigm of social innovation (see also Nicholls, 2010a).

However, there are strong signs that interest is growing in this insti-tutional space where innovative thinking and models can address both problems of social welfare efficiency or distribution and imbalances and inequalities in social structures and relations. Moreover, inter-est in this field appears to cut across governments, civil society and even mainstream businesses and investors. It has also become a topic for scholarly enquiry and research (see e.g., Nicholls and Murdock, 2012). This book aims to explore the multiple dimensions of social innovation – both theoretically and empirically – in order to advance research and contribute to shaping the formation of its boundaries and to advancing a wider recognition of the opportunities and challenges of this new phase.

1

In particular, this volume aims to challenge some of the emerging normative assumptions about the 'promise of social innovation', namely a general acceptance that it is an unproblematic and consistently positive phenomenon without drawbacks or unintended consequences. Thus, this collection explores the implications of social innovation in cross-sector collaborations and hybrid forms, across several contexts and in multiple country settings to highlight a range of issues across social innovation models. The research presented here deliberately ranges across different socio-structural levels and units of analysis – from micro to macro – in order to offer multiple insights into the various contexts in which social innovation can operate effectively. Much of the work here also has strong policy implications: by codifying and analysing practice, its objective is to inform future policy making in social innovation across countries. This book also aims to contribute to the critical field-building project of social innovation that is already underway across a range of researchers and institutions by augmenting the existing body of knowledge on this subject with work on new trends and case examples. In the process, the hope is that the work published here will also support the building of a community of researchers looking at social innovation by adding its own, modest legitimacy to working on this subject. The contents and structure of this volume are considered in more detail below.

Definitions

At its simplest, social innovation can be seen as 'new ideas that address unmet social needs – and that work' (Mulgan *et al.*, 2007, p. 2). In practice, social innovations can take the form of specific ideas, actions, frames, models, systems, processes, services, rules and regulations as well as new organisational forms. However, more specifically, there are two interlinked conceptualisations of social innovation, focused on either new social *processes* or new social *outputs and outcomes*. The first emphasises changes in social relations and often has a focus on rebalancing power disparities of economic inequalities in society (see Moulaert *et al.*, 2014a). For example, Mumford (2002, p. 253) suggested that:

> Social innovation refers to the generation and implementation of new ideas about how people should organize interpersonal activities, or social interactions, to meet one or more common goals.

Westley and Antadze (2010, p. 2) subsequently expanded upon this by noting that:

> Social innovation is a complex process of introducing new products, processes or programs that profoundly change the basic routines, resource and authority flows, or beliefs of the social system in which the innovation occurs. Such successful social innovations have durability and broad impact.

Second, social innovation can be seen as the answer to social market failures in the provision of vital public goods. This is reflected in the OECD's definition of social innovation, which also includes a reference to the process dimensions of social innovation (2011, p. 1):

> Social innovation is distinct from economic innovation because it is not about introducing new types of production or exploiting new markets in itself but is about satisfying new needs not provided by the market (even if markets intervene later) or creating new, more satisfactory ways of insertion in terms of giving people a place and a role in production.

In addition to these two meta-definitions, three levels of social innovation can be identified (see Table I.1). First, there is *incremental* innovation in goods and services to address social need more effectively or efficiently. This is the objective of many successful charities and not-for-profits, as well as some so-called 'Bottom of the Pyramid' (Prahalad, 2006) commercial firms. From this perspective, social innovation may simply be a good business opportunity. Second, there is *institutional* innovation that aims to harness or retool existing social and economic structures to generate new social value and outcomes. Examples such as Fair Trade (Nicholls and Opal, 2005) or mobile banking typically exploit or modify existing market structures to deliver new or additional social value. Finally, *disruptive* social innovation aims at systems change. This is typically the realm of social movements and self-consciously 'political' actors, groups and networks aiming to change power relations, alter social hierarchies and reframe issues to the benefit of otherwise disenfranchised groups. Disruptive social innovation can be characterised by structured mass participation in political parties or formal membership schemes of social movements, on the one hand, or loose coalitions of individuals and interests united by an evanescent issue or technology such as social media, on the other. Policy entrepreneurs from within

Table I.1   Levels of social innovation

Level	Objective	Focus	Examples
Incremental	To address identified market failures more effectively	Products	Kickstart (low-cost irrigation foot pump)
Institutional	To reconfigure existing market structures and patterns	Markets	M-PESA (mobile banking)
Disruptive	To change cognitive frames of reference to alter social systems and structures	Politics	Tostan (human rights)

Source: Nicholls and Murdock (2012).

Table I.2   Dimensions of social innovation

Dimension	Social process	Social outcome
Individual	Co-Production (Southwark Circle)	Lost-cost Healthcare (Aravind Eye Hospital)
Organisation	Wiki-Production (Wikipedia)	Work Integration Social Enterprise (Greyston Bakery)
Network/ Movement	Open Source Technology (Linux)	Non-Traditional Training and Education (Barefoot College)
System	Microfinance (Grameen Bank)	Mobile Banking (MPESA)

Source: Nicholls and Murdock (2012).

state structures can also drive disruptive social innovation by focussing on reforming democracy and enlarging or deepening citizens' roles within it.

Social innovation can also be defined in terms of the level of its action or impact from the individual to the systems level (micro-, meso- or macro-level). Such levels or dimensions can be mapped against the two main definitions of social innovation focused either on new social processes or on new social outcomes (see Table I.2). These differing levels of impact point to the complexity of performance measurement on social innovation and emphasise the need for clarity about the unit of impact of a social innovation.

Social innovation can also be considered in the context of the more institutionalised fields of social entrepreneurship (Dees, 1998; Nicholls, 2006) and social enterprise (Alter, 2006; Nyssens, 2006). In this setting, social innovation can be seen as the biggest field of action encompassing any new idea or model that addresses a social (or environmental) need. Social entrepreneurship can, then, be seen as a subset of social innovation – the organisational enactment of social innovation ideas and models.

Finally, drawing upon theory from design thinking, Murray *et al.* (2010) set out the key stages of the development of a social innovation as a nonlinear process. This model is characterised by a series of key inflection points where the development of an innovation moves first from prompts and proposals to prototyping (an important part of the design process), then to sustainability and, finally, to scale.

It should also be acknowledged that social innovation is not, in and of itself, a socially positive thing. Social innovation may have a 'dark side'. This could be evidenced in several ways:

- Socially divisive or destructive objectives and intentions (e.g., secret societies or extreme political parties)
- Deviant or unintended consequences that achieve negative social effects (e.g., by excluding some groups from the focus of social goods, services or change)
- Operational failure, mission drift or strategic co-option by an external party (e.g., Tracey and Jarvis, 2006)

It is well understood within innovation studies that innovations will create value for some and destroy it for others. This underlies Schumpeter's (1942) notion of 'creative destruction'. In the context of social innovation, however, the idea that social innovations might create winners and losers is rarely, if ever, articulated. Phills *et al.* (2008) appeared to recognise the potential for a dark side of social innovation in a definition that emphasises *improvement* rather than *change* as a central feature:

> A novel solution to a social problem that is more effective, efficient, sustainable, or just than existing solutions and for which the value created accrues primarily to society as a whole rather than private individuals. (p. 36)

Moreover, this conceptualisation also highlights a potential bifurcation of value creation and value appropriation within social innovation that renders the interests of the individual (social) innovator secondary to wider social value creation (see Nicholls, 2010b, for a similar argument in the context of social investment).

Clearly, social innovation is a complex and multi-faceted institutional space that is still subject to competing discourses and definitions. Moreover, as is illustrated in this collection, social innovation can have a 'dark side' that challenges normative assumptions that (social) innovation is always positive (i.e., improvement rather than just change). It is important, therefore, to be aware that social innovation from one stakeholder perspective may look and feel very different from another – social benefit is always contingent. As such, in terms of this collection, social innovation can be seen as:

> Varying levels of deliberative novelty that bring about change and that aim to address suboptimal issues in the production, availability, and consumption of public goods defined as that which is broadly of societal benefit within a particular normative and culturally contingent context.

Drivers

As Moulaert *et al.* (2014b) noted:

> Socially innovative actions, strategies, practices and processes arise whenever problems of poverty, exclusion, segregation and deprivation or opportunities for improving living conditions cannot find satisfactory solutions in the 'institutionalized field' of public or private action. (p. 2)

As such the growth of interest in social innovation as a field or set of tools and models reflects the failure – for at least some sections of society – of established systems (technology, markets, policy, governance, etc.) to deliver well-being and economic prosperity. This can be seen, fundamentally, as a distribution problem in terms of both mainstream innovation policy and democratic reform. Social innovation can be viewed, therefore, as partly a response to patterns of modernity that have marginalised certain populations and that see the individual citizen as essentially an economic/consuming actor, not as an active participant in collective decision-making. From this perspective social innovation is a sense-making process that, first, frames key issues and then proposes alternative worldviews (functioning much like the classic social movement: see Davis *et al.*, 2005). This reading of the drivers of social innovation emphasises addressing sub-optimal configurations of social relations via new models of empowerment, engagement or political mobilisation.

Of course, social innovation is also driven by simple welfare need. The increasing challenges of global warming, growing inequality (if not absolute poverty), demographics (notably a growing ageing population), migration, pandemics and terrorism have been compounded by the effective nationalisation by governments of the private sector financial crisis after 2008. Thus, the age of public sector austerity will likely stretch forward into the 2020s and beyond in many developed countries and this will continue to severely constrain welfare budgets. As a consequence, in both developed and developing country contexts, there will be a need for social innovation to address shortfalls and market failures in the provision of basic, universal, welfare services.[1]

One account of the increased focus on social innovation in recent years casts it as a response to an acceleration of global crises and so-called 'wicked problems' characterised by multiple and contradictory analyses and diagnoses (Rittel and Webber, 1973; Rayner, 2006; Mulgan *et al.*, 2007; Murray *et al.*, 2010), such as: climate change; social breakdown; rising life expectancy and associated health and social care costs; growing cultural diversity within and across countries; growing inequality; rising incidences of chronic long-term conditions and pandemics; behavioural problems associated with the 'challenge of affluence' (Offer, 2006); difficult transitions to adulthood; endemic reductions in individual happiness and indices of well-being. The rise of social innovation also demonstrates a collapse in trust in the status quo – as established models and social relations have increasingly failed to deliver well-being for many. In this context, intractable problems are seen as highlighting the failure of conventional solutions and established paradigms, entrenched in institutional settings across all three conventional sectors of society. This is evident through private sector market failures, public sector siloed thinking and a lack of scale in and fragmentation across civil society.

An important subset of these 'wicked problems' concerns welfare reform. After World War Two a new model of welfare provision emerged across many developed economies with the state delivering universal public services largely free at the point of access, funded by taxation and compulsory individual 'national' insurance. The centrepiece of many welfare states has been the development of powerful public healthcare systems. However, demographic and societal changes combined with the economic realities of rising welfare costs and worsening public finances have led to radical innovation in the provision of welfare goods and services in recent years (Leadbeater, 1997). In many cases this has involved a retreat from centralised state-led provision and an engagement with new 'partnership' models involving both the private and civil society sectors. A key objective has been increased economic efficiency, but there has also been a realisation that innovation and reform offer the opportunity to improve the effectiveness of services.[2] For example, in both the United Kingdom and elsewhere there has been a clear move in public policy towards enabling greater 'choice' and control for the recipient of welfare services (Bartlett, 2009a and 2009b). Indeed, policy reform offers an important mechanism by which social innovation can be both incubated and enacted as a part of 'reinventing government' (Osborne and Gaebler, 1992). At the same time, there has been a crisis in the legitimacy of the democratic process in many developed countries with the consequence that social innovation is also being used as a set of processes to improve citizen engagement within the policy-making process.

In developing country contexts, public welfare has typically not developed in this way. Large welfare states are not present here. Nevertheless, social innovation models of mixed provision, co-creation and deep citizen participation in welfare – that are becoming entrenched in the developed nations – are also playing a role in emergent welfare states elsewhere (Nicholls, 2013). This is discussed further below.

An alternative view of this new phase of social innovation sees it as a necessary (but not always automatic) companion to rapid technological change and economic innovation (Hämäläinen and Heiskala, 2007). This conceptualisation presents social innovation as a process of reshaping social relations to maximise productivity and economic development, often framed by the (perhaps optimistic) assumption that the benefits of these changes will be shared equally across society. Such a reading also suggests that social entrepreneurship represents the reconciliation of an historical division between private and public sector mechanisms of productivity growth (Drayton, 2002). These approaches are at a systems level of analysis that relates most clearly to a disruptive vision of social innovation.

Common to all these drivers are a series of complex and multifaceted social contexts that drive innovation not only in processes and outcomes but also, increasingly, as boundary-blurring activity across the conventional sectors of society. As Murray *et al.* (2010) wrote:

> Social innovation doesn't have fixed boundaries: it happens in all sectors, public, non-profit and private. Indeed, much of the most creative action is happening at the boundaries between sectors. (p. 3)

Each of the three sectors of society – civil society, public and private – has its own internal logic of action and defining features. Taken together, these three ideal-type sectors can be conceptualised as a triad represented in stability as a triangle. Between each of the three ideal-type points lies a spectrum of hybrid institutions and organisations that represent sites for social innovation as a boundary-blurring activity (see Figure I.1). Thus, between the civil society sector and the private sector are social enterprises that combine business logics and models with social objectives and ownership structures (Alter, 2006). Some examples along this spectrum will be closer to the logic of business (i.e., businesses with a social purpose: see also Corporate Social Innovation, Moss Kanter, 1999) and some to that of civil society (i.e., not-for-profit organisations that have an earned income stream). In the spectrum between the private and public sector ideal types are hybrids such as public–private partnerships that aim to provide new models of welfare provision outside of, but in tandem with, the state (Bovaird, 2006). Finally, between the state and civil society ideal types lies the 'shadow state' in which civil society organisations function as a surrogate state, providing welfare where there is a public sector market failure. For example, in Bangladesh, BRAC and the network of Grameen organisations act as quasi-state providers of education, health, employment and

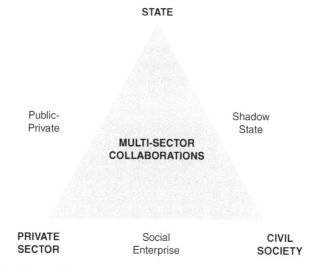

Figure I.1   The social innovation triad
Source: Nicholls and Murdock (2012).

financial services across the country in and around institutional voids at the policy and market levels (Mair and Marti, 2009).

There are multiple, often sector-specific, drivers behind the growing relevance of social innovation across sectors. For the private commercial sector, there is an increasing recognition of social innovation as offering a model for new roles of business in society (e.g., the 'Shared Value' model, Porter and Kramer, 2012). For the state, social innovation links with traditions of welfare reform based on increased efficiency and effectiveness, also reflecting a move from a focus on New Public Management to Public Value and, more recently, New Public Governance. It may also challenge the governance status quo in societies by aiming to transform the power structures across social relations that allocate goods and services ineffectively or unequally. For civil society, social innovation may involve both internal processes of organisational change (such as new legal forms, collaborations and income strategies) and novelty in external outputs and outcomes (such as new products and services).

Research themes

To date, the research literature that focuses on social innovation specifically is limited, albeit growing. A review of this body of work reveals three clusters of research themes. Each is now considered in turn.

Innovation in social relations

The largest and most well-developed body of work on social innovation specifically focuses on innovation that addresses various dimensions of changes in social relations. This literature can be subdivided into five categories of scholarship:

1. Research Design Challenges: Early work on social innovation developed from within behavioural science with a particular interest in devising 'social change' approaches to tackle key, contemporary social problems, often at a community level (Fairweather, 1967).[3]
2. Changes in Social Structures: Hämäläinen and Heiskala (2007) argued that it is social innovation processes that ultimately determine the economic and social performance of nations, regions, and industrial sectors and organisations: 'Social innovations are changes in the cultural, normative or regulative structures of society which enhance its collective power resources and improve its economic and social performance' (2007, p. 59).

3. Changes in Patterns of Work (or workplace innovation): Holt (1971) focused on social innovation within organisations, conceived of as new social patterns of employee interaction. This work was echoed in the activities of the Netherlands Centre for Social Innovation 30 years later (see Pot and Vaas, 2008).
4. Diffusion of Social Change: From within sociology, there are analyses of the micro-level structures of innovation and diffusion that affect society – for example, how medical innovations spread across groups of clinicians – that have been classed as social innovation. Henderson (1993) was interested in the relationship between social innovation and political change in terms of diffusion processes. He explored how citizen movements catalyse social innovation – conceptualised as distinct from dominant cultural norms – from fluid positions outside of conventional societal structures.
5. Urban Studies: There is a significant cluster of work within urban studies exploring innovative responses to social exclusion as social innovation under the heading of Integrated Area Development. Much of this work centres on innovation within social relations in urban contexts, and as a body of work, it explores the potential of public, private and civil society models, interventions and interactions. In 2007, Moulaert *et al.* characterised social innovation as 'a polymorphic constellation of counter-hegemonic movements and initiatives' (p. 196) engaged in active processes of social struggle and change.

Innovation to address social market failures

This stream of work relates to the outcome-driven model of social innovation already discussed above and focuses on innovation as the means by which new products and services can be provided to underserved market segments. At the macro level, this includes the mechanisms by which new markets are created in weak institutional spaces or to address market failures. The latter is conceived of as encompassing failures not only in commercial markets but also in public sector 'markets', where the state fails to provide public goods, and civil society 'markets', where charities, not-for-profits and NGOs fail to provide effective goods and services to their beneficiaries (Nicholls, 2006). High-profile examples include developments focused on the Bottom of the Pyramid (Prahalad, 2006) or frugal innovation (Jugaad) models (Zeschky *et al.*, 2011). However, while such failures typically provide innovation opportunities, they can also offer challenges in terms of reconciling potentially competing institutional logics (Battilana and Dorado, 2010).

Resilience theory

A third strand of social innovation theory has emerged recently focusing on its relationship with the overall sustainability and, particularly, the resilience of the larger ecosystem within which it evolves. The overall resilience of a system may be examined through the lens of the adaptive cycle, which is graphically represented by an infinity loop encompassing four phases: release, reorganisation, exploitation and conservation. The exploitation and conservation phases in the 'front' loop represent periods of growth and resource accumulation, where change is routine and almost always adaptive, while the release and reorganisation phases in the 'back' loop can represent the introduction of novelty, either transformative (radical) or adaptive change, and renewal of the system. The back loop, therefore, represents a precarious moment from the point of view of whether the system remains stable, adapting and learning but not transforming, or whether it is pushed close to a threshold that tips the system into a new stability domain. The new domain may share characteristics with the old stability domain but will have radically different feedback loops, and hence different relationships between the phases (Moore and Westley, 2011). Resilience theory offers a systems-level model of the emergence and dissemination of patterns of social innovation.

That social innovation occurs in multiple contexts of praxis serves to reinforce the need for theoretical particularity in the analysis and presentation of the phenomenon (Moulaert *et al.*, 2014a). Thus, each case of social innovation in healthcare, education, economic development, agriculture, urban development or governance and political transformation will need its own epistemology and set of boundaries and logics if it is to be understood clearly. This is, of course, a methodological, as well as theoretical, challenge for researchers.

Objectives of this book

This collection aims to contribute to the small but growing research literature on social innovation. In particular, it attempts to challenge some of the emerging normative assumptions concerning the 'promise' of social innovation via critical analyses, extending and testing relevant theory, and via new empirical contributions. One important contribution of this volume is to test the assumption that social innovation is somehow inherently 'good' or socially positive in all contexts. As noted above, it is easy to imagine a 'dark side' to social innovation (as highlighted here by McGowan and Westley). However, even self-evidently positive social innovation may not benefit all relevant stakeholders equally and may, indeed, create negative effects for some. Moreover, the disruptive effects of some social innovation may undermine important institutional norms whilst still delivering substantial benefits to target populations. For example, some analyses of the role of social innovation in welfare services delivery would emphasise that this simultaneously undermines the roles and responsibilities of the state (and, therefore, citizens' democratic rights) as it delivers measurably positive benefits to target populations (see Evers and Ewert here). Unger also notes the need for social innovation to 'aim high' by acknowledging – and confronting – political and power issues across societies. The danger, otherwise, is that social innovation becomes absorbed into existing systems – tamed into irrelevance.

This collection also intends to help build a global community of researchers in social innovation by bringing together a range of perspectives and examples from around the world. The authors included here range across a variety of disciplines – management, political science, not-for-profit studies, sociology and economics – making this volume an avowedly multi-disciplinary endeavour. This is not only intellectually interesting but also reflects the reality of praxis in social innovation that is often characterised by cross-sector collaboration and organisational hybridity.

This book offers examples and insights from multiple geographical contexts and reflects many different cognitive frames, discourses and debates concerning the nature and enactment of social innovation. The innovation within this book itself lies in its presentation of new cases, new theories and new methodologies allied to different levels and units of analysis across its chapters.

Finally, this collection hopes to contribute meaningfully to emergent policy debates across countries concerning the role and functioning of social innovation across the commercial, not-for-profit and public sectors (and in the blurred institutional spaces between them). The contributions here serve to codify and analyse practice in a way that can inform better public policy decision-making. Academic research can play a significant role in this regard since it often explores models and issues that sit ahead of current policy debates and agendas. It is the ambition of this collection to offer such insights.

Key themes

The various contributions in this collection have a number of common themes and topics.

First, this volume offers a number of new observations concerning the *practice and process of researching social innovation.* A foundational question asked here is: Is there a need for specific theories of social innovation or is social innovation simply a phenomenon that can be observed and made sense of using existing theoretical frameworks? Moreover, if the latter is true, then which disciplines best suit this analytic purpose? Partly to answer this, the chapters in this volume offer a rich and broad range of theoretical approaches to framing and analysing social innovation. They also touch on several important methodological issues. There are three chapters that present detailed case material from different countries (Brazil, South Korea and India): each offers new and rich empirical evidence of social innovation in context.

Second, and perhaps unsurprisingly, there is a clear focus on exploring the *nature of social innovation.* Overall, the research presented here situates social innovation as a 'quasi-concept' characterised by its fluidity in terms of its meanings and attendant discourses. This, of course, is a contingent effect of the widely observed tendency of social innovation to occupy hybrid institutional spaces and organisational forms. Specifically, the approaches to the nature of social innovation set out here include discussions of definitions with particular emphasis on the implications of social innovation at different socio-structural levels and at different stages of the innovation lifecycle from emergence to institutionalisation and, ultimately, entropy and re-invigoration as a new cycle begins (within the resilience model). The analysis of lifecycle issues also focuses on process questions around the dissemination, diffusion, growth and scaling of social innovation in various contexts.

Several chapters explore the nature of social innovation in terms of the complex interactions between individual actors and the systems in which they are located – this work reflects the central sociological debates concerning the roles of agency and structure in determining the shape and functioning of social action. This book also highlights examples of cross- or multi-sector collaboration (often in network settings) as defining features of successful social innovation. Research here demonstrates how successful examples of cross-sector partnerships also need to be carefully calibrated to their socio-cultural contexts.

A final focus of this collection is on the *effects of social innovation.* Within this topic there is a strong interest in democratic and public sector reform. This is manifest in social innovation aimed at citizen engagement and improved political accountability and transparency, on the one hand, and examples of innovative public service reform, on the other. The former is also analysed in terms of practical examples of innovations in governance and accountability mechanisms and models. Connected to these themes is research here that explores social innovation directed towards disrupting the (unjust) status quo of power structures via an explicit social change agenda. This theme also acknowledges the significance of community-level innovation and action. Another research focus examines how social innovation shapes, is shaped by and interacts with market structures and models. This set of work lies in stark contrast to the public sector focus noted elsewhere and provides a useful counterpoint to it, enriching the overall scope and argument of the book as a whole.

Structure of the book

The collection opens with some reflections by Mulgan on the future of social innovation research. He argues that social innovation rests on an idea about possibility, rather than being a field with clearly defined boundaries. As such, social innovation research cannot be simply a detached, empirical social science; it is inevitable – and healthy – that research is coupled with practice.

After this introduction, the book is divided into three parts: researching social innovation; blurring boundaries and reconfiguring relations; and producing social innovation through new forms of collaboration.

Part I examines a range of issues concerning the research of social innovation. This section explores new methodological approaches that can help to understand the roles of particular social innovation actors and to identify broader patterns and trends regarding the relationship between social innovation, social change and societal transformation.

The theoretical foundations of the concept of social innovation remain relatively weak and much research in this area is descriptive or evaluative. To further develop the theory underpinning social innovation research, one potential approach is to revisit the works of social theorists whose frameworks and models can help to make sense of critical issues within social innovation discourses. In Chapter 1, Howaldt, Kopp and Schwarz revisit the work of Gabriel Tarde and make a case for using his social theory in developing a theoretically grounded concept of social innovation. Tarde's basic idea is to explain social change 'from the bottom up'. Countless and nameless inventions and discoveries change society and its practices through equally countless acts of imitation, and only as a result do they become a true social phenomenon. By identifying the practices and laws of imitation as central to social innovation and social change, the authors propose shifts of perspective relevant to contemporary social innovation policy and discussions about the diffusion of social innovations.

Another approach to researching social innovation, exemplified in Chapter 2, is the use of comparative historical case studies. McGowan and Westley introduce a theoretical and methodological framework based on three propositions: first, that new social phenomena create the opportunity for changes to social relations and structures by enabling glimpses into the 'adjacent possible'; second, that agents' behaviour and roles within social innovation can be divided into three categories – poets, debaters and designers – whose efforts are complementary; and finally, that to achieve broad, lasting change, the innovation in question must cross multiple scales – from the niche (micro) level to the (macro) landscape level. The authors explore these frameworks through a case study on the emergence of the intelligence test. This illustrates the three elements within the authors' theoretical framework and also shows how social innovation is culturally contingent. The ideas that inspired the development of the intelligence test, such as Social Darwinism, are now widely viewed as profoundly perverse.

In 2011, the Centre de recherche sur les innovations sociales (Center for Research on Social Innovations – CRISES) started to build a database of social innovations. In Chapter 3, Bouchard *et al.* examine the uses and the challenges of building such a database. Since research on social innovation is generally conducted through case studies, it is difficult to carry out macro-sociological analysis of the social transformations that accompany these innovations, and results cannot be generalised. The database of social innovations aims to fill this gap and to enable the longitudinal, sectoral and spatial analysis of social innovation in the context of Quebec. The process of building a database represents an innovative approach to the research of social innovation, and the authors point to a number of methodological, theoretical and episte-mological challenges associated with such a task.

Part II explores some of the ways in which social innovations recon-figure relations between civil society, the state and the market. Indeed, the boundaries between these sectors are becoming increasingly porous and one of the striking features of social innovations is their ability to combine the traditionally disparate logics of the private, public and civil society sectors.

In Chapter 4, Jenson examines some of the varied meanings of the 'quasi-concept' of social innovation, and argues that one of its major contributions is to provide a novel way to reorganise market relations in the post-neoliberal world. The 'welfare diamond' is a heuristic device that illustrates the mixed sources of well-being, which include the market, the state, the family and the community. Each is a potential source of well-being. Increasing reliance on social entrepreneurs and social enterprises to achieve social innovations in social policy implies a reconceptualisation of relations within the welfare diamond, often by explicitly exposing and developing a reliance on non-market dimensions (such as community engagement and public policy) in the processes of market making and in quasi-markets.

Chapter 5, by Evers and Ewert, looks at the welfare diamond from a different perspective. The chapter describes and analyses approaches and instruments used in a range of innovative welfare projects from twenty cities and ten countries across Europe. Analysing these reveals recurring approaches and instruments in relation to various dimensions of welfare systems. The chapter reflects on the relationship between social innovation in the welfare field and welfare reform, and raises challenges for both. The economic precariousness caused by flexible labour markets, together with growing levels of in-work poverty, high levels of unemployment and squeezes to welfare entitlements and pensions, probably creates more significant social problems than could ever be addressed through socially innovative services that empower citizens and communities. This raises questions about the ability of social innovation to live up to its 'promise', and shows that, in order for social innovations to have real impact, engaging with political processes is essential.

Chapter 6 provides empirical evidence of the ways in which social innovations reconfigure market relations and blur boundaries between sectors, in this case between the market and civil society. Cipolla, Melo and Manzini describe the development and emergence of a new type of 'collaborative service' in a pacified favela in Rio de Janeiro. The pacification process enabled a local energy company to start offering services in the favela, but residents found it difficult to pay their bills. To overcome these challenges, the energy company developed 'Light Recicla', a service that reduced residents' electricity bills by exchanging recyclable materials for energy credits. Based on this case study, the authors discuss the possibility of building a new type of service based on vertical, experiential interactions between service providers and service users in informal settlements such as favelas.

While Part II explores issues about *structure* in generating social innovation, Part III examines some of the key issues around *agency*. In particular, it looks at the roles played by social innovation actors – such as social entrepreneurs, citizens and public sector managers – and explores how these roles can be strengthened in order to support the generation of social innovation. The chapters in this section underline the importance of collaboration in producing social innovation, even while some also highlight the roles of key individuals in the process, such as Mayor Park in Seoul. In this way, the chapters in this section echo arguments made by Howaldt *et al.* and McGowan and Westley, which emphasise the roles of different actors within the social innovation process.

In Chapter 7, Sørensen and Torfing argue that multi-actor collaboration in networks, partnerships and inter-organisational teams can spur public innovation. They argue that the principles of New Public Management are giving way to 'New Public Governance', and that the enhancement of collaborative innovation has now become a key aspiration of many public organisations around the world. However, collaborative and innovative processes are difficult to trigger and sustain without proper innovation management and a supportive cultural and institutional environment. Arguing strongly that innovation is produced through collaboration and not through the actions of 'heroic individuals', the authors describe the roles for public innovation managers that are necessary to enhance innovation through collaboration.

In Chapter 8, Han, Kim, Rim and Park provide an empirical case study from Seoul. Led by Mayor Park, a famous social innovator, Seoul Metropolitan Government has developed various communication channels, both online and offline, which have enabled new forms of consultation and engagement between the city administration and citizens. The chapter outlines three communication tools and programmes that reflect the current administration's approach and values, and presents a case study of a particular challenge that the city government solved through engaging with citizens. New communication tools often have a limited reach, and the methods currently being used only contribute to solving a limited range of social problems. Nevertheless, Seoul Metropolitan Government's approach offers valuable lessons to other cities that are ambitiously planning to initiate and drive social innovation.

In Chapter 9, Tjornbo examines whether the wisdom of crowds can be harnessed to generate social innovation. The development of modern information and communication technologies has led to a renewed interest in the phenomenon of collective intelligence, defined here as the capacity to mobilise and coordinate the knowledge, skills and creativity possessed by large groups of individuals, and combine them into a greater whole. Social innovation is deeply reliant on the capacity to combine the ideas, knowledge and resources possessed by disparate groups, something collective intelligence can do well. However, it is also clear that collective intelligence has serious limitations when it comes to dealing with complex problems that are politically contested and require careful coordination. This chapter provides a framework for examining how collective intelligence might support social innovation and explores three existing collective intelligence platforms that have promoted social innovation: Innocentive, Open Source Ecology and TED.

Chapter 10 examines how successful social entrepreneurs use networks to build their businesses. Focusing on social entrepreneurs as a particular sub-group of social innovators, Sonne maps the individual networks of three innovative social enterprises in India. Analysing these networks helps to improve understanding of to whom social entrepreneurs turn for access to knowledge and financial and non-financial support in order to innovate, build and grow their businesses and develop social capital. The author also explores the way in which social entrepreneurs build the relationships that form the basis of their networks and the ways in which important networks change over time.

In the book's conclusion, Roberto Mangabeira Unger offers a manifesto for the social innovation movement: he explores the impulses driving the movement and argues for a view of what its agenda and methods can and should be. In this 'maximalist' view, the task of the social innovation movement is to challenge the worldwide 'dictatorship of no alternatives' by addressing 'the whole of society, of its institutional arrangements, and of its dominant forms of consciousness'. The best way to carry out this task is to take small-scale experimental initiatives that both mark a path for society and represent first steps for treading it. For Unger, the overriding mission of the social innovation movement is the enhancement of agency – our power, as individuals and as collectivities, to reshape our world. It is to help create a society of innovators.

Conclusions

This chapter has set the context for the remainder of the volume and has summarised the key contributions of the research featured here. However, there are several important and interesting topics of relevance to social innovation that would benefit from future research. Six such topics are sketched out below.

An important feature of social innovation that has sometimes been overlooked in the literature to date is political disruption. The social movements literature suggests that truly systemic change only comes about through struggle and changing the dominant cognitive frames that frame social issues. Such activity typically comes up against strong vested interests and can encounter (sometimes violent) resistance. As a consequence, the politicisation of social innovation research offers an important new lens through which systemic change can be understood: recognising the political dimension of social innovation is not merely a research opportunity, but it also raises significant practical questions and challenges. Political action often prompts a reaction and can lead to institutional confrontation or even danger. Further, when social innovation addresses public welfare issues or aims to drive political change, it typically does so as private action that lacks any formal democratic legitimacy. This is particularly problematic in cases where social innovation acts as a 'shadow state' substituting for what would otherwise be the welfare responsibilities of the elected state. Such a democratic deficit challenges rights-based models of citizens' relationship to their government. There is also the more general issue of who is included in, and who is excluded from, social innovation impacts.

A second issue concerns the public legitimacy of social innovation. Many social innovations that aim to address institutional voids may initially lack legitimacy to key populations. This is because they often take the form of interventions that combine otherwise distinct institutional logics and models of action in innovative forms and that challenge normative notions of the roles and responsibilities of the discrete sectors. Such hybrid forms of action typically blend the logics and rationales of two or more established sectors to build new organisational structures (i.e., 'social' business), processes (i.e., work integration models) or goods and services (i.e., user-led welfare models) that correspond to complex sets of needs and demands in late modern societies better than conventional interventions do. The logics and rationales of action of each conventional sector are quite different and even contradictory at the normative level. As a consequence, the public legitimacy of social innovation (at both normative and cognitive levels: see Suchman, 1995) can often be compromised, with new models variously seen as attempts to privatise the social, dismantle the state or undermine civil society (Nicholls and Cho, 2006). The reaction to the social enterprise/social business hybrid model within social innovation has been particularly hostile since this challenges fundamental principles of the state and civil society as not-for-profit sectors in many countries. Such loss of public legitimacy can have serious consequences in terms of access to resources, market competitiveness, policy support and staff recruitment.

Third, there are challenges in scaling up social innovation. The stated objective of much social innovation is to bring about systemic change. However, genuine systems change is a very ambitious objective and typically requires a combination of scale, geographical spread and political support. Bloom and Chatterji (2009) acknowledged these factors when they established the SCALERS model as a guide to key activities needed to achieve scale in social innovation, notably in terms of staffing, communicating, alliance building, lobbying, earnings generation, replicating and stimulating market forces. Elsewhere research has focused on the institutional, rather than organisational, aspects of achieving scale, particularly in terms of building social innovation 'ecosystems' (Bloom and Dees, 2008). However, there is relatively little evidence as yet of social innovation delivering systems change without government support – which begs important questions about the public–private dimensions of scaling social innovation.

Fourth, social innovation is often limited by access to market – or even discretionary – commercial finance at the start-up and growth phase (Nicholls, 2010b). There are several reasons for this. First, as was noted above, social innovation often occupies hybrid institutional spaces that span the logics of the state and the for-profit and not-for-profit sectors. This creates difficulties in terms of assessing risk and return within conventional financial modelling. Furthermore, given its explicit social focus, social innovation 'ventures' may not aim at maximising their financial bottom line, focusing instead on creating 'blended value' (Emerson, 2003) that combines social and financial performance. A third challenge is investor exit – there is currently no fully functioning secondary market in which social innovation investments can be realised. The emergence of an impact investing market (O'Donohoe *et al.*, 2010) over recent years may partly address this capital gap – but it seems likely that, going forward, public and philanthropic finance will remain important to develop and grow social innovation.

Fifth, there are, as yet, no agreed measurement mechanisms or standard units of analysis for social innovation impact and performance. Welfare economics and the large range of bespoke social impact measurement approaches developed within the not-for-profit or social entrepreneurship sectors offer a set of models that can be used in different contexts, but no dominant standard has emerged (Mulgan, 2010; Ebrahim and Rangan, 2010). As a consequence, exploring the comparative performance of social innovation remains a challenge. This has profound implications for access to capital and policy making.

Related to the problems of measuring social innovation impact is a sixth challenge. As has already been suggested, social innovation may have problematic unintended or accidental consequences or externalities. There are four issues to be considered here. First, social innovation can have negative social effects by excluding some groups from the focus of its provision of social goods and services or its campaigns for social change. Second, another unintended set of consequences can arise from different framings or perceptions of the hybrid nature of social innovations that blend social and financial objectives. From one point of view such activities are exploitative and represent the 'privatisation' of the social, as critiques of the high interest rates offered by many micro-finance organisations have pointed out. Third, social innovation could be hijacked for socially divisive or destructive objectives and intentions, for example by secret societies or extreme political parties. Finally, social innovation can achieve perverse effects in cases of operational failure (e.g., Tracey and Jarvis, 2006). Since social innovation is often expressed organisationally in the form of innovative start-ups in weak institutional spaces, it is inherently risky. As a result, it is reasonable to expect that much social innovation will fail, with potentially damaging effects for vulnerable populations.

Finally, it is important to note that social innovation is often highly contingent and contextually sensitive. It will therefore look quite different in different countries. Thus, outside of the United States and Europe, social innovation has very different political-economic contexts (see Kerlin, 2009). For example, in the transition countries of Eastern Europe after the fall of communism, weak market structures, significant injections of international aid and a rejection of centralised organisational forms led to the development of social innovation focused on creating small businesses that rejected the co-operative and mutual form due to cultural-political reasons of history. In Latin America, after the financial crisis of the late 1990s, market, state and international aid structures were severely weakened. In this context, social innovation evolved, first, as a mechanism of social solidarity built from the grass roots up (Klein, 2002) and, then, as mechanisms to rebuild jobs and regenerate economies (see, e.g., NESsT, 2005). In Africa, social innovation emerged at the intersection of state and market failures (sometimes bordering on actual collapse) and was often driven by high levels of extreme poverty and large inflows of international development aid. Particularly significant here was the provision of micro-credit for small businesses, as well as the emergence of innovative organisations in health, education and farming. More recently, there has been a strong focus on environmentally sustainable businesses and enterprises, particularly in green technology, often funded by international investors.

Finally, in parts of South and South East Asia – notably Bangladesh and India – social innovation has emerged to address a combination of minimalist state welfare structures and growing welfare failures. This did not reflect state failure or welfare crises on an African scale, but rather was the product of a context in which the relationship between the private individual and the state was often remote and problematic. In the case of the Grameen Bank and BRAC in Bangladesh, for example, social innovation reached a national scale, with these two organisations functioning as a shadow state delivering financial services, employment, health and education to many more citizens than the elected state.

Social innovation offers an exciting space for research and debate, but it also offers the potential to bring about substantive changes in the alignment of resources, policy and societal structures to address the major issues of modernity across many different countries. This is very much a dynamic project – a constantly renewing work-in-progress that has an in-built self-reflexivity and self-critique – working across many sectors (and their interfaces) and at many socio-structural levels. The empirical project to test and map the impact and effectiveness of social innovation is only at an early stage of development, but a better understanding of the trends, blueprints, challenges and opportunities is emerging. It is to this vibrant and international conversation that this book hopes to contribute.

Notes

1. There are two additional issues here. First, there is a growing disconnect between traditional services and new needs – health services, for example, were originally designed to deal with acute rather than chronic disease, but it is chronic disease which is becoming more prevalent across many societies. Second, it has proved difficult to offset growing demands on services through cost savings and efficiencies.
2. Broadly known as New Public Management (Hood, 1991), this new paradigm in public administration was based on the idea that if applied to the public sector, private sector management tools and techniques and the creation of quasi markets or internal markets to enable choice and competition could drive innovation and efficiency savings and increase user satisfaction.
3. Some of these themes have been further developed more recently by the Design for Social Innovation and Sustainability (DESIS) Network: http://www.desis-network.org [Accessed 26 November 2014].

References

Alter, K. (2006) 'Social Enterprise Models and Their Mission and Money Relationships', in A. Nicholls (ed.), *Social Entrepreneurship. New Models of Sustainable Social Change.* Oxford: Oxford University Press, pp. 205–32.

Bartlett, J. (2009a) *At Your Service: Navigating the Future Market in Health and Social Care*. London: Demos.

Bartlett, J. (2009b) *Getting More for Less: Efficiency in the Public Sector*. London: Demos.

Battilana, J. and Dorado, S. (2010) 'Building Sustainable Hybrid Organizations: The Case of Commercial Microfinance Organizations', *Academy of Management Journal*, 53 (6): 1419–40.

Bloom, P. and Chatterji, A. (2009) 'Scaling Social Entrepreneurial Impact', *California Management Review*, 51: 114–33.

Bloom, P. and Dees, J.G. (2008) 'Cultivate Your Ecosystem', *Stanford Social Innovation Review*, 6: 46–53.

Bovaird, T. (2006) 'Developing New Forms of Partnership with the "Market" in Procurement of Public Services', *Public Administration*, 84 (1): 81–102.

Davis, G., McAdam, D., Scott W.R. and Zald, M. (eds) (2005) *Social Movements and Organization Theory*. Cambridge: Cambridge University Press.

Dees, J.G. (1998) *The Meaning of Social Entrepreneurship*, available at: http://www.caseatduke.org/documents/dees_sedef.pdf [Accessed 26 November 2014.]

Drayton, W. (2002) 'The Citizen Sector: Becoming As Entrepreneurial and Competitive As Business', *California Management Review*, 44 (3): 120–32.

Ebrahim, A. and Rangan, K.V. (2010) 'The Limits of Nonprofit Impact: A Contingency Framework for Measuring Social Performance', Harvard Business School General Management Unit Working Paper, 10–99.

Emerson, J. (2003) 'The Blended Value Proposition: Integrating Social and Financial Results', *California Management Review*, 45 (4): 35–51.

Fairweather, G. (1967) *Methods for Experimental Social Innovation*. Hoboken, NJ: John Wiley.

Hämäläinen, T. and Heiskala, R. (eds) (2007) *Social Innovations, Institutional Change and Economic Performance: Making Sense of Structural Adjustment Processes in Industrial Sectors, Regions and Societies*. Cheltenham, UK: SITRA and Edward Elgar.

Henderson, H. (1993) 'Social Innovation and Citizen Movements', *Futures*, April: 322–38.

Holt, K. (1971) 'Social Innovations in Organizations', *International Studies of Management and Organization*, 1 (3): 235–52.

Hood, C. (1991) 'A Public Management for All Seasons?', *Public Administration*, 69 (1): 3–19.

Kerlin, J. (ed.) (2009) *Social Enterprise: A Global Comparison*. Medford, MA: Tufts University Press.

Klein, N. (2002) *Fences and Windows*. London: Flamingo.

Leadbeater, C. (1997) *The Rise of the Social Entrepreneur*. London: Demos.

Mair, J. and Marti, I. (2009) 'Entrepreneurship In and Around Institutional Voids: A Case Study from Bangladesh', Journal of Business Venturing, 24 (5): 419–35.

Moore, M. and Westley, F. (2011) 'Surmountable Chasms: Networks and Social Innovation for Resilient Systems', *Ecology and Society*, 16 (1): 1–5.

Moss Kanter, R. (1999) 'From Spare Change to Real Change: The Social Sector as *Beta* Site for Business Innovation', *Harvard Business Review*, May–June: 122–32.

Moulaert, F., Martinelli, F., Gonzalez, S. and Swyngedouw, E. (2007) 'Introduction: Social Innovation and Governance in European Cities', *European Urban and Regional Studies*, 14 (3): 195–209.

Moulaert, F., MacCallum, D., Mehmood, A. and Hamdouch, A. (eds) (2014a) *The International Handbook on Social Innovation: Collective Action, Social Learning and Transdisciplinary Research*. Cheltenham: Edward Elgar.

Moulaert, F., MacCallum, D., Mehmood, A. and Hamdouch, A. (2014b) 'General Introduction: The Return of Social Innovation as a Scientific Concept and a Social Practice', in Moulaert, F.,Mulgan, G. (2010) 'Measuring Social Value', *Stanford Social Innovation Review*, Summer: 38–43.

Mulgan, G., Tucker, S., Ali, R. and Sanders, B. (2007) *Social Innovation: What it is, why it matters and how it can be accelerated*. Oxford: Skoll Centre for Social Entrepreneurship.

Mumford, M. (2002) 'Social Innovation: Ten Cases from Benjamin Franklin', *Creativity Research Journal*, 14 (2): 253–56.

Murray, R., Caulier-Grice, J. and Mulgan, G. (2010) *The Open Book of Social Innovation*. London: Young Foundation.

NESsT (2005) *Risky Business: The Impacts of Merging Mission and Business*. Santiago: NESsT Learning Series.

Nicholls, A. (ed.) (2006) *Social Entrepreneurship: New Models of Sustainable Social Change*. Oxford: Oxford University Press.

Nicholls, A. (2010a) 'The Legitimacy of Social Entrepreneurship: Reflexive Isomorphism in a Pre-Paradigmatic Field', *Entrepreneurship Theory and Practice*, 34 (4): 611–33.

Nicholls, A. (2010b) 'The Institutionalization of Social Investment: The Interplay of Investment Logics and Investor Rationalities', *Journal of Social Entrepreneurship*, 1 (1): 70–100.

Nicholls, A. (2013) 'The Social Entrepreneurship–Social Policy Nexus in Developing Countries', in Walker, D. and Surrender, R. (eds), *Social Policy in a Developing World: A Comparative Analysis*. Oxford: Oxford University Press, pp. 183–216.

Nicholls, A. and Cho, A. (2006) 'Social Entrepreneurship: The Structuration of a Field', in Nicholls, A. (ed.), *Social Entrepreneurship: New Models of Sustainable Social Change*. Oxford: Oxford University Press, pp. 99–118.

Nicholls, A. and Murdock, A. (eds) (2012) *Social Innovation: Blurring Boundaries to Reconfigure Markets*. Basingstoke: Palgrave Macmillan.

Nicholls, A. and Opal, C. (2005) *Fair Trade: Market-Driven Ethical Consumption*. London: Sage.

Nyssens, M. (2006) *Social Enterprise*. Basingstoke: Palgrave Macmillan

OECD (2011) *LEED Forum on Social Innovations*.

Offer, A. (2006) *The Challenge of Affluence*. Oxford: Oxford University Press.

O'Donohoe, N., Leijonhufvud, C. and Saltuk, Y. (2010) *Impact Investments: An Emerging Asset Class*. New York: JP Morgan Global Research and the Rockefeller Foundation.

Phills, J., Deiglmeier, K. and Miller, D. (2008) 'Rediscovering Social Innovation', *Stanford Social Innovation Review*, Fall: 34–43.

Osborne, D. and Gaebler, T. (1992) *Reinventing Government: How the Entrepreneurial Spirit Is Transforming the Public Sector*. Reading, MA: Addison-Wesley.

Pot, F. and Vaas, F. (2008) 'Social Innovation, the New Challenge for Europe', *International Journal of Productivity and Performance Management*, 57 (6): 468–73.

Porter, M. and Kramer, M. (2011) 'Creating Shared Value', *Harvard Business Review*, January–February, 89 (1/2): 62–77.

26 *Alex Nicholls, Julie Simon and Madeleine Gabriel*

Prahalad, C.K. (2006) *The Fortune at the Bottom of the Pyramid*. Upper Saddle River, NJ: Pearson.
Rayner, S. (2006) *Wicked Problems: Clumsy Solutions – Diagnoses and Prescriptions for Environmental Ills*. Jack Beale Memorial Lecture on Global Environment.
Rittel, H. and Webber, M. (1973) 'Dilemmas in a General Theory of Planning', *Policy Sciences*, 4: 155–69.
Schumpeter, J.A. (1942) *Capitalism, Socialism and Democracy*. New York: Harper and Row.
Suchman, M. (1995) 'Managing Legitimacy: Strategic and Institutional Approaches', *Academy of Management Review*, 20 (3): 571–610.
Tracey, P. and Jarvis, C. (2006) 'An Enterprising Failure: Why a Promising Social Franchise Collapsed', *Stanford Social Innovation Review*, Spring: 66–70.
Westley, F. and Antadze, N. (2010) 'Making a Difference: Strategies for Scaling Social Innovation for Greater Impact', *The Innovation Journal: The Public Sector Innovation Journal*, 15 (2): 1–19.
Zeschky, M., Widenmayer, B. and Gassmann, O. (2011) 'Frugal Innovation in Emerging Markets', *Research-Technology Management*, 54 (4): 38–45.

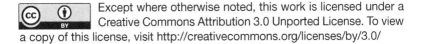

Part I
Researching Social Innovation

This page intentionally left blank

Social Innovations as Drivers of Social Change – Exploring Tarde's Contribution to Social Innovation Theory Building

Jürgen Howaldt, Ralf Kopp and Michael Schwarz

Introduction

In the context of seemingly intractable social challenges such as climate change, environmental destruction, youth unemployment and social exclusion, social innovation has emerged as a potentially sustainable solution. It is often assumed that social innovation can lead to social change (see, for example, Cooperrider and Pasmore, 1991; Mulgan *et al.*, 2007; BEPA, 2010). However, the relationship between social innovation and social change remains underexplored:

> Rather than being used as a specifically defined specialist term with its own definable area of studies, social innovation is used more as a kind of descriptive metaphor in the context of phenomena of real world problems, social change, and the modernisation of society. (Howaldt and Schwarz, 2010, p. 49)

There is still no consistent or coherent concept of social innovation grounded in social theory that is suitable for empirical research (Mulgan, 2012; European Commission, 2013, p. 26). The result is 'an incoherent body of knowledge on social innovation with the consequence that there is a lack of clarity of the concept of social innovation' (Rüede and Lurtz, 2012, p. 2). The scientific discussion on social innovation is polarised between an actor-centred, individualistic, attitude-orientated perspective on the one hand and an implicit, structuralist perspective on the other. Social innovations are either attributed to individualistic acts or considered as deterministic results of external context (Cajaiba-Santana, 2014; European Commission, 2013). Given the fact that social theory does not yet play an important role in social innovation research

(Howaldt and Schwarz, 2010; Mulgan, 2012; Moulaert *et al.*, 2013; European Commission, 2013), its possible contributions are worthy of exploration.

In light of the increasing importance of social innovation, this chapter focuses on a conception of social innovation that is grounded in social theory, as a precondition for the development of an integrated theory of socio-technological innovation in which social innovation is more than a mere appendage, side-effect and result of technical innovation. Against this background, social innovation is defined here as a new combination[1] or configuration of practices in areas of social action, prompted by certain actors or constellations of actors with the ultimate goal of coping better with needs and problems than is possible by using existing practices (Howaldt and Schwarz, 2010, p. 54). An innovation is, therefore, 'social' to the extent that it varies social action and is socially accepted and diffused in society (be it throughout society, through large parts of it or only in certain societal sub-areas). Depending on the circumstances of social change, interests, policies and power, social ideas and successfully implemented social innovations may be transformed and, ultimately, institutionalised as regular social practice, that is, made routine. From this perspective, social innovations can be seen as actions that spread through society as a result of imitation, bringing about social change: a 'process of change in the social structure of a society in its constitutive institutions, cultural patterns, associated social actions and conscious awareness' (Zapf, 2003, p. 427). Only by taking into account the unique properties and specifications of social innovation will it be possible to understand the systemic connection and interdependence of social and technological innovation processes to analyse the relationship between social innovation and social change.

This chapter aims to outline how Gabriel Tarde's social theory can be of benefit in developing a theoretically grounded concept of social innovation and how it can be reinterpreted in terms of practice theory.[2] In comparison with action, system and structural theories, this perspective on social innovation is based upon a modified understanding of the 'social' as social practices and their reconfiguration as a core element of social innovation (Shove *et al.*, 2012). Practice theories overcome the dichotomies between structure and action, subject and object, rule and application, society and the individual, that arbitrarily define micro and macro levels or sociological 'reality rules' (Latour and Lépinay, 2010, p. 114). Tarde focuses on social practices as the central theoretical and analytical category and last unit of sociality. The social world is, therefore, composed of specific, although interdependent practices: practices of governance; practices of organising; practices of partnership; practices of negotiations; practices of self (Reckwitz, 2003); practices of comfort, cleanliness and convenience (Shove, 2003); practices of working and nurturing (Hargraves *et al.*, 2011) and practices of consumption (Brand, 2011; Warde, 2005).

By defining social innovation 'as a new combination or configuration of practices', an approach can be found in recent social theory that focuses on the social practices and dynamics of change. In the conclusion of their paper analysing definitions of social innovation from various disciplines, Rüede and Lurtz (2012) recognised the potential for future research in practice theory. As part of the 'practice turn' in the field of social sciences (Schatzki *et al.*, 2001; Reckwitz, 2003), practice theories – for example those of Bourdieu, Giddens and Latour – can be seen as important components of a theory of social innovation (Howaldt and Schwarz, 2010), essential for analysing 'the dynamics of social practice' (Shove *et al.*, 2012). In this sense, social innovation can be:

> Interpreted as a process of collective creation in which the members of a certain collective unit learn, invent and lay out new rules for the social game of collaboration and of conflict or, in a word, a new social **practice**, and in this process they acquire the necessary cognitive, rational and organizational skills. (Crozier and Friedberg, 1993, p. 19) [emphasis added]

Social innovation encompasses new practices (concepts, policy instruments, new forms of cooperation and organisation), methods, processes and regulations that are developed and/or adopted by citizens, customers and politicians, in order to meet social demands and to resolve societal challenges in a better way than existing practices.

This chapter starts with a short review of Ogburn's concept of social change, which laid the foundation for a specialised sociology of change. Ogburn's concept provided important input into a better understanding of technological *and* social innovation on the one hand and social change on the other. However, it is only through recourse to the social theory of Tarde that the opportunities arising from a sociology of innovation for the analysis of social change become apparent. This is the subject of the following section. For Tarde, social macrophenomena such as social structures, systems and social change are 'easy to describe, but hard to explain, because the true complexity resides in the microphenomena' (Gilgenmann, 2010, p. 2). His basic idea was to explain social change from a 'post-foundationalism' (Marchart, 2013) perspective and not objectivistically (like Durkheim) from the top down, in terms of social facts and structures (Gilgenmann, 2010, p. 7), or subjectivistically, following the approaches of social phenomenology, symbolic interaction or ethno-methodology (Marchart, 2013, p. 45). Recourse to Tarde helps to overcome the restriction of the concept of innovation to purely economic aspects. Taking his micro sociological approach as a starting point, key implications are outlined in the final section of this chapter. This analysis allows a theoretically grounded understanding of social innovation on which innovation policy can be built.

Theoretical foundations for social innovation

Theories of social change have been at the core of sociology since its beginning. So far, however, no consistent theory has emerged. In particular, theory has difficulties with social change that is not continuous and linear (Weymann, 1998, p. 17). In so far as sociological theories deal with processes of change, they do so almost universally from the perspective of the reproduction, and not the transformation of social order. Social change in the sense of fundamental transformations at the macro (structural) level – that function as 'mega trends' or as a sequence of phases separated by (epochal) upheavals – belongs to the field of the sociological diagnosis of epochs. This can manage completely without social theory and at the same time is often mistaken for it (Osrecki, 2011).

Social innovation, as an analytical category, has remained, at best, a secondary topic in both classical and modern social theory – often in relation to concepts such as social differentiation and social integration, social order and social development, modernisation and transformation. The social sciences refuse to a large extent to 'present and list as social innovations the relevant social changes' that they have discovered and studied (Rammert, 2010, p. 26).[3]

Ogburn theorised the basis for a comprehensive theory of innovation. Ogburn made 'cultural lag' – the difference in the time it takes for the comparatively slow, non-material culture to catch up with the faster developing material culture – his analytical starting point. He systematically differentiated between technological and social innovations (and inventions) as critical factors in social change. He also explained that the use of the term 'inventions' is not restricted to the technological but can also be used to include 'social inventions', such as the League of Nations:

> Invention is defined as a combination of existing and known elements of culture, material and/or non-material, or a modification of

one to form a new one. [...] By inventions we do not mean only the basic or important inventions, but the minor ones and the improvements. Inventions, then, are the evidence on which we base our observations of social evolution. (Ogburn, 1969, p. 56 ff.)

Thus, Ogburn was convinced that in the interplay between invention, accumulation, exchange and adaptation, he had discovered the basic elements of 'cultural development' and hence – like Darwin for biological evolution – had developed a model to explain social evolution.

Although Ogburn's approach allowed for the analysis of social innovations as drivers of social change, the debate in the field of the sociology of technology concerning the relationship between technological and social innovation and social change has tended to conceptualise the former as independent from technological development.[4] Ogburn started by exploring the interrelationship between the 'material' and 'non-material elements of culture'. He assigned to 'innovations in the non-material field' the character of 'secondary changes' in the sense of an 'adaptation to a change in the material field' (Ogburn, 1969). This was further conceptualised as an 'invention in the field of technology or a discovery in applied science' that can have an extraordinarily large effect 'with great likelihood in changes in other cultural fields' or even in the 'formation of completely new social institutions' (ibid., p. 67). In this original interpretation, social change was understood as a process of the diffusion of innovations and, hence, as the imitation or adoption of a (technological or social) invention by others – sometimes as an emergent innovation process in which social innovations are primarily ascribed the function of a (delayed) adaptation in the sense of a 'cultural lag' (Ogburn, 1969, p. 64).

At the same time, it is overlooked that in his later work, Ogburn referred to an important misunderstanding of his concept. In an essay published in 1957, he wrote:

In most of the examples I gave at that time, the starting point was a technological change or a scientific discovery, and the lagging, adaptive cultural element generally was a social organisation or an ideology. These examples led some researchers to think the cultural lag theory was a technological interpretation of history. Yet when the cultural lag theory was published, I pointed out that the independent variable could just as well be an ideology or other non-technological variable [...]. So the fact that the technological changes always came first was simply due to the fact that at a particular point in time, only certain observations were available; but it is not an inherent part of the theory (Ogburn, 1969, p. 139).[5]

Yet, these aspects of Ogburn's theory – that could have formed the basis for a comprehensive theory of innovation – remained largely ignored in a wider theoretical context in which there was a one-sided focus on the relevance of technology for social change (Freeman, 1974; OECD, 1997).

Only in recent years has a new understanding of the innovation process become more important, in which openness towards society is central (FORA, 2010, p. 15 ff.). Individual aspects of this development are reflected in terms and concepts such as 'open innovation', 'customer and user integration', '(innovation) networks', 'multi-stakeholder dialogues' and 'the new power of the citizenry' (Marg *et al.*, 2013). The development of 'robust design concepts' (Gross *et al.*, 2005) and institutions that combine research and innovation with 'post-conventional forms of participation' (Marg *et al.*, 2013, p. 8) are explicitly the subject matter of, for example, transition management, transdisciplinary sustainability research, governance research and, particularly, network research (for example, Powell and Grodal, 2005). Thus, at the same time, social innovation has started to be seen as a type of innovation that is distinguishable from technological innovation with its own subject area, sphere of influence and field of application (Howaldt and Schwarz, 2010).

However, it is not possible to define social innovations solely by referring to a distinct social sphere or to socially desirable outcomes as their key purpose (Rammert, 2010, p. 40). Rather, what is at issue is the substantive core of the innovation. With social innovations, the new does not manifest itself in the medium of technological artefacts, but at the level of social practices. If it is accepted that the invention and diffusion of the steam engine, the computer or the smartphone should be regarded differently from the invention and social spread of a national system of healthcare provision, the concept of corporate social responsibility (CSR) or a system of micro lending, then it stands to reason that there is an intrinsic difference between technological and social innovations. While it is true that all innovations, regardless of their object, can be viewed as a social phenomenon, this does not obviate the need empirically to research the commonalities and differences between these two types of innovation. Even if, in reality, both types closely connect with each other in socio-technological systems, the need for analytical distinction does not disappear. This is all the more urgent given that existing sociological innovation research, that has emanated mainly from the sociology of technology, centres on the investigation of technological innovations:

> If one asks what are the relevant innovations of the last 100 years or if one reads lists of the most important innovations, the answer usually is a series of technological inventions. (Rammert, 2010, p. 25)[6]

From this perspective, it becomes more important to devote greater attention to social innovation as a mechanism of change residing at the micro and meso levels. There are two main reasons for this. First, the shortcomings of older models of social change – and of an economically and technologically focused innovation model – have become increasingly apparent when dealing with the key social challenges (Howaldt and Schwarz, 2010). Second, new forms of social self-management, of the 'criticism that actually takes place in society' (Vobruba, 2013, p. 160), are becoming increasingly evident.

In the context of broader debates about sustainable development, there is a question about the relationship between social innovation and the transformative change of existing structures, policies, institutions and behaviours that aim to improve the quality of life. How can processes of transformative social change (Moore and Westley, 2011) be initiated which link social innovations from the mainstream of society with the intended social transformation processes? This

> refers to moving an innovation into a broader system and creating transformation through the linking of opportunities and resources across scales. Quite often, to effect transformative change in a broader system, the innovation will be reconfigured into an entirely new form to suit that context. (Moore and Westley, 2011)

Tarde's analysis of social change

Recourse to Tarde may be helpful in gaining a better theoretical understanding of the relationship between social innovation and social change (Howaldt *et al.*, 2014). Instead of explaining social change objectivistically or subjectivistically, he argued in terms of social practices of invention and imitation. Tarde's contribution to the understanding of a sociology of innovation can be used for developing a concept of social innovation as a social mechanism of change residing at the micro and meso levels. This seems all the more necessary given that Tarde's social theory – in terms of its implications and usefulness in the analysis of innovation – has been little explored until now.[7]

Revisiting Tarde's social theory – which, at its core, is a sociology of innovation – allows a widening of perspective on the nature of social innovation. This goes beyond the economic and technological innovations noted by Schumpeter (1964) and, after him, by the sociology of technology focused either on the social consequences of technology (Ogburn, 1937) or on the 'social shaping of technology' (MacKenzie and Wajcman, 1985; Williams and Sörensen, 2002) or 'social construction of technological systems' (Bijker, Hughes and Pinch, 1987). At the same time, this new focus reveals the blind spots of a narrow economic view. Because Tarde places the laws of the practices of imitation at the centre of his theory of social development, the associated micro foundations of social phenomena provide vital input into an integrative theory of innovation. It enables a discovery of how social phenomena – conditions and constructs – come into being and how they change. The key to this discovery is to analyse the development of social inventions and innovations as well as the associated social practices of their imitation.

Unlike Schumpeter, for whom the innovator – namely the 'entrepreneur' – is the focus of interest, Tarde is concerned with the *inventions* that are understood to be the central driver of social change. For Tarde, these are the many small inventions and ideas,

> which were difficult or easy to arrive at and mostly went unnoticed at the time of their arising, which therefore are usually almost exclusively inglorious and nameless. (Tarde, 2009b, p. 26)

These countless inventions can change society and its practices through multiple acts of imitation, and only as a result of imitation do these inventions become an innovation and a true social phenomenon: 'In the realm of the social, everything takes place as invention and imitation, with imitation forming the rivers and inventions the mountains' (ibid, p. 27). For Tarde, imitation is the central mechanism of social reproduction and of social change:

> All similarities of social origin that belong to the social world are the fruits of some kind of imitation, be it the imitation of customs or fashions through sympathy or obedience, instruction or education, naïve or carefully considered imitation. (ibid, p. 38)

According to Tarde, imitations always involve variations and simultaneously bring about innovations in social structures and practices.

Added to this are individual initiatives and rebellions against prevailing morals, customs, rules – interruptions or crossings of 'imitation streams' – that are transferred and imitated from person to person, leading to social innovations.

'Researching the "many small inventions", according to Tarde, is a matter for a sociology which "has become a truly experimental science"' (Balke, 2009, p. 151). Social change must be viewed as a contingent phenomenon that resists any general (macro) theory. Because of the basic interdependence between social structures and social negotiation (Joas, 1992, p. 60), in every reproduced action there exists simultaneously the momentum of creation, change and transformation. The benefit of conceptualising a micro foundation of the social realm consists in decoding the recursive processes based on many small social inventions, ideas, initiatives and innovations as drivers of social change.

If social micro units are accorded constitutive importance for the dynamics of society, it becomes possible to describe social change not simply as a trend in the sense of a transition from one state at time t to another at time t_1, but to see it as an independent non-deterministic reality. Thus, social innovation can be understood as a 'starting point for creating social dynamics behind technological innovations' (Geels, 2006, p. 6), that is, as change that arises as a result of constant changes by inventive and imitating actors (Tarde, 2009c, p. 67). With Tarde, social change can be traced back to the effects of small and micro units. Change is explained from the bottom up in current discourse on social transformation processes, as a fundamental prerequisite for substantial change (Paech, 2012). Its emergence from unintended and intentional deviations from the ideal of imitation provides the possibility of linking micro and macro perspectives (Gilgenmann, 2010, p. 7) – connecting a view of individuals in their society with a view of the society as a whole.

While the macro perspective looks at how social facts and constructs impact on social life, that is, it refers to the power of structures, institutions etc. to shape actions (see, for example, Hasse and Krücken, 2005, p. 17), the micro perspective on the social realm focuses on the 'law of their formation' (Tarde, 2009a, p. 101) and discovers how they emerge and transform, that is, it enables a micro foundation of social change. The key to analysis, therefore, lies in identifying social innovations that spread through society as a result of imitation to bring about social change: a 'process of change in the social structure of a society in its constitutive institutions, cultural patterns, associated social actions and conscious awareness' (Zapf, 2003, p. 427). These are non-teleological and highly contingent processes.

Tarde devised and pursued an analytical agenda that made social innovation the starting point for understanding social conditions and how they change. Accordingly,

> the real causes of change consist of a chain of certainly very numerous ideas, which however are different and discontinuous, yet they are connected together by even far more numerous acts of imitation, for which they serve as a model. (Tarde, 2009b, p. 26)

For Tarde, there was only one decisive factor driving the constitution of society: the mutual imitation of individuals, kept moving by innovations of others (Keller, 2009, p. 233).

Development and change are enabled by invention, by successful initiatives that are imitated, and hence become (social) innovations: 'Social transformations are explained by the individual initiatives which are imitated' (Tarde, 1902, p. 1; as quoted by Michaelides and Theologou, 2010, p. 363). These are the directing, determining and explanatory force, the 'key drivers of social transformation processes' (Moebius, 2009, p. 269).

A new understanding of innovation and a new innovation policy?

Based on Tarde's concept of innovation, key conclusions can be drawn with regard to a new understanding of innovation that contributes to its theoretical foundations and to the policy concepts associated with it.

Social innovation as a driver of social change

Social innovation is a central driver and element of social change. Hence, it is not surprising that it occupies a key position in debates concerned with how best to address major social challenges. It is important here to look at the findings of research on the genesis of technology and, in particular, at those approaches that tackle questions of transition management and sociotechnical system change (cf. Geels and Schot, 2007). Geels and Schot pursued a multi-level approach (MLP) by distinguishing three levels: niche innovations, the sociotechnical regime and the sociotechnical landscape. They understood 'transitions as outcomes of alignment between developments at multiple levels' or 'as changes from one sociotechnical regime to another' (ibid., p. 399). Starting from these basic assumptions, the authors developed a typology of transformation processes that differentiated between available resources (internal/external) and the degree of coordination. Whereas 'endogenous renewal' is performed by actors within an existing regime – in the form of consensus-oriented and planned efforts as a response to perceived pressure using resources internal to the regime – the 'reorientation of trajectories' results from a shock. In contrast, an 'emergent transformation' results from uncoordinated pressure from outside of the system boundaries, while 'purposive transition' is initiated from outside the existing regime as an intended and coordinated transformation process (ibid., p. 401).

These considerations allow for a closer inspection of the relationship between social innovation and social change. Seen in the light of Tarde's approach, new practices of social action would, first, be discovered and invented at the micro level, in social niches. From there, they could be imitated and spread by particular actors or networks of actors,[8] changing themselves in this process. Furthermore, new social practices can develop outside of the prevailing imitation streams. Together with changes in the sociotechnical landscape – that exert pressure on the predominant sociotechnical system (for example, through environmental changes such as climate change) – or systemic dysfunctions (financial crisis, unemployment, social inequality, etc.), these developments can result in the destabilisation of the system and open up windows of opportunity for creating and spreading out niche innovations leading to transformation and, ultimately, the institutionalisation of new social practices.

With regard to the need for a comprehensive transformation of the dominant economic growth model, Meadows *et al.* (1972, p. 173) pointed out 'that social innovation can no longer lag behind technological innovation'. Likewise, the directed, rapid and far-reaching transformation that is demanded by the notion of sustainable development explicitly addresses radical changes at the level of political governance and social practices that go far beyond technological innovations. Transformative social change here is no longer understood to be a largely uncontrolled outcome of gradual evolutionary developments (cf. Osterhammel, 2011) but as something that can, in principle, be shaped by society – 'by the actors and their innovations' (Schneidewind, 2013, p. 123). To rely on new technologies alone to achieve this is regarded as insufficient on account of the problem-shifting, secondary, consequences and rebound effects that may frequently accompany them. The necessary transformation – that is already emerging in many areas, yet at the same time is also comprehensively blocked in others – needs to be shaped by society and demands new concepts of welfare, diverse social innovation, and an as yet unattained level of international cooperation (cf. WGBU, 2011).

This makes it necessary to place the transformation of ideas and initiatives as an independent form of innovation at the centre of processes of social self-organisation and real-life experiments embedded in them, as well as imitation processes going beyond them, and, relating to this, at the centre of a 'truly experimental science' (Tarde, 2009a, p. 101).

The importance of successful imitation to disseminate social innovation

Tarde's approach can also be used to bring about an important shift in perspective. Rather than constantly producing new individual inventions, it seems more meaningful creatively to reconfigure the opportunities presented by existing inventions through social practice:

> The qualities that in any age and in any land make a man superior are those which make him better able to understand the discoveries already made and exploit the inventions already devised. (Tarde, 2009b, p. 251)

In this context, the wealth of a nation, for Tarde, was rooted in its ability to 'use the knowledge of its time in a particular way' (ibid., p. 254). If, like Tarde, a situation is explained from the imitation practices of people, then the specific cultural frameworks need to be decoded.

At the same time, inventions can also be adopted from other cultural groups. Not only Tarde, but later Ogburn too, emphasised:

> The inhabitants of a cultural group can also come into possession of inventions, without making inventions themselves, by importing them from other countries. In fact, most inventions found within a specific area are imported [...] (Ogburn, 1969, p. 62)

Ogburn also pointed to the Renaissance in Italy, which owed its creativity to the inflow of ideas from antiquity.

With the shift in perspective from inventions to social practices of imitation, the key question in the context of diffusion is how new social practices come into being from the imitation of social practices. The concept of imitation underpins an understanding of innovation that focuses on social practices. Practices of organisation, consumption, production and so forth become the central object of Tarde's conception of imitation. This includes the production and consumption of technological artefacts. The spread of social ideas or initiatives through imitation tends to combine with other inventions to form increasingly complex and more widely acting social innovations. Imitation always involves variation and, to this extent, imitations constantly bring about innovations in social structures and constructs.

The diffusion of social innovation

With regard to the debate surrounding the importance of social innovation (cf. Franz, Hochgerner and Howaldt, 2012), the question of the possibilities for its (fast and sustained) spread or diffusion has become important. Rogers, who has decisively influenced research on the diffusion of innovations, also regarded Tarde as a source of inspiration for his own ideas and believed him to have been far ahead of his time (cf. Rogers, 2003, p. 41). Rogers' approach to diffusion, which is still dominant in business contexts, exhibited a series of links to Tarde that can assist in understanding the mechanisms by which social innovation can spread. At the same time, however, Rogers' reinterpretation of Tarde has contributed to a problematic narrowing of diffusion research. His references to Tarde are by no means 'slightly different concepts' (Rogers, 2003, p. 41), rather, they are a serious change of perspective. Whereas Tarde's sociology is interested in the genesis of the new as social practice, Rogers took innovation (as rational problem-solving produced by science and technology) for granted and focused on its transfer into different areas of application. Thus, Rogers severed the direct connection between invention and innovation – through which an invention becomes an innovation – and reduced the creative process of imitation to its adaptive function. According to Rogers' definition, the innovation precedes the diffusion process. Diffusion refers to the acceptance and adoption of the innovation by the relevant individuals – namely, the innovation gains acceptance instead of being produced.

The associated diffusion research asks, with regard to the intended target groups, how the innovation can be substantively modified and prepared for information and communication purposes, so that the adoption rate can be increased and/or accelerated. It attempts to develop 'push strategies' aimed at speeding up the introduction of solutions into society (outside-in processes). Diffusion research is highly affected by a pro-innovation bias. It is guided by the conviction that the innovation is effective, with the assumption that the main problem is how to convince various target groups to adopt it. Diffusion research, therefore, generates an asymmetrical communication relationship between the developers and the users of problem solutions or innovations. Society itself – as the original source of innovation and creativity – is a blind spot in diffusion research. On the other hand, that which Rogers defines as the diffusion of an idea, technology and so on would be described in Tarde's terms as a process which initiates new acts of imitation and triggers cultural learning processes, while interrupting existing imitation streams and advancing social change. Inventions open up new opportunities, expose problems and shortcomings in established practices, initiate processes of learning and reflection, and ultimately enable new social practices to emerge. To this extent, for any invention, it is necessary to enquire about its potential to trigger such imitation and learning processes and, hence, generate new social practices. Only through the development of new social practices or changes to existing practices do their effects unfurl and inventions become innovations and, hence, social facts. In reality, therefore, the process of diffusion is a process centred on changing patterns of behaviour that sets social learning processes in motion that are triggered by new inventions.

The internal logic of these processes of imitation and social learning, that Tarde made the focus of his attention, determine the innovation process. The unpredictable dynamics of the self-organised interaction of heterogeneous actors dealing in various ways with innovations requires 'more realistic assumptions about decision-making processes' (Schröder *et al.*, 2011, p. 28) and an approach that ultimately inverts Rogers' perspective. Whereas traditional diffusion research offers *ex-post* explanations of how individual innovations have ended up in social practice, the goal here is to develop approaches to understanding the genesis of innovations from the broad range of social practice. This focuses on the extent to which they are concerned not so much with the transfer and modification of isolated singular innovation offerings but, rather, with multiple innovation streams, fed by an evolutionary interplay of invention and imitation: the 'cycle of interlinked and recurring (repeating with variations) actions' (Tarde, 2009a, p. 73).

The wisdom of the crowds and new forms of governance

Tarde's proposition that any invention is embedded in a dense network of imitation streams shows that social innovations are, first and foremost, ensemble performances, requiring interaction between many actors. Above all, they need the 'wisdom of crowds'. As 'open' innovation – meaning the engagement of users, citizens and consumers in the innovation process – is a key characteristic of the new innovation paradigm (cf. Howaldt and Kopp, 2012, p. 45), there is also greater experimentation in innovation processes both in the world of scientific laboratories and in society (Krohn, 2005). Social innovators challenge established rules, routines, pathways and models in politics, business and society – such as the economisation of all areas of life and an inevitable link between prosperity and growth (Leggewie and Welzer, 2009; Jackson, 2012; WBGU, 2011) – and call them into question. In doing so, they lead the way to changed, alternative social practices and lifestyles that are the basis and relevant drivers of transformative social change (cf. for example, Jonker, 2012). The perspective of a conception of social innovation founded in social theory, therefore, focuses on the interfaces between the self-referencing social sectors of government, business and civil society – that are distinct, and largely shielded, from each other – and on their respective rationales of action and regulatory mechanisms, their limited problem-solving capacities, and other associated problems. Regarding the governance question of how these interfaces could be reconfigured, established patterns of control and coordination may be added to, expanded and remoulded via processes such as self-organisation, inter-sectoral cooperation, networks and new forms of knowledge production. The associated processes of 'cross-sector fertilisation' (Phills, Deiglmeier and Miller, 2008, p. 40 ff.) and convergence of sectors (Austin *et al.*, 2007) increasingly enable a kind of *blended value creation* (Emerson, 2003) and, in some cases, promote a 'moralisation of markets' (Stehr, 2007). Such cross-sector fertilisations and convergences require and enable far-reaching social innovations that set in motion and spur the blurring of sector boundaries. In view of the complex interdependencies between the different social sectors, system levels and levels of action, social innovations are necessarily separate from, and in addition to, technological and economic innovations 'in order to reach systemic synergies, productivity growth, increasing returns and steadily growing incomes' (Hämäläinen and Heiskala, 2007).

Social practices are basic operations whose execution and repetition drives stability and instability, order as well as the emergence of something new. Changing social practices usually involves a drawn-out, contingent and self-organised process that, as Tarde pointed out, is subject to its own 'laws' – the laws of imitation. Previous policy attempts to manage the implementation of new practices (for example, in organisations, in mobility and in health systems) have generally proven to be difficult. A comprehensive innovation policy agenda would, in addition to supporting new technologies, also focus on social innovation by enabling actors 'to suspend established routines and patterns, as only then can new ideas and behaviours thrive' (Adolf, 2012, p. 40). Such an agenda would foster the necessary freedom to do this and the opportunities 'to share objectified and personal (implicit) knowledge' (ibid., p. 41).

One of the key tasks in this regard is a redefinition of the relationships between policy and the 'new power of the citizenry' (Marg *et al.*, 2013), civil society engagement, the many and diverse initiatives and movements 'for the transformation of our type of industrial society' (Welzer, 2013, p. 187):

> A central element here is to enable citizens [in the sense of empowerment – authors' note] to share in responsibility for the future, which should not be equated with personal responsibility in the neoliberal sense. (Rückert-John, 2013, p. 291)

This demands a change in perspective from a logic of transfer to a logic of transformation. The question is not about how to introduce solutions into society, but rather how to transform existing solutions to better arrangements. The means of doing this is multi-stakeholder dialogue that enables actors to articulate ideal outcomes and identify actions for their realisation and implementation.

Conclusion

As shown above, the emerging concept of social innovation suffers as a result of its poor social theoretical foundations with the consequence that there is a lack of clarity, especially concerning the relationship between social innovation and transformative social change. By defining social innovation as 'a new combination or configuration of practices', a more effective approach can be found in social practice theories because they focus on social practices as *the* central theoretical and analytical category and last unit of sociality. It has been suggested here that an important point of reference is Tarde's micro-sociological and poststructuralist approach. For Tarde, in the social everything occurs through invention and imitation (cf. Tarde, 2009b, p. 27). Tarde's concept of imitation provides important insights for analysing how practices are created and institutionalised. Tarde devised and pursued an analytical agenda that made social innovation the starting point for understanding social conditions and how they change. As such, a theoretical foundation of social innovation can fundamentally benefit from Tarde's social theory. Taking his micro sociological approach as a starting point, key implications can be outlined for a theoretically grounded understanding of social innovation and for an innovation policy that builds upon this.

By reference to Tarde's social theory it is possible to develop a robust and comprehensive concept of social innovation and its relationship to social change. It also allows for the analysis of the relationship between social and technological innovation and a better understanding of the most appropriate conditions for introducing, implementing, diffusing and establishing social innovation as a new social practice.

Starting from the interdependent relations between the elements of social practices, social innovations can be seen as central drivers and elements of social change. The internal logic of these processes of imitation and social learning, that is the focus of Tarde's attention, determines the innovation process. Whereas traditional diffusion research offers *ex-post* explanations of how individual innovations have ended up in social practice, the goal here is to develop approaches to understanding the genesis of innovations from the broad range of social practice with special attention paid to multiple innovation streams, fed by an evolutionary interplay of invention and imitation: the 'cycle of interlinked and recurring (repeating with variations) actions' (Tarde, 2009c, p. 73). If Tarde's perspective is followed in pointing to the social embeddedness of any invention in a dense network of imitation streams, then social innovations are first and foremost *ensemble* performances, requiring the interaction of many actors and, therefore, cross-sector analyses of the dynamics of social practices and the corresponding governance of transition in practice.

If the question of the relationship between social innovation and social change is to become a core issue for public and policy discussion, then recourse to Tarde highlights a wider set of issues within a non-deterministic explanation of social change as a key element of social transformation processes. Because Tarde placed the practices of imitation at the heart of his theory of social development, reference to the associated micro foundations of social phenomena can provide useful input into an integrative theory of innovation. As a robust scientific conceptualisation of active social life (cf. Toews, 2013, p. 401), it enables an analysis of how social phenomena, conditions and constructs come into being and how they change.

A sociologically grounded innovation theory can examine many and varied imitation streams and help decode their logics and laws. From this perspective, the focus is always on social practices, since it is only via social practices that diverse inventions make their way into society and, thus, become the object of acts of imitation. Social practice is a central component of a theory of transformative social change, in which a wide variety of everyday inventions constitutes stimuli and incentives for reflecting on – and possibly changing – social practices. It is only when these stimuli are absorbed, leading to changes in existing social practices that spread through society and construct social cohesion via acts of imitation, that they drive social transformation. Thus, new perspectives open up on an understanding of innovation that fully captures the diversity of innovations in society.

The great challenge for contemporary innovation policy lies in exploiting these possibilities. Nearly seventy years ago, in his 1945 report to President Roosevelt, Vannevar Bush directed the pioneering spirit towards exploring the 'endless frontiers' of natural science research, hoping that this would promote social welfare (Bush, 1945).

Today, there is a need for a fundamental broadening of perspective. First, challenges are present on a global scale and overcoming them requires a global perspective. Second, the major challenges are in the social sphere. The Vienna Declaration (2011) stated:

> The most urgent and important innovations in the 21st century will take place in the social field. This opens up the necessity as well as possibilities for Social Sciences and Humanities to find new roles and relevance by generating knowledge applicable to new dynamics and structures of contemporary and future societies.

In the middle of the last century, conditions were created – based on systematic innovation policy – that allowed exploration of the possibilities of the natural sciences to make them usable for society. In a similar way, there is now a need for a pioneering spirit in the search for new social practices that enable a secure future and allow people to live 'a richer and more fulfilled human life' (Rorty, 2008, p. 191).

The observations set out in this chapter make it clear that increased attention to social innovation is necessary to develop the potential for new social practices beyond the current, dominant, economic growth model. To this extent, a new model for innovation policy is required that directs its focus from technologies onto social innovations and systemic solutions and onto a corresponding empowerment of actors, thus transforming it into a comprehensive social policy.

Notes

1. The term relates to the Schumpeterian terminology, defining innovations as 'new combinations of production factors' (Howaldt and Schwarz, 2010; Hochgerner, 2012).
2. First mentioned by anthropologist Sherry B. Ortner (Ortner, 1984).

3. Important exceptions are, for example, Mulgan, 2012, and Hochgerner, 2009.
4. It centres on the question of whether social innovations are a prerequisite for a phenomenon that is concomitant with, or a consequence of, technological innovations (cf. Zapf, 1989; Gillwald, 2000, p. 38 ff.; Freeman, 1996; Meyer-Krahmer, 1998).
5. Duncan also highlighted this clarification in his introduction to Ogburn's works: 'It is wrong to characterize Ogburn's theory of social change as a "cultural lag theory". He did not regard the cultural lag theory as a "fundamental element of the theory of social evolution"' (Duncan, 1969, p. 21). He goes on to state: 'Ogburn makes it quite clear that one should in no way assume that all lags are initiated by technological inventions, to which social forms must subsequently sooner or later adapt. This statement results only from a generalization of empirical findings for a particular historical period, and even for this period it is not said to be valid without exception' (ibid., p. 22).
6. For many years, this one-sided technology orientation has found expression in an innovation policy that concentrates on supporting leading-edge technologies. The many reasons for this trend are founded, for example, in the various models of economic growth theory (cf. Hirsch-Kreinsen, 2010).
7. A recent article by Palmås (2012) explores the implications of Tarde's theories for the study of social entrepreneurship.
8. 'Niche innovations are carried and developed by small networks of dedicated actors, often outside the fringe actors' (Geels and Schot, 2007, p. 400).
9. '[...] Without scientific progress no amount of achievement in other directions can insure our health, prosperity, and security as a nation in the modern world' (Bush, 1945, p. 11).
'The Government should accept new responsibilities for promoting the flow of new scientific knowledge and the development of scientific talent in our youth. These responsibilities are the proper concern of the Government, for they vitally affect our health, our jobs, and our national security. It is in keeping also with basic United States policy that the Government should foster the opening of new frontiers and this is the modern way to do it. For many years the Government has wisely supported research in the agricultural colleges and the benefits have been great. The time has come when such support should be extended to other fields' (Bush, 1945, p. 8).

References

Adolf, M. (2012) 'Die Kultur der Innovation. Eine Herausforderung des Innovationsbegriffs als Form gesellschaftlichen Wissens', in Hilty, R.M., Jaeger, T. and Lamping, M. (eds), *Herausforderung Innovation. Eine interdisziplinäre Debatte*. Berlin, Heidelberg: Springer.
Austin, J.E., Gutierrez, R., Ogliastri, E. and Reficco, E. (2007) 'Capitalizing on Convergence', *Stanford Social Innovation Review*, 5 (4): 24–31.
Balke, F. (2009) 'Eine frühe Soziologie der Differenz: Gabriel Tarde', in Borch, C. and Stäheli, U. (eds), *Soziologie der Nachahmung und des Begehrens. Materialien zu Gabriel Tarde*. Frankfurt a.M.: Suhrkamp.
BEPA (2010) *Empowering People, Driving Change. Social Innovation in the European Union*. Brussels: Bureau of European Policy Advisers and European Commission.

Bijker, W.E., Hughes, T.P. and Pinch, T.J. (eds) (1987) *The Social Construction of Technological Systems. New Directions in the Sociology and History of Technology.* Cambridge, MA: MIT Press.

Brand, K.W. (2011) 'Umweltsoziologie und der praxistheoretische Zugang', in Gross, M. (ed.), *Handbuch Umweltsoziologie.* Wiesbaden: VS-Verlag für Sozialwissenschaften.

Bush, V. (1945) *Science, the Endless Frontier. A Report to the President by Vannevar Bush.* Washington, DC: Director of the Office of Scientific Research and Development.

Cajaiba-Santana, G. (2014) 'Social Innovation: Moving the Field Forward. A Conceptual Framework', *Technological Forecasting & Social Change*, 82: 42–51.

Cooperrider, D.L. and Pasmore, W.A. (1991) 'Global Social Change: A New Agenda for Social Science?' *Human Relations*, 44: 1037–55.

Crozier, M. and Friedberg, E. (1993) *Die Zwänge kollektiven Handelns – Über Macht und Organisation.* Frankfurt a.M.: Hain.

Duncan, O.D. (1969) 'Einleitung', in Ogburn, W.F., *Kultur und Sozialer Wandel. Ausgewählte Schriften. Herausgegeben und eingeleitet von Otis Dudley Duncan. Soziologische Texte, 56.* Neuwied, Berlin: Luchterhand.

Emerson, J. (2003) 'The Blended Value Proposition. Integrating Social and Financial Returns', *California Management Review*, 45 (4): 35–51.

European Commission (2013) *Social innovation research in the European Union. Approaches, findings and future directions. Policy Review.* Brussels: European Commission.

FORA (2010) *New Nature of Innovation. Report to the OECD.* Copenhagen.

Franz, H.W., Hochgerner, J. and Howaldt, J. (2012) *Challenge Social Innovation. Potentials for Business, Social Entrepreneurship, Welfare and Civil Society.* Berlin, New York: Springer.

Freeman, C. (1996) 'The Greening of Technology and Models of Innovation', *Technological Forecasting and Social Change*, 53 (1): 27–39.

Freeman, C. (1974) *The Economics of Industrial Innovation.* Harmondsworth: Penguin.

Geels, F.W. (2006) 'Multi-level Perspective on System Innovation', in Olsthoorn, A. and Wieczorek, A.J. (eds), *Understanding Industrial Transformation: Views from Different Disciplines.* Dordrecht: Springer.

Geels, F. W. and Schot, J. (2007) 'Typology of sociotechnical transition pathways', *Research Policy*, 36(3):399–417.

Gilgenmann, K. (2010) 'Gabriel Tarde oder die Erfindung und Nachahmung eines Klassikers', *Soziologische Revue*, 33 (3): 261–86.

Gillwald, K. (2000) *Konzepte sozialer Innovation. WZB paper: Querschnittsgruppe Arbeit und Ökologie.* Berlin.

Gross, M., Hoffmann-Riem, H. and Krohn, W. (2005) *Realexperimente. Ökologische Gestaltungsprozesse in der Wissensgesellschaft.* Bielefeld: transcript.

Hämäläinen, T.J. and Heiskala, R. (2007) *Social Innovations, Institutional Change and Economic Performance. Making Sense of Structural Adjustment Processes in Industrial Sectors, Regions and Societies.* Cheltenham, Northampton: Edward Elgar.

Hargraves, T., Haxeltine, A., Longhurst, N. and Seyfang, G. (2011) Sustainability transitions from the bottom up: Civil society, the multi-level perspective and practice theory, CSERGE Working Paper 2011–01. Available at: http://www.cserge.ac.uk/publications/cserge-working-paper/2011-01-sustainability-transitions-bottom-civil-society-multi-level [Accessed 5 November 2014.]

Hasse, R. and Krücken, G. (2005) *Neo-Institutionalismus*. Bielefeld: transcript.

Hirsch-Kreinsen, H. (2010) 'Die "Hightech-Obsession" der Innovationspolitik', in Howaldt, J. and Jacobsen, H. (eds), *Soziale Innovation. Auf dem Weg zu einem postindustriellen Innovationsparadigma*. Wiesbaden: VS.

Hochgerner, H.-W. (2012) 'New Combinations of Social Practices in the Knowledge Society', in Franz, H.-W., Hochgerner, J. and Howaldt, J. (eds), *Challenge Social Innovation. Potentials for Business, Social Entrepreneurship, Welfare and Civil Society*. Berlin, New York: Springer.

Hochgerner, J. (2009) 'Innovation Processes in the Dynamics of Social Change', in Loudin, J. and Schuch, K. (eds), *Innovation Cultures. Challenge and Learning Strategy*. Prague: Filosofia.

Howaldt, J. and Kopp, R. (2012) 'Shaping Social Innovation by Social Research', in Franz, H. W., Hochgerner, J. and Howaldt, J. (eds), *Challenge Social Innovation. Potentials for Business, Social Entrepreneurship, Welfare and Civil Society*. Berlin, New York: Springer.

Howaldt, J. and Schwarz, M. (2010) *'Soziale Innovation' im Fokus. Skizze eines gesellschaftstheoretisch inspirierten Forschungskonzepts*. Bielefeld: transcript.

Howaldt, J., Kopp, R. and Schwarz, M. (2014) *Zur Theorie sozialer Innovationen. Tardes vernachlässigter Beitrag zur Entwicklung einer soziologischen Innovationstheorie*. Weinheim und Basel: Beltz Juventa.Jackson, T. (2012) *Wohlstand ohne Wachstum. Leben und Wirtschaften in einer endlichen Welt*. Bonn: Bundeszentrale für Politische Bildung.

Joas, H. (1992) *Die Kreativität des Handelns*. Frankfurt a.M.: Suhrkamp.

Jonker, J. (2012) *Sustainable Thinking and Acting. An Inspirational Book for Shaping Our Common Future*. Deventer: Kluver.

Keller, F. (2009) 'Das endgültige soziale Rom. Tarde, Saussure und darüber hinaus', in Borch, C. and Stäheli, U. (eds), *Soziologie der Nachahmung und des Begehrens. Materialien zu Gabriel Tarde*. Frankfurt a.M.: Suhrkamp.

Krohn, W. (2005) 'Einleitung', in Gross, M., Hoffmann-Riem, H. and Krohn, W. (eds), *Realexperimente. Ökologische Gestaltungsprozesse in der Wissensgesellschaft*. Bielefeld: transcript.

Latour, B. and Lépinay V. (2010) *Die Ökonomie als Wissenschaft der leidenschaftlichen Interessen. Eine Einführung in die ökonomische Anthropologie Gabriel Tardes*. Frankfurt a. M.: Suhrkamp.

Leggewie, C. and Welzer, H. (2009) *Das Ende der Welt, wie wir sie kannten. Klima, Zukunft und die Chancen der Demokratie*. Frankfurt a.M.: Fischer.

MacKenzie, D. and Wajcman, J. (eds) (1985) *The Social Shaping of Technology*. London: Open University Press.

Marchart, O. (2013) *Das unmögliche Objekt. Eine postfundamentalistische Theorie der Gesellschaft*. Berlin: Suhrkamp Verlag

Marg, S., Geiges, L., Butzlaff, F. and Walter, F. (2013) *Die neue Macht der Bürger. Was motiviert Protestbewegungen? BP-Gesellschaftsstudie*. Reinbek: Rowohlt.

Meadows, D.L., Meadows, D.H. and Zahn, E. (1972) *Die Grenzen des Wachstums. Bericht des Club of Rome zur Lage der Menschheit*. Stuttgart: Deutsche Verlags-Anstalt.

Meyer-Krahmer, F. (ed.) (1998) *Innovation and Sustainable Development. Lessons for Innovation Policies*. Heidelberg: Physica.

Michaelides, P.G. and Theologou, K. (2010) 'Tarde's Influence on Schumpeter: Technology and Social Evolution', *International Journal of Social Economics*, 37 (5): 361–73.

Moebius, S. (2009) 'Imitation, differentielle Wiederholung und Iterabilität. Über eine Affinität zwischen Poststrukturalistischen Sozialwissenschaften und den "sozialen Gesetzen" von Gabriel Tarde', in Borch, C. and Stäheli, U. (eds), *Soziologie der Nachahmung und des Begehrens. Materialien zu Gabriel Tarde*. Frankfurt a.M.: Suhrkamp.

Moore, M.-L. and Westley, F. (2011) 'Surmountable Chasms: Networks and Social Innovation for Resilient Systems', *Ecology and Society*, 16 (1): 5.

Moulaert, F., MacCallum, D., Mehmood, A. and Hamdouch, A. (eds) (2013) *The International Handbook on Social innovation. Collective Action, Social Learning and Transdisciplinary Research*. Cheltenham: Edward Elgar.

Mulgan, G. (2012) 'Social Innovation Theories: Can Theory Catch Up with Practice?' in Franz, H.W., Hochgerner, J. and Howaldt, J. (eds), *Challenge Social Innovation. Potentials for Business, Social Entrepreneurship, Welfare and Civil Society*. Berlin, New York: Springer.

Mulgan, G., Tucker, S., Ali, R. and Sanders, B. (2007) *Social Innovation: What It Is, Why It Matters and How It Can Be Accelerated*. Oxford: Skoll Centre for Social Entrepreneurship.

Ogburn, W. F. (1969) *Kultur und sozialer Wandel. Ausgewählte Schriften. Herausgegeben und eingeleitet von Otis Dudley Duncan. Soziologische Texte, 56.* Neuwied, Berlin: Luchterhand.

Ogburn, W. F. (1937) *Technological Trends and National Policy. Including the Social Implications of New Inventions*. Washington, DC: United States Government Printing Office.

OECD (1997) *Oslo Manual: Proposed Guidelines for Collecting and Interpreting Technological Innovation Data*. Paris: Organisation for Economic Co-operation and Development.

Ortner, S. B. (1984) 'Theory in Anthropology since the Sixties', *Comparative Studies in Society and History*, 26(1): 126–66.

Osrecki, F. (2011) *Die Diagnosegesellschaft. Zeitdiagnostik zwischen Soziologie und medialer Popularität*. Bielefeld: transcript.

Osterhammel, J. (2011) *Die Verwandlung der Welt. Eine Geschichte des 19. Jahrhunderts*. Munich: Beck.

Paech, N. (2012) *Befreiung vom Überfluss. Auf dem Weg in die Postwachstumsökonomie*. Munich: oekom.

Palmås, K. (2012) 'Re-assessing Schumperian Assumptions Regarding Entrepreneurship and the Social', *Social Enterprise Journal*, 8 (2): 141–55.

Phills Jr., J., Deiglmeier, K. and Miller, D. (2008) 'Rediscovering Social Innovation', *Stanford Social Innovation Review*, 6 (3): 33–43.

Powell, W.W. and Grodal, S. (2005) 'Networks of Innovators', in Fagerberg, J., Mowery, D. C. and Nelson, R.R. (eds), *The Oxford Handbook of Innovation*. New York: Oxford University Press.

Rammert, W. (2010) 'Die Innovationen in der Gesellschaft', in Howaldt, J. and Jacobsen, H. (eds), *Soziale Innovation. Auf dem Weg zu einem postindustriellen Innovationsparadigma*. Wiesbaden: VS.

Reckwitz, A. (2003) 'Grundelemente einer Theorie sozialer Praktiken. Eine sozialtheoretische Perspektive', *Zeitschrift für Soziologie*, 32 (4): 282–300.

Rogers, E. M. (2003) *Diffusion of Innovations*. New York: Free Press.

Rorty, R. (2008) *Philosophie als Kulturpolitik*. Frankfurt a.M.: Suhrkamp.

Rückert-John, J. (2013) 'Die Nachhaltigkeit der Debatte um soziale Innovationen – Innovationsschub für den nachhaltigen Wandel', in Rückert-John, J. (ed.), *Soziale Innovationen und Nachhaltigkeit*. Wiesbaden: Springer VS.

Rüede, D. and Lurtz, K. (2012) Mapping the various meanings of social innovation: Towards a differentiated understanding of an emerging concept. EBS Business School Research Paper Series 12-03, Oestrich-Winkel.

Schatzki, T. R., Knorr-Cetina, K. and Savigny, E. von (eds) (2001) *The Practice Turn in Contemporary Theory.* London, New York: Routledge.

Schneidewind, U. (2013) 'Wandel verstehen – Auf dem Weg zu einer "Transformative Literacy"', in Welzer, H. and Wiegandt, K. (eds), *Wege aus der Wachstumsgesellschaft.* Frankfurt a.M.: Fischer Taschenbuch.

Schröder, T., Huck, J. and Haan, G. de (2011) *Transfer sozialer Innovationen. Eine zukunftsorientierte Fallstudie zur nachhaltigen Siedlungsentwicklung.* Wiesbaden: VS.

Schumpeter, J.A. (1964) *Theorie der wirtschaftlichen Entwicklung.* Berlin: Duncker & Humblot.

Shove, E. (2003) 'Converging Conventions of Comfort, Cleanliness and Convenience', *Journal of Consumer Policy,* 26: 395–418.

Shove, E., Pantzar, M. and Watson, M. (2012) *The Dynamics of Social Practice. Everyday Life and How It Changes.* London: Sage.

Stehr, N. (2007) *Die Moralisierung der Märkte. Eine Gesellschaftstheorie.* Frankfurt a.M.: Suhrkamp.

Tarde, G. (2009a) *Die sozialen Gesetze. Skizze einer Soziologie* (1899). Marburg: Metropolis.

Tarde, G. (2009b) *Die Gesetze der Nachahmung.* Frankfurt a.M.: Suhrkamp.

Tarde, G. (2009c). *Monadologie und Soziologie.* Frankfurt a.M.: Suhrkamp.

Toews, D. (2013) 'Tarde's Sociology of Difference: Its Classical Roots and Contemporary Meanings', *Journal of Classical Sociology,* 13 (3): 393–401.

Vienna Declaration (2011) *The Most Relevant Topics in Social Innovation Research. Concluding resolution provided by the conference 'Challenge Social Innovation. Innovating Innovation by Research – 100 Years after Schumpeter'.* Available at: http://www.socialinnovation2011.eu/ [Accessed 5 November 2014.]

Vobruba, G. (2013). 'Soziologie und Kritik', *Soziologie,* 42 (2): 147–68.

Warde, A. (2005) 'Consumption and Theory of Practice', *Journal of Consumer Culture,* 5 (2): 131–53.

WBGU (Wissenschaftlicher Beirat der Bundesregierung) (2011) *Globale Umweltveränderungen 2011: Welt im Wandel. Zusammenfassung für Entscheidungsträger. Gesellschaftsvertrag für eine Grosse Transformation.* Berlin.

Welzer, H. (2013) *Selbst denken. Eine Anleitung zum Widerstand.* Frankfurt a.M.: Fischer.

Weymann, A. (1998) *Sozialer Wandel: Theorien zur Dynamik der modernen Gesellschaft.* Weinheim, Munich: Juventa.

Williams, R. and Sörensen, K. (2002) *Social Shaping, Guiding Policy. Concepts, Spaces, and Tools.* Edinburgh: Edward Elgar.

Zapf, W. (2003) 'Sozialer Wandel', in Schäfers, B. (ed.), *Grundbegriffe der Soziologie.* Opladen: Leske Budrich.

Zapf, W. (1989) 'Über soziale Innovationen', *Soziale Welt,* 40 (1/2): 170–83.

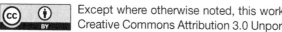

2
At the Root of Change: The History of Social Innovation

Katharine McGowan and Frances Westley

Introduction

This chapter explores the roots and developments of social innovation through comparative historical case studies. Specifically, this chapter introduces a theoretical and methodological framework for this historical discussion. It then goes on to discuss trends observed from a preliminary analysis of several historical cases of social innovation and offers a more detailed discussion of one specific case – the emergence of the intelligence test. This research contributes findings around three key trends and dynamics: how new ideas shift the intellectual landscape and create the space for novel combinations; the complimentary and overlapping efforts of 'poets', 'debaters' and 'designers' (different roles for agents); and the importance of agents functioning at both the niche and landscape level.

This chapter, as part of a larger project based at the Waterloo Institute for Social Innovation and Resilience (WISIR), Canada, examines the life cycle of a social innovation using historical examples. Throughout this chapter, social innovations are defined as new products, processes, procedures, policies and designs that seek profoundly to change authority and resource flows and eventually tip entire systems towards greater resilience and sustainability (Westley, Zimmerman and Patton, 2006). This cycle begins with the discovery and definition of new social phenomena (discrete new values or ideas about society, nature, technologies, processes and/or the individual that have credibility and legitimacy, with people acting as though they believe them to be true). These new social phenomena offer a glimpse of the 'adjacent possible' – the scope of possible social arrangements one degree removed from current realities (Kaufmann, 2000). By doing so, new social phenomena

spark wider exploration and provide the opportunity for the creation of clusters of inventions and innovations. These innovations can ultimately shift an entire system, potentially moving it to a place of greater social resilience and rooting those new social phenomena as core ideas in the new iterations of the system in question (Westley *et al.*, 2011). Wallerstein (1974) argued truth changes because society changes, but this chapter suggests that as new 'truths' emerge and compete for dominance, they create the space for society to follow.

Mulgan (2006) pointed to the 'radical innovation' origins of much of modern life. Although Mulgan saw social innovation as a response to modernity's twin pillars – industrialisation and urbanisation – many radical ideas that have changed society emerged long before the 18th and 19th century. Some of these are still embedded in society, while others have been displaced or abandoned over time. History allows the observation of patterns and disruptions across multiple timescales post hoc. This type of analysis is the goal of many contemporary studies of resilience and complexity (see Van der Leeuw *et al.*, 2011). A well-constructed historical narrative can provide insights into events and trends to a far greater extent than can be done in the moment (Byrne, 1998, p. 26).

Berkes and Folke (1998) argued that the characteristics of complex systems require a case study-based approach for their analysis. Several excellent studies have employed historical cases in their research into complex systems (Gunderson *et al.*, 1995; Berkes and Folke, 1998; Ommer, 2007; Redman and Foster, 2008; Bures and Kanapaux, 2011). Despite the dangers of historicism (imposing the perspective of inevitability on events), history can provide a rich resource for those looking to understand social processes. However, there is an equal risk of over-emphasising detail, context and specificity, as there is of imposing rigid theory on the messy complexity of human systems. In complex systems, information and behaviours do not necessarily scale up; activity at the micro level does not simply add up to produce outcomes at the macro level and one does not necessarily explain the other, hence the benefit of conducting multiple cases, with replication in questions and design, to allow for cross-case comparison (Yin, 2003). Multiple cases of equal and significant depth hopefully allow the researcher to differentiate context and phenomena, as individual details must be 'always considered within the broader concerns of the overarching research question' (Ommer, 2007, p. 26).

This chapter is based on research carried out during the initial stages of a comparative historical project at WISIR. Since social innovation is

defined here as including products as well as deliberative processes and policies that are transformative in their outcome with respect to building greater social resilience (Westley, Zimmerman and Patton, 2006), the case selection focused initially on these disruptions and then worked backwards. This approach revealed unexpected combinations, incredible innovations and sometimes no ultimate innovation at all. Cases also focused on those products and processes that sought to shift systems towards greater inclusion, greater resilience and greater prosperity, although it became clear that such objectives do not always translate into their desired outcomes. Additionally, wider social changes can ultimately cause a great innovation with an admirable social goal to fail. Two such examples of failed social innovation are included in the overall set of cases analysed. After extensive discussion of possible examples of historical social innovations, cases were selected that represented a broad spectrum of innovations and disruptions in different domains and temporal spaces, including the American national parks system, the World Wide Web, financial derivatives, contraception, intelligence testing and the Dutch spice trade. At this early stage of the project, breadth was preferred to test the hypothesis in different contexts.

The research aimed to find out whether there were common mechanisms or trends across disparate disruptive shifts. The first step was to identify significant institutional shifts (such as the introduction of a new law). Looking at these discrete moments, the goal(s) (rather than the results) of these new pieces of legislation or institutional changes were explored and the windows of opportunity that made change possible were identified. Therein, this research looked for new ideas: it considered both the description and discovery of new ideas and the convergences of new and existing ideas and trends, and investigated whether any of these new ideas constituted a new social phenomenon.

A framework for analysis

Social innovation is of increasing interest in exploring 'wicked problems', limited resources and ingenuity gaps (Rittel, 1972; Westley, Zimmerman and Patton, 2006; Bason, 2010; Homer-Dixon, 1995). Despite the apparent novelty of social innovation as a construct or set of discourses, humans have experimented and achieved disruptive and durable social change repeatedly over time. This research suggests that social innovation is a common dynamic of human history, although the way in which sustainability and resilience are defined at specific historical moments is not a constant. This is especially important from

an analytical standpoint, as including a range of historical examples considerably increases the pool of social innovations that can be studied, allowing researchers to test multiple theories and look for overarching patterns and commonalities across cases. The theoretical framework employed here to explore historical social innovation is composed of three broad elements: the driving force of new (and new combinations of) ideas into the adjacent possible, the compilation of different agents' activities within a specific case and the importance of understanding the obstacles and opportunities at the niche and landscape level.

New ideas; novel combinations

Combination of two or more existing ideas, theories or products is commonly acknowledged as a key driver of technological innovation and scientific discovery, and similarly is seen as a key mechanism of innovation generally (van den End and Kemp, 1999; Becker *et al.*, 2006; Arthur, 2009; Biggs *et al.*, 2010; Thagard, 2012). Arthur (2009) suggested new technologies and technological domains emerge as the result of the discovery of new naturalistic phenomena, as well as through the combination of existing technologies within and across domains. Similarly, looking at 100 scientific discoveries and 100 technological innovations, Thagard (2012) sought common features of how individuals involved in those breakthroughs had perceived and/or created novelty. Thagard credited combinations of mental representations (ideas that combine two or more distinct concepts, products, etc.) as the most common, compelling explanation for the creative process.

This research considers a social dimension of the combination hypothesis of invention. It examines how the emergence of new social phenomena – discrete new ideas about society, nature, technologies, processes and/or the individual – can create the opportunity for new perceptions of or re-interpretations of social arrangements and of human behaviour, individually or collectively. These new social phenomena allow for glimpses of the adjacent possible, the range of alternative social arrangements just beyond the horizon of prevailing practice (Kauffman, 2000; Johnson, 2010). Translating this glimpse into action, agents create new processes, products, programmes and, eventually, policies, all or any of which can produce deep shifts in complex social systems (this assertion is hypothesised from arguments in Arthur (2009), as well as the description of social innovations' potential as described in works like Westley, Zimmerman and Patton, 2006). The exploration of the adjacent possible is a key dynamic of social innovation.

This chapter proposes three general categories of social phenomena: naturalistic, constructed and technological. Naturalistic phenomena are primarily discovered in the realm of science. An example of a new and transformative naturalistic phenomenon was the discovery of the microbial cause of cholera, which replaced the miasma hypothesis and arose from discrete observations strengthened by careful data collection (Johnson, 2006). For example, Dr John Snow tracked an entire, and very deadly, outbreak of cholera in 19th-century London, clearly demonstrating that the only common thread between disparate victims was a single contaminated water pump. The weight of such evidence pushed key thinkers and decision-makers away from believing in bad air and towards an understanding of bad microbes as cholera's cause (Johnson, 2006).

Constructed phenomena are concepts that a discrete group (a culture, a sect or a political group) believes to be true and that guides their behaviour accordingly. These reflect an earlier sociological concept, the 'social fact', namely ideas, rules and beliefs that are real in their effects (if not always strictly tangible or falsifiable), and constrain or direct our activities (Durkheim, 1912; 1968).

Technological phenomena consist of both individual technologies (e.g., a car or computer or the subsidiary technologies of which they are composed) and technology regimes. New technologies can enhance people's ability to engage with the natural world or achieve insights into the workings of their own bodies. Similarly, new technologies or technology regimes – such as the World Wide Web – can affect how societies live and how citizens interact and organise their economies, as well as affecting the larger flows of power. The emergence of each type of phenomenon can trigger or create space for social innovations that can ultimately change an entire social system; a new idea can, thus, lead to further opportunities for transformative innovation.

The heterogeneity of agency

The social innovation process is often the result of the interaction of agency and institutional dynamics (North, 1990; McCallum *et al.*, 2009). This chapter's exploration of historical social innovation further distinguishes agents' behaviour and roles into three categories (adopted from Himelfarb, 2013): the 'poet', the 'designer' and the 'debater'. These are agent 'roles' (an agent can transition between roles), and this chapter argues that the success of a disruptive social innovation relies on the cooperation or compilation of their efforts at specific moments and over time. The poet shapes or expresses the new idea or social phenomenon, the designer converts the phenomenon into an innovation (a policy agenda, a programme, a product, etc.) and the debater advocates either for the innovation, the new phenomenon, or both.

The debater is the historical social or systems entrepreneur, who champions an innovation through the system, convening different stakeholders and interest groups; 'finding the opportunities to leverage innovative ideas for much greater system impact' (Westley, 2013). However, the roles of designer and poet are not directly translatable to the existing concepts of the social entrepreneur defined or discussed in the business or social change literature (Peredo and McLean, 2006; Mair and Marti, 2006; Bornstein, 2007; Gunn and Durkin, 2010; Abu-Saifan, 2012). Perhaps this is a function of the difference in breadth between the concepts. The poet, who first observes and/or describes a new social phenomenon, is not necessarily tied to the social innovation or social change process. Instead, that role falls on the designer, who sees the opportunities created through the adjacent possibles that are opened up by the description and specification of this new phenomenon.

For instance, the early 19th-century romantic artists and explorers who first praised the 'pristine' and distinctive quality of America's interior did not themselves decide that large public parks were the appropriate means to protect and share that experience. Their celebration of wilderness was the inspiration for the creation of the first national park at Yosemite during the American Civil War. It took the combined work of men like landscape architect Frederick Law Olmsted (a designer who wrote a manifesto for parks) and businessman-turned-environmentalist John Muir (co-founder of the Sierra Club) to lobby the public and government to create a system of parks open to the entire American population. Thus, poets, designers and debaters built on the work of each other to create disruptive change.

Scale

To achieve broad, lasting change, social innovations must cross multiple scales (Westley *et al.*, 2011). Actors can work across scales and can influence rules and structures: 'action is constrained and enabled by structure, but through reflexive feedback, structures are also changed by agency' (MacKay and Tambeau, 2013, p. 676). In this research study, cross-scale, cross-case comparison initially proved problematic. The DRIFT group used a framework consisting of three scales – niche, regime and landscape – in their interesting examinations of socio-technical transitions (Geels, 2006; Geels and Schot, 2007). However, since the historical cases considered in this study represented highly variant problem domains, geographical domains (regional, national and international) and temporal scales, defining a common 'regime' or a similar meso-level of analysis was difficult. Exploring the landscape (macro) and niche (micro) scales, however, proved critical in understanding the ways in which ideas open up adjacent possibles.

The landscape scale comprises the 'backdrop that sustains society' (Geels and Schot, 2007, p. 403), ranging from the physical environment to the 'political constellations, economic cycles, and broad societal trends' (Westley *et al.*, 2011). Borrowing from the Resilience Alliance's heuristic discussion of resilience, this chapter uses the concept of 'basins of attraction', defined as the factors within a given landscape that contribute to the stability of a specific system or set of arrangements (Folke *et al.*, 2004). These are deepened by landscape conditions – the collection of resources and the influence of overarching 'big ideas' (such as democracy, capitalism and scientific progressivism) that maintain stable states within that broader landscape. It also identifies the importance of historical niches or micro-level sites – protective spaces where agents exchange ideas, experiment and explore relative possibilities.

Building on the assertion that a disruptive innovation can trigger the transition of a system from one basin of attraction to another, and that an institutional or systems entrepreneur can also lower the thresholds between proximate basins (Hwang and Christensen, 2008; Westley *et al.*, 2011), historical examples of this dynamic were sought within the cases. The analysis showed how agents were able to travel between the niche and landscape level to aid critical transitions and advocate for their particular innovation. In the case of the World Wide Web, designers (frequently programmers) often considered what could be done technologically (working in research institute niches, for instance), and also what *should* be done. The latter question was a landscape-level concern, as designers like Ted Nelson (*The Computer Manifesto*) sought to create an open, egalitarian web, which reflected their political and social values broadly.

Hence, the theoretical framework developed here encompasses both the interplay of agency and structure, and the idea that innovation and exploration can be both spontaneous and contingent as well as deliberate and thoughtful. This analysis sought to understand not just the conditions that favour disruptive change but also the behaviours that encourage it, and to identify the important actors and milestones in the lifecycle of an idea from possibility to innovation to disruption to orthodoxy.

The intelligence test: an explanatory case study

The creation of the intelligence test was a specific solution to a concern about how to arrange people in an emerging modern meritocracy and industrial economy, grounded in the growing faith in scientific progressivism to improve society and individuals. The particular scientific – or pseudo-scientific – basis for the tests relied on a combination of theories of genetic inheritance and Social Darwinism, as well as new scientific techniques that facilitated repeatable mass testing. There were two 'poets', Sir Francis Galton (the creator of Social Darwinism) and Alfred Binet, who articulated mental capacity as 'intelligence'. Binet himself was also a 'designer'. He created the first reliable test of children's cognitive abilities, although other designers experimented with the potential of testing mental capacity two decades before Binet debuted his test in 1911, and continued to refine Binet's test for years to come. Two key 'debaters' advanced the idea of testing in America: Henry Herbert Goddard, a psychologist who worked with people labelled 'feebleminded', and Robert Yerkes, a psychologist whose chairmanship of the National Research Council during the First World War allowed him to successfully advocate for testing for all American army recruits. Although Goddard and Lewis Terman (another designer in this story) began work in their respective laboratory/academic settings, as debaters, they were able to see the policy implications of their work and read signals of potential landscape shifts as opportunities to advance the use of the intelligence test.

New ideas, new combinations and adjacent possibles

Two key new naturalistic phenomena (re)discovered in the 19th century had foundational effects on the education and treatment of children. The first was Darwin's description of natural selection, which, he argued, 'works solely by and for the good of each being, all corporeal and mental endowments will tend to progress towards perfection' (Chitty, 2007, p. 25). The second was the rediscovery of Mendel's rules of genetic inheritance, specifically heredity.

So emerged an adjacent possible: if features such as eye colour and height could be explained by genetic differences, some reasoned the same could be said for character, for intelligence and achievement, as well as for social problems such as crime and poverty (O'Brien, 2011). Darwin's second cousin, Francis Galton (an example poet for scientific progressivism's ability to improve society, and rank humanity according to measurable merit), applied the concept of natural selection to explain social stratification: those who enjoyed the spoils of society were closer to 'perfection' than their lesser fellows (Chitty, 2007; Dudziak, 1986). This 'Social' Darwinism mixed scientific and social validation of a class-based society (inequality of situation and opportunity), combining naturalistic and constructed phenomena. This in turn created a new adjacent possible: specifically, might heredity and science build a better population? These views defined the intellectual niche of Eugenics, the so-called 'science' of improving the quality of humanity (Chitty, 2007). 'Better' here meant racial purity and was usually seen from a middle- or upper-middle-class Protestant perspective, borrowing elements from Malthusian and Darwinian theory (Dudziak, 1986; Zenderland, 1998).

Many who were concerned with social improvement in the late 19th and early 20th century considered the 'menace of the feebleminded' to be a significant threat to public safety and social progress (Samelson, 1987, p. 114). If 'better' was possible, so too it must be possible to eliminate society's least desirable, specifically those labelled 'feebleminded'. According to this view, 'the feebleminded' posed a several-pronged threat (reflecting in part the confused and flexible definition of 'feeblemindedness'): they were incompetent (and idle), so they did not and could not contribute to the productive economy, and collectively and individually, they represented a threat to public health and morals as they were liable to commit such sins as 'promiscuity, adultery, incest, crime and alcoholism' (Dudziak, 1986, p. 845; Zenderland, 1998). Thanks to the combination of these social views with new understandings of the naturalistic phenomenon of inheritance, negative behaviours were perceived as the result of bad genes and, therefore, fixed more than environmental.

The intelligence test: a social innovation

The belief that the differences among people, including ability, character and intelligence, were measurable and determinate opened up a new adjacent possible for educators. Progressives had campaigned for decades for technical and scientific expertise in designing, implementing and evaluating public policy (Cravens, 1987). Within this broader debate about the direction and content of the public realm, the education regime in North America and Western Europe was undergoing a fundamental pedagogical shift, from philosophy to psychology (Blanton, 2000; Cravens, 1987). Education had become the state's purview in many Western countries, and education officials sought to take advantage of new scientific quantitative measurements methods effectively and definitively to test and stream their student bodies (Chitty, 2007).

As part of the view that schools were the avenues to change or build society, several niches of experimentation presented new innovations to scale across the system. As an example, to address the concerns of 'feeblemindedness' in schools, an association of American teachers established special education programmes in 1902, where instruction would be tailored to the academic limitations or specific needs of a class of students (Zenderland, 1998). But to educate the 'feebleminded', there needed to be an effective, reliable method of sorting the student population. Education officials sought to take advantage of the emerging statistical study of human populations (a new technological process), especially the permanent census (Ramsden, 2003). The ability to collect and process large amounts of data about a state's population informed many aspects of the state's growing responsibilities, including the management of the classroom. There was competition between different types of tests and different assumptions of how hereditary intelligence could be measured, but most failed to scale beyond the small niches in which they developed (Sokal, 1987).

In the last decades of the 19th century, psychological laboratories emerged in universities. While these laboratories were ideal niches for experimentation, they had failed to produce workable, scalable innovations. Charles Spearman – a key poet in the development of intelligence testing – lamented the first decades of his discipline as failing to achieve its promised impact on such fields as education, or on life more broadly. In an artistic flourish, he remarked that the laboratory results had yet to bridge the divide between academia and society: 'the results of all good experimental work will live, but as yet most of them are like hieroglyphics awaiting their deciphering Rosetta stone' (Spearman, 1904, p. 204). In this 1904 treatise (surprisingly replete with such bold illustrations), Spearman reported on a correlation he observed: people who did well on one form of mental test did well on all forms of mental tests (Bartholomew, Allerhand and Deary, 2013). Spearman hypothesised that there existed a 'general mental ability' which he labelled g: 'Spearman speculated that its [g] biological basis was some general aspect of how brains varied between people' (Bartholomew, Allerhand and Deary, 2013, p. 223).

The most important poet (and designer) in the case of the intelligence test was Alfred Binet. He sought a practical way to capture 'g' or his equivalent: importantly, this test must be 'a work of administration, not a work of science' (Binet and Simon, 1905, trans. Kite, 1916). Binet devised the first reliable test of children's cognitive capabilities, based on the twin assumptions that ability is based on genetic inheritance rather than environmental factors and that it can be mapped systematically over time. Binet and his colleague Theodore Simon devised the first practical test to distinguish the mentally incapable from those failing for environmental rather than genetic reasons (Spearman, 1904; Chitty, 2007; Zenderland, 1998). Those children whom the test 'objectively' indicated were 'feebleminded' could be institutionalised, a separation believed to be in their best interest and as well as the interest of society generally (Blanton, 2000, p. 1016).

Scaling towards a tipping point and mass adoption

In this case, one key debater who scaled Binet's test in the United States and who argued for intelligence as a naturalistic phenomenon was Henry Herbert Goddard. Goddard was a psychologist and Director of Research at the Vineland Training School for Feeble-Minded Girls and Boys in New Jersey, a niche that allowed him to experiment with different tests. A vociferous advocate for intelligence testing and the role of psychology in education, Goddard successfully shifted the narrative of 'feeblemindedness' in America to a question of intelligence (Zenderland, 1998). Binet had developed his test for the French school system (Binet and Simon, 1905, trans. Kite, 1916), and his ideas and practices were largely limited to Europe until the spring of 1908 when Goddard, as the latter wrote later, 'made a visit to Europe in the interests of the work [of the Vineland Laboratory]' and 'learned of the tests', from a Dr Decroly in Brussels, who had recently completed his own tests using the Binet-Simon method (Goddard, in Binet and Simon, 1905, trans. Kite, 1916, p. 5). Goddard advocated for the theory that 'feeblemindedness' was the result of a lack of intelligence, and that a simple test could differentiate these children from the broader class. He was able to convince American doctors working in institutions for the 'feebleminded' to 'redefine mental deficiency in terms of intelligence' (Zenderland, 1998, p. 104).

At first, the proposed solution to 'feeblemindedness' was institutional segregation. Advocates believed that a good institution could even train the 'feebleminded' to 'go out into the world and support themselves', but that should only be allowed if the 'feebleminded' could be sterilised to remove 'the terrible danger of procreation' (Zenderland, 1998, pp. 81–182; Dudziak, 1986). If 'feeblemindedness' was inherited, then removing any question of genetic transmission could remove the major threat the 'feebleminded' apparently posed to society.

Disruptions and social shifts

The intelligence test quickly facilitated another form of social control over those deemed 'feebleminded', as new medical technology allowed for safe sterilisation. Beginning with Indiana in 1907, twenty-eight states introduced compulsory sterilisation laws (although it was not until the case of Carrie Buck in 1925 that any of these laws were upheld at the state supreme court level) (Dudziak, 1986). Mass testing was also used to 'validate' assumptions about the hierarchy of races. Binet explicitly did not want his test to be used to rank people, beyond separating those who fell below a certain level and could benefit little from conventional education (Blanton, 2000). Once the process was available, however, it was quickly seized on by others who aimed to differentiate people based on intelligence and race.

Lewis Terman expanded the scale of Binet's test to a wider range of age categories, including adults in 1916, which facilitated the work of Robert Yerkes, another key debater in the adoption of the intelligence test. Like Goddard, Yerkes was an American psychologist. Yerkes believed science could validate and inform a merit-based hierarchy of people based on their ability and potential contribution to the economy (Kevles, 1968). Yerkes was the Chairman of the National Research Council in the United States, a position that put him in direct contact with key powerful individuals within the American military.

America joined the Allies in the First World War in 1917, and needed to raise a large (mainly civilian) army quickly. Yerkes saw this as an opportunity for psychology generally and intelligence tests specifically to demonstrate their utility in evaluating human potential rapidly and efficiently. He convinced the Surgeon General of the Army of the potential of testing its new recruits as the country quickly expanded its forces for combat in France (Kevles, 1968). Half a million men underwent the test. Although this process was not without problems[1] (Blanton, 2000; Pinter, 1926), tests on this massive scale were seen to validate both the test and the concept behind it – intelligence. In 1919, the *Lancet* declared, 'Intelligence, of course, is only one of the factors in military efficiency, but it is probably the most important single factor', and that, thanks to the war, intelligence tests had given 'clear indications of their future value in the work of human selection and vocational training' (p. 539).

The rush of tests during the war may not have resulted in many privates being raised to officers, as Terman and others had argued they would. However, the war did allow the test to scale out from niche laboratories very quickly, reflecting the Lancet's confidence that the test would change vocational training. The war was a proof of process, that testing could be done on a mass scale, and produce results in which the testers had confidence. As a result, schools increasingly adopted the tests

(Watson, 1953; Blanton, 2000). Simultaneously, Goddard introduced internships for consulting psychologists at his Vineland school, further reinforcing the tests' role in psychology as new entrants were trained at this centre of Binet-based testing (Watson, 1953).

The link between Eugenics and race was central to the perverse logics of Nazi Germany, but it is hardly the only example. One particularly well-documented example was the mass I.Q. testing that the state educational establishment of Texas used to affirm their belief in a hierarchy of racial intelligence (Blanton, 2000). The testers wanted to find differences between Caucasian, Hispanic and African American children. When the results strongly pointed to an urban–rural divide instead, they hypothesised (and then concluded) that this reflected a difference in the children's skin tone – something for which the children were never tested (Blanton, 2000). Chitty (2007) has argued that the link between fixed intelligence and class was reflected in the ongoing differentiation of academic and vocational education that began in the late 19th century: 'we need to educate the middle class but merely to train the working class'. Although credible accusations of racism and classism remain, nevertheless tests of intellectual capacity opened up educational opportunities for lower-income children, beginning in the 1950s (Blanton, 2000).

Conclusion

Given much of the current interest, verging on excitement, surrounding social innovation, it is an ever-present risk that the concept becomes a normative label for the products, processes and procedures that are valued today – such that novelty is inherently seen as better than past arrangements and ideas. History is rich with examples of such hubris and, although it is a useless (and often inaccurate) truism to say history repeats itself, this chapter suggests that the study of social innovation is richer for a consideration of historical examples, especially when those examples reflect both on the process of change but also its risks. This is not to recommend a paralysis among social entrepreneurs – not all social innovations are the equivalent of the intelligence test – but to support the acknowledgement of actors' part in complex systems. Social innovation is not a process through which to achieve a Whiggish ideal future but rather an ongoing re-evaluation and exploration of systems as needs and values change.

The story of the intelligence test is not a celebratory one, but it was certainly an attempt better to serve the marginalised (in this case 'serve' must be interpreted through the cultural lens of the time) and to build a more resilient society through scientific–social partnerships. The big ideas of scientific progressivism created opportunities for innovation: concepts of intelligence generated the possibility of a test for ability and theories of inheritance, for sterilisation based on the tests. Poets created and described this opening to the adjacent possible, designers created tests that could bring the current reality into line with that future and debaters made the necessary connections (political, medical and institutional/educational) to bring the intelligence test from its niche in laboratories and small-scale schools to become a key element of the meritocracy in pre-war America.

The history of social innovation offers a glimpse of process, of agency and of perspective: indeed, of the entire lifecycle of the innovation process. As an example of WISIR's ongoing research project into social innovation, the intelligence test highlights the importance of landscape-level events, particularly the World Wars, as massively disruptive, creating multiple, and sometimes surprising, windows of opportunity for agents like Yerkes who can align their networks and campaign for their particular project or product. Additionally, the emergent professional and educational bodies important in the story of the intelligence test appear increasingly relevant in many of the research cases, especially those in the increasingly merit-based 20th and 21st century. Individual innovations aside – and these can be systems shifting too – it is the dynamics of the social, economic and political systems that emerge so powerfully in historical cases and, when stripped of specific context, offer great potential to inform current study of social innovation as an increasingly important and self-conscious phenomenon.

Note

1. Terman's results reflected his own racial assumptions and tested individuals' level of education rather than their capability. His views were also clearly demonstrated in his hope to reduce the number of children born to non-white Americans.

References

Abu-Saifan, S. (2012) 'Social Entrepreneurship: Definition and Boundaries', *Technology Innovation Management Review*, 2 (2): 227.
Arthur, B. (2009) *The Nature of Technology: What It Is and How It Evolves.* New York: Free Press.

Bason, C. (2010) *Leading Public Sector Innovation: Co-Creating for a Better Society.* Bristol: Policy Press.

Bartholomew, D., Allerhand, M. and Deary, I. (2013) 'Measuring Mental Capacity: Thomson's Bonds Model and Spearman's *g*-model compared', *Intelligence*, 41: 222–33.

Becker, M., Knudsen, T. and March, J. (2006) 'Schumpeter, Winter and the Sources of Novelty', *Industrial and Corporate Change*, 15: 353–71.

Berkes, F. and Folke, C. (eds) (1998) *Linking Social and Ecological Systems: Management Practices and Social Mechanisms for Building Resilience.* New York: Cambridge University Press.

Biggs, R., Westley, F. and Carpenter, S. (2010) 'Navigating the Back Loop: Fostering Social Innovation and Transformation in Ecosystem Management', *Ecology and Society*, 15 (2): 9.

Binet, A. and Simon, T. (1905, trans. 1916). *The Development of Intelligence in Children (The Binet–Simon test)* trans. Elizabeth Kite. Baltimore: Williams and Wilkins.

Blanton, C.K. (2000) '"They Cannot Master Abstractions, but They Can Often Be Made Efficient Workers": Race and Class in the Intelligence Testing of Mexican Americans and African Americans in Texas during the 1920s', *Social Science Quarterly*, 81 (4): 1014–26.

Bornstein, D. (2007) *How to Change the World.* Oxford: Oxford University Press.

Bures, R. and Kanapaux, W. (2011) 'Historical Regimes and Social Indicators of Resilience in an Urban System: The Case of Charleston, South Carolina', *Ecology and Society*, 16 (4): 16.

Byrne, DS. (1998) *Complexity Theory and the Social Sciences: An Introduction.* London: Routledge.

Chitty, C. (2007) *Eugenics, Race and Intelligence in Education.* London: Continuum.

Cravens, H. (1987) 'Applied Science and Public Policy: The Ohio Bureau of Juvenile Research and the Problem of Juvenile Delinquency, 1913–1930', in Michael Sokal (ed.), *Psychological Testing and American Society, 1890–1920.* New Brunswick: Rutgers University Press.

Dudziak, M. (1986) 'Oliver Wendell Holmes As a Eugenics Reformer: Rhetoric in the Writing of Constitutional Law', *Iowa Law Review*, 71: 833–67.

Durkheim, E. (1912, 1968) *Les formes elementaires de la vie religious.* 5th Ed. Paris: Presse universitaires de France.

Folke, C, Carpenter, S., Walker, B., Scheffer, M., Elmqvist, T., Gunderson, L. and Holling, C.S. (2004) 'Regime Shifts, Resilience and Biodiversity in Ecosystem Management', *Annual Review of Ecology, Evolution and Systematics*, 35 (2004): 557–81.

Geels, F. (2006) 'The Hygienic Transition from Cesspools to Sewer Systems (1840–1930): The Dynamics of Regime Transformation', *Research Policy*, 35: 1069–82.

Geels, F and Schot, J. (2007) 'Typology of Sociotechnical Transition Pathways', *Research Policy*, 36: 399–417.

Gunderson, L., Holling, C.S. and Light, S. (1995) *Barriers and Bridges: To the Renewal of Ecosystems and Institutions.* New York: Columbia University Press.

Gunn, R. and Durkin, C. (2010) *Social Entrepreneurship: A Skills Approach.* Bristol, UK: Policy Press.

Himelfarb, A. (2013) 'The Means Test: How We Measure Success'. Blog Entry at afhimelfarb.wordpresscom/2013/01/03/the-mean-test/ 3 January.

Homer-Dixon, T. (1995). 'The Ingenuity Gap: Can Poor Countries Adapt to Resource Scarcity?' *Population and Development Review*, 21 (3): 587.

Hwang, J. and Christensen, C. (2008) 'Disruptive Innovation in Health Care Delivery: A Framework for Business-Model Innovation', *Health Affairs*, 27 (5): 1329–35.

Johnson, S. (2006) *The Ghost Map: The Story of London's Most Terrifying Epidemic – and How It Changed Science, Cities, and the Modern World*. New York: Riverhead Books.

Johnson, S. (2010) *Where Good Ideas Come From: The Natural History of Innovation*. New York: Penguin.

Kauffman, S. (2000) *Investigations*. Oxford: Oxford University Press.

Kevles, D. (1968) 'Testing the Army's Intelligence: Psychologists and the Military in World War I', *The Journal of American History*, 55 (3): 565–81.

MacCallum, D., Moulaert. F., Hillier, J. and Vicari Haddock, S. (2009) *Social Innovation and Territorial Development*. Aldershot: Ashgate.

MacKay, B., and Tambeau, P. (2013) 'A Structuration Approach to Scenario Praxis', *Technological Forecasting and Social Change*, 80 (4): 673–86.

Mair, J. and Marti, I. (2006) 'Social Entrepreneurship Research: A Source of Explanation, Prediction and Delight', *Journal of World Business*, 41 (1): 36–44.

Mulgan, G. (2006) 'The Process of Social Innovation', *Innovations*, (Spring): 145–62.

North, D. (1990). *Institutions, Institutional Change and Economic Performance*. Cambridge: Cambridge University Press.

O'Brien, G. (2011) 'Eugenics, Genetics, and the Minority Group Model of Disabilities: Implications for Social Work Advocacy', *Social Work*, 56 (4): 347–54.

Ommer, R. (2007) *Coasts Under Stress: Restructuring and Social-Ecological Health*. Montreal: McGill-Queen's University Press.

Peredo, A.M. and McLean, M. (2006). 'Social Entrepreneurship: A Critical Review of the concept', *Journal of World Business*, 41 (1): 56–65.

Pinter, R. (1926) 'Intelligence Tests', *Psychological Bulletin*, 23 (7): 366–81.

Ramsden, E. (2003) 'Social Demography and Eugenics in the Interwar United States', *Population and Development Review*, 29 (4): 547–93.

Redman, C and Foster, D. (2008) *Agrarian Landscape in Transition: Comparisons of Long-Term Ecological and Cultural Change*. Oxford: Oxford University Press.

Rittel, H. (1971) 'Some Principles for the Design of an Education System for Design', *Journal of Architectural Education*, 25 (1/2): 16–27.

Samelson, F. (1987) 'Was Early Mental Testing: (a) Racist Inspired, (b) Objective Science, (c) A Technology for Democracy, (d) The Origin of the Multiple Choice Exams, (e) None of the Above? (Mark the RIGHT Answer)', in Sokal, M. (ed.), *Psychological Testing and American Society, 1980–1930*. New Brunswick: Rutgers University Press.

Sokal, M. (1987) 'James McKeen Cattell and Mental Anthropometry: Nineteenth-Century Science and Reform and the Origins of Psychological Testing', in Sokal, M. (ed.), *Psychological Testing and American Society, 1890–1930*. New Brunswick: Rutgers University Press.

Spearman, C. (1904). 'General Intelligence: Objectively Determined and Measured', *The American Journal of Psychology*, 15: 201–92.

Thagard, P. (2012) 'Creative Combination of Representation: Scientific Discovery and Technological Innovation', in Proctor, R. and Capaldi, E.J. (eds), *Psychology of Science: Implicit and Explicit Processes*. Oxford: Oxford University Press, pp. 389–405.

The Lancet, *Intelligence Test*, 9 September 1919, p. 539.

Ven den Ende, J. and Kemp, R. (1999) 'Technological Transformations in History: How the Computer Regime Grew Out of Existing Computing Regimes', *Research Policy*, 28 (8): 833–51.

Van der Leeuw, S., Kubiszewski, I., Downy, C., Aulenbach, S., Brewer, S., Burek, M., Cornell, S., Costanza, R., Crumley, C., Dearing, J., Graumlich, L., Hegmon, M., Hibbard, K., Jackson, S., Sinclair, P., Sörlin, S., Steffen, W. and Heckbert, S. (2011) 'Towards an Integrated History to Guide the Future', *Ecology and Society*, 16 (4): 2.

Wallerstein, I. (1974) *The Modern World*. New York: Academic Press.

Watson, R. (1953) 'A Brief History of Clinical Psychology', *Psychological Bulletin*, 50 (5): 321–46.

Westley, F. (2013) 'Social Innovation and Resilience: How One Enhances the Other', *Stanford Social Innovation Review*, Summer: 6–8.

Westley, F., Olsson, P., Folke, C., Homer-Dixon, T., Vredenburg, H., Loorbach, D., Thompson, J., Nilsson, M., Lambin, E., Sendzimir, J., Banerjee, B., Galaz, V. and Van der Leeuw, S. (2011) 'Tipping Toward Sustainability', *AMBIO*, 40: 719–38.

Westley, F., Zimmerman, B. and Quinn Patton, M. (2006) *Getting to Maybe: How the World Is Changed*. Toronto: Random House.

Yin, R. (2003) *Case Study Research: Design and Methods*. 3rd Edition. Thousand Oaks, NY: Sage.

Zenderland, L. (1998) *Measuring Minds: Henry Herbert Goddard and the Origins of American Intelligence Testing*. Cambridge: Cambridge University Press.

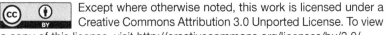

3

A Relational Database to Understand Social Innovation and Its Impact on Social Transformation

Marie J. Bouchard, Catherine Trudelle, Louise Briand, Juan-Luis Klein, Benoît Lévesque, David Longtin and Mathieu Pelletier

Introduction

Research on social innovation has, to date, mainly been carried out through case studies. This is due to the unique character of innovations, at least when they emerge, and the fact that the concept of social innovation is still poorly codified. Case studies are typically used to explore new research areas for which existing theory seems inadequate. A case study approach is the prescribed methodology to explore phenomena that are not easily distinguishable from their context and to document them thoroughly by referring to multiple information sources (Yin, 1994).

A cross-analysis of many case studies can shed light on the links between different forms of social innovation and their configurations, evolution and distribution in time and space. However, the ultimate value of such an analysis is quickly exhausted due to the limited amount of information that can be processed in a qualitative way. Moreover, cross-analyses are likely to fail to establish links between much of the data from case studies, which impedes knowledge building.

These observations prompted a team of researchers from the Centre de Recherche sur les Innovations Sociales (CRISES) to build a data warehouse – the CRISES Database on Social Innovations – dedicated to the analysis of data that has so far been limited to the case method. The working hypothesis is that a quantitative analysis of a large number of cases will reveal aspects of social innovation that have not previously been observed while also generating information on the relationship between social innovation and social transformation. The CRISES Database on Social Innovations initially focuses on an existing body of research on social innovation that was produced in the province of Québec (Canada). However, the goal is eventually to expand the work to include other provinces and countries. To allow for this type of research, which requires multivariate statistical analyses of a large volume of information, the data warehouse must be able to offer flexible data storage options.

This chapter discusses the different stages of building a data warehouse based on case studies (n ≥ 500) on social innovations, in particular those emerging from the social economy, conducted in Québec over a period of over twenty years (1986 to 2011). With a focus on the methodological, theoretical and epistemological challenges of such an undertaking, this chapter also discusses the potential scientific contribution that such an initiative will provide to the study of social innovation and social transformation. Beyond the work of CRISES, this project will provide the research community with a conceptual thesaurus on social innovation and a relational database model to analyse case studies, facilitating inter-regional comparison. This new way of gathering data will reinforce the capacity to develop theories about social innovations.

The formalisation of a research field

Social innovation is often the product of improvisation, serendipity and tacit knowledge acquired through experience (Bouchard, 1999). In addition, most social innovations are often not labelled as such. In that context, one of the primary functions of research is to identify and recognise these innovations, referred to as codification and formalisation. For this task, the preferred methodology of CRISES researchers has been based, since the founding of the Centre in 1986, on case studies. It has also tended to be the main methodology of other large social innovation research projects, such as several of those funded by the European Commission's Seventh Framework Programme.[1]

Nevertheless, the case study methodology has certain limitations. First, case studies seek to understand a particular phenomenon occurring in a given context. In epistemological terms, this means that they generally follow an *idiographic* rather than *nomographic* perspective.[2] Such an approach helps to understand the meaning of a specific phenomenon but is not intended to establish evidence on – or formulate general and causal laws about – an object under study. For this reason, this methodology does not lend itself to the generalisation of knowledge. Secondly, works conducted in a multidisciplinary research centre such as CRISES reflect a diverse range of interests and theoretical stances

(Tardif, 2005). This calls for the formalisation and systematisation of the research results in order to advance knowledge.

As a relational database compiled of source material from case studies, the CRISES Database on Social Innovations aims to serve as a complementary tool for creating new research opportunities and for overcoming these limitations, at least in part. A database is a collection of data that is structured in a certain way. A database model determines that structure. The most commonly used database models include the hierarchical, network, object and relational models. The CRISES Database on Social Innovations is based on the relational model. A relational database is a database that stores information both about the data and how it is related. It enables data to be structured in a way that formalises the logical relations, or interdependencies, between the data. Queries can be made to the relational database, which would enable associating data in a number of ways, unlike a flat database that only offers a single table, with a determined relation between the rows and the columns.

The creation of a relational database proceeds in three stages of modelling: conceptual, logical and physical. The first stage, laying the foundation of the overall process, is the creation of the conceptual model, or schema, for the formal and systematic organisation of data.[3] It also involves the defining of entities, or core concepts, used to describe phenomena related to social innovation. In the subsequent stage of creating the logical model, these entities are then operationalised through a series of attributes, in turn allowing for the retrieval of data from the case studies and for them to be organised on the basis of logical links and relationships. The third stage consists of the actual programming of the database into a physical model.

The creation of a relational database is an iterative process in which changes made at a later stage, such as during the development of the logical model, may lead to a revision of work done at an earlier stage, such as during the building of the conceptual model (Mata-Toledo and Cushman, 2002, p. 257). In the case of CRISES, the conceptual modelling led to the creation of a code book compiling some fifty-nine entities of three to fourteen attributes each, all of which are linked together through relations. In fact, relations underpin the basic concept of the relational model and represent the association of elements from the real world. The logical relations or links are based on relational algebra and allow detailed mathematical calculations to be performed.

The CRISES Database on Social Innovations is based on case studies that have already been conducted, so the design methodology differs slightly from the process described above in that the conceptual model was deduced from theory in addition to being induced from empirical data. Many steps mark the process of building the relational database on social innovations.

The formalisation allows for the transformation of qualitative data, which is textual in the case studies, into quantifiable data (i.e., nominal, ordinal, interval or ratio) that can then be subjected to statistical analyses. For example at CRISES, trained researchers have to go through and code each case study using the conceptual thesaurus on social innovation. Thus, the database can perform multidimensional comparative analyses on social innovation using both descriptive and explanatory statistical methods. For the corpus of existing case studies, the codification process occurs *a posteriori* but will in the future be implanted *a priori*, in the case study research design. In this sense, this project will impact future case study research on social innovation at CRISES, and potentially that of other researchers who adopt a similar view.

The CRISES Database on Social Innovations will enable the measurement of innovation from three spatial-temporal components, namely location, time and theme (Sinton, 1978). To study a phenomenon, one of these components is fixed, the second is varied in a controlled manner and the third is measured. Given the structural framework of the data, the relational data model allows for quantitative analyses that can capture all of these types of profiles to be performed. Multidimensional comparative analysis opens up the possibility of studying social innovation in a systematic way and to spot or confirm trends that were difficult to identify using the case study method. However, the results generated by this systematic quantitative analysis may also be counterintuitive or run counter to prevailing ideas in the field of social innovation and social transformation.

The challenges of database design

Given the nature of the sources – namely case studies based on non-probabilistic sampling and not designed for integration into a database – a hybrid approach that was both inductive and deductive was adopted to identify, define and operationalise the key concepts relevant to the study of social innovation. This approach made it possible to base the conceptual model on theories mobilised in the framework of CRISES research[4] (deductive approach) and to delimit the data that was effectively provided by the case studies (inductive approach).

This approach raised the challenge of building, *a posteriori*, a coherent conceptual model. Despite their convergence and complementarity, the conceptual tools used in CRISES studies had not been fully integrated into a common framework (Tardif, 2005). Building the conceptual model of the database thus strengthened this theoretical integration. Building the conceptual model prompted CRISES researchers to reflect more deeply on notions they had used in previous research and to address points of divergence between different approaches. Nevertheless, many challenges remained with regard to the definition of concepts and their operationalisation using attributes allowing the retrieval and correlation of data from case studies.

One of the difficulties was the polysemic nature of certain concepts that had more than one meaning (e.g., *market* can mean an actual place where goods are sold, and it can also mean a group of consumers for an organisation's products, or the meeting of the offer and demand forces within the economy). The meaning of concepts also can depend on context (e.g., *democratic control* has a different significance in a consumers' cooperative than is has in the workplace or in the public sphere). Some concepts, such as social innovation or social economy, still have an open-ended theoretical basis. Research has also advanced conceptually, such as by developing the notion of *regressive* social innovation, which emerged more recently in some CRISES work (Hodgson and Briand, 2013). Other concepts have multiple theoretical anchor points, such as the concept of *governance*, used in the standard economic and financial approaches as well as in institutional sociology and social geography. Here as well, more recent studies have contributed different meanings of the concept (Cornforth, 2004; Bernier, Bouchard and Lévesque, 2002). One impact of building a relational database was the clarification of the scope and limits of the conceptual field of CRISES. In the process, the conceptual approach to social innovation at CRISES became more rigorous and in depth (Bélanger and Lévesque, 1992; Favreau and Lévesque 1995; Favreau, 1995; Lapointe 2000a; 2000b; Comeau *et al.*, 2001; Klein and Champagne, 2011; Bouchard and Lévesque, 2013).

Concepts associated with social innovation are diverse, ranging from *collective action* to *public policy, beliefs and cognitive scheme, interorganisational relationships*, and many more. A further task concerned determining the relationships between concepts such that these are clear and unambiguous. Here, some concepts may have some degree of redundancy, albeit without lending themselves to be classified into categories and subcategories. For example, the concept of *partnership* could be synonymous with the concept of *network* in the case of public policy networks that involve the participation of civil society organisations in the delivery or co-production of services (White *et al.*, 1992). However, *partnership* may also be conceived of as a system of governance for a territory or sector that engages government and non-governmental actors in the co-design and co-construction of public policies, or alternatively as hierarchical, community-based, corporate or competitive types of governance systems (Enjolras, 2008). Some concepts may also appear as sub-categories of more than one concept (or category). Thus, a *network* might be a form of organisation (e.g., the Desjardins Movement, a large cooperative federation) or a form of governance (distributed power networks). Choices must, therefore, be made such that the conceptual model permits a continuous and coherent analysis of the data without a critical loss of their analytical significance.

Finally, each of the categories used in codifying data must be described with attributes that are sufficiently accurate to be unambiguously identifiable in the data, as well as mutually exclusive so that their classification is done uniformly, irrespective of the person who did the codifying. This requires specifying the concrete factual and observable dimensions of the mobilised concepts rather than attributing them to a single concept. For example, when codifying 'triggers of social innovation', a researcher may choose to group problems that were perceived or experienced at a collective level (e.g., decay of a territory or the high school dropout rate) into the 'problems' category; problems experienced by people (such as need for housing or employment) into the 'needs' category; and wishes for change at the values scale (such as self-management), self-realisation (empowerment) or social demands (e.g., justice or fairness) into the 'aspiration' category. These choices must be coherent throughout the operationalisation of the database and comply with the principle of relevance, calling for coherence with the original nature of the material analysed, from the case studies. Training the researchers on the codification manual and asking different researchers to codify the same text in order to reach interrater agreement helped to ensure consistency.

While the work of creating the CRISES Database on Social Innovation is not yet completed, it is already clear that this approach will have an impact on the renewal of the conceptual, analytical and programmatic framework of CRISES, not only by clarifying and refining it but also by expanding its analytical potential. The methodology, rendered available to researchers outside CRISES, will also potentially impact social innovation research at a larger scale. For example, the conceptual thesaurus, being (to the authors' knowledge) the first extensive repertoire of concepts on social innovation, will be available as a reference to be used – criticised and extended – in new case studies and in other database projects. The utilisation of CRISES' relational database model will also permit research teams in other regions to populate their own databases in a similar fashion, enabling cross-territorial comparison.

The database also has limitations that must be taken into account. The first concerns the source of the data. The case studies were conducted according to analytical frameworks that, although sharing a common basis, often varied from one research team to another or evolved over time (three to four data collection templates have been used in the various research programmes at CRISES over time). As indicated earlier, the conceptual model of the database reflected the many meanings and notions associated with the nature of social innovation (such as 'new governance') as well as the evolution of the overall analytical framework (e.g., the economic 'crisis' of the 1980s was experienced at the time as economic recession and institutional reforms but is interpreted today as a global phenomenon). A second limitation concerns the fact that the data, largely based on interviews and organisational document analysis, had already been filtered and codified by researchers. In other words, the database on social innovations is populated with 'real world' data that has been selected and filtered on the basis of a specific research objective. This systematic data analysis reveals the subtle evolution of the CRISES research programme since its creation in the 1980s. That said, the CRISES research programme has led to the development of a set of analytical tools that enable social innovation to be studied in a variety of ways (manufacturing companies, social economy, public policy networks, etc.).

In addition, the majority of case studies developed by CRISES were based on non-probabilistic sampling of social innovations. Essentially, the cases were composed of a series of non-random samples based on criteria that varied depending on the research programme. Hence, serious caution needs to be taken in the interpretation of the data, considering the sample and coding biases inherent to this methodology (see Biernaki, 2012). Given this limitation, care must be taken in interpreting the comparative analyses, the results of which cannot be generalised to all social innovations produced in Québec (or indeed beyond Québec). However, this does not detract from the ability of comparative analyses to identify trends, which, as spatial, temporal or sector phenomena, could not be detected otherwise. The comparative analyses will enable typologies, possibly even models, to be built and tested with a hypothetical-deductive method. In this way, the generalisability of results is increased relative to the case study method.

Potential contributions: from micro to meso and macro

The concept of social innovation has a variety of meanings, from new social relations, to solutions, to complex social and environmental problems (Nicholls and Murdoch, 2012). Research studies conducted by CRISES have been inspired by different approaches to social innovation that highlight organisational (Schumpeter, 1932), institutional (North, 1990; Scott, 1995) and governance-related (Enjolras, 2008) innovations, national systems (Freeman, 1991; Lundvall, 1992; Nelson, 1993) and innovation regimes (Nelson and Winter, 1982), as well as social entrepreneurs (Caulier-Grice *et al.*, 2010; Young, 1983) and social enterprises (Defourny and Nyssens, 2013), in particular within social (Vienney, 1994) and solidarity-based (Laville, 1994) economies. Moreover, innovations are identified as social based on their purpose (responding to aspirations and to social, cultural territorial needs), their processes (new social relations, new combinations) and their reach (having been taken up within institutions). Lastly, studies conducted by CRISES on social innovations are correlated to development paths or paradigms. In other words, social innovation is conceived of with the view towards social transformation (Klein *et al.*, 2013).

The link between social innovation and social change or social transformation is explained either as a pattern of dissemination and growth supported by inter-organisational relations (e.g., Dees *et al.*, 2004; Mulgan *et al.*, 2007) or by the capacity to connect to societal challenges and dynamics (Howaldt and Schwarz, 2010), suggesting new institutional frameworks or development paradigms (Klein, Laville and Moulaert, 2014). New methods for researching social innovation are needed to explore how social innovation and transformation are related, leading to strengthening the theoretical foundation of social innovation. CRISES' approach proposes that social innovations and social transformations take shape along three dimensions – method of organisation, institutional form and social relationships – and that within these dimensions, the three levels of analysis, macro, micro and meso, are correlated. The macro level pertains to social structures and regulations; micro to social agency, identity rationales and action; and meso to organisations and networks.

These three dimensions are usually analysed in a contingent manner, with social innovation (micro or meso) being driven by social movements in times of crisis (macro) in a given territorial, sectoral and historical context (meso or macro). The CRISES case studies have, indeed, been conducted mainly at the local level on organisations that implement innovations. According to Tardif (2005, p. 25), the approach is based on the notion of the emergence of social innovation:

> As a localized process initiated by different actors who seek to change the interactions taking place between themselves as well as with their organizational and institutional environment – the whole with the aim to counteract the impact of crises while attempting to reconcile the different levels of individual interest, public interest and common good.

The statistical analysis of data will make it possible to move from a micro to a meso and macro approach to studying social innovation. The assumption is that there are objects of study of relevance for social innovation that are not observable at the micro scale. At the meso level of analysis, such a database will allow for a new reading of social innovations in terms of the mechanisms, configurations, evolution and modes of dissemination in time and across locations and sectors of activity. The approach will, moreover, make it possible to focus on phenomena hitherto little studied in the Québec context, such as the emergence and dissemination of innovation clusters, including their patterns and paths of institutionalisation or even their configuration into an innovation system, and to examine their impacts on social transformation, in particular with regard to the Québec development model. This framework, once applied to Québec, may be extended to other areas in order to conduct international comparisons.

There are, indeed, times and territories where social innovations tend to multiply, taking the form of innovation clusters, especially at the onset of crises or in economies with plural tendencies (Klein *et al.*, 2013). Innovations are, then, oriented along emerging socio-technical paradigms, such as new representations of problems and possible solutions or experiments that were successfully carried out in organisations and local communities. For example, during the 1980s and 1990s in Québec, when the crisis of Fordism and the welfare state became apparent, social innovations arose in the areas of labour, people services, collective enterprises, public policies and local development (the areas that CRISES focuses on). Using the CRISES Database on Social Innovations, it will be possible to trace the dynamics of the emergence of these innovations as well as their spread into clusters and their wider impacts on society. For example, a researcher might study the proximity effect, which is a phenomenon that promotes collective dynamics with the potential to modulate or reject the dominant forms of social control or even to propose innovative institutional solutions for a given organisation, industry or territory (Gilly and Pecqueur, 1995).

Using the database it will be possible to study the processes leading to the institutionalisation of social innovations. These issues have been addressed through various approaches, including institutionalist and neo-institutionalist theories, theories of regulation as well as economic sociology inspired by theories of conventions and social movements (Lévesque *et al.*, 2001). The idea of an innovation system draws from the institutionalist approach to building national and regional innovation systems (see Lundvall, 1992). The neo-institutionalist approach places emphasis on the effects of dependencies that limit institutional changes (path dependency), explaining institutionalisation as adaptation and diffusion (Nelson and Winter, 1982; 2002; Schumpeter, 1932; Porter, 1990). However, the notion of path-building, that refers to the ability of collective actors to break up the regulatory framework in order to create a new one, can complement the notion of dependency. Path-building also reveals how social innovations can serve as tools for social transformation (Klein *et al.*, 2013, p. 382; Fontan *et al.*, 2008). Theories of regulation, for their part, have insisted on the deterministic relation between institutions and innovations at the organisational level, albeit characterising institutions as historical and political organisations that result from contingent conflicts between social actors (Aglietta, 1998; Boyer, 1986). The theories on social movements have taken into account the effects of institutions on collective mobilisation and conflict. Among these are the political opportunity structure (McAdam, 1982), the repertoire of collective action (Tilly, 1976; 1986), the agency of social actors and actionalist approaches (Touraine, 1997; Mellucci, 1985) and the resource mobilisation theory (McCarthy and Zald, 1973). Finally, theories on conventions have studied the dynamics of building compromises that lead to the institutionalisation of innovations (Boltanski and Chiapello, 1999; Boltanski and Thévenot, 1991). These theoretical approaches, thereby, offer a variety of explanations of the institutionalisation process of social innovations, ranging from adaptation to institutional constraints, changes in the face of conflict dynamics, to the compromises between actors on the basis of conventions. The statistical analysis of a large amount of data will reveal patterns in the processes of institutionalising innovations and the relationships between these patterns and different governance regimes.

Finally, at the macro-analytical level, the relations between social innovation and the Québec development model can be examined. Often referred to as an 'innovation system', the Québec model is characterised by partnership governance, civil society's participation in the design and implementation of public policies, and the establishment of a plural, mixed, economy (Klein *et al.*, 2013). This analysis would lead to a more in-depth understanding of the characteristics of this model, including its evolution over time, as well as the effects of social innovations on social transformation. Social innovation could even be examined with regard to its possible capacity to influence or transform the development model itself (Lipietz, 1989), and conversely, the effects of such a modified model on social innovation. It would also be possible to study regional innovation systems in the context of smaller territories or sector-based innovation systems (Lévesque, 2011).

There are many other possible lines of research that could be addressed by the CRISES Database on Social Innovation, including:

- To what extent does the state-institutional framework (public policy, governance schemes, etc.) influence the means – collective action and social innovations – used by organisations to respond to civil society's needs and aspirations? An answer to this question might be found in the analysis, for a given territorial context, of the relationships between the legal and regulatory framework in which organisations operate; the public policies and government programmes that apply to organisations; and the factors of emergence of social innovations, in particular the needs and aspirations leading to collective action.
- How does geographic proximity influence the development of social innovation clusters and which sectors of activity are the most conducive to the development of such clusters?
- To what extent do the different types of interactions between organisations have an influence on the development of certain types of social innovation? This pertains to the question of networking between organisations, and a network analysis calls for a spatio-temporal analysis of data. More concretely, the composition and structure of networks, as manifested in interactions, can be studied by means of visualisations and associated analytical methods. In fact, graphs are the most widely used theoretical tool for modelling and identification of properties of structured sets (Beauquier *et al.*, 1992). They are essential to anyone wishing to study and represent a set of links between elements of a finite set of objects (Xuong, 1992). In the CRISES Database on Social Innovations, a detailed analysis of networks of organisations will be realised on the basis of spatio-temporal measurements of the density, eccentricity and centrality of

these networks. The characteristics of organisations and interactions (relations) will serve as discriminating factors for providing a better understanding of certain types of social innovations.

Thus, by expanding the level of analysis and by allowing for comparative analyses, the database can strengthen and build the existing links between social innovation and social transformation. In this way, it will allow for a thorough examination of a central assumption of CRISES, namely that room for innovation and experimentation widens when the macro-social regulations (market, state, collective agreements) are in flux. In such a context, micro-systems can serve as places from which to identify the processes in which new social patterns emerge. By building clusters (Schumpeter, 1932; Porter, 1990) and by institutionalising along different logics, they can form systems and eventually shape new national trajectories of growth (Hollingsworth and Boyer, 1997; Strange, 1996; Crouch and Streeck, 1996).

Conclusion

The decision to develop a database on social innovation was prompted by the limitations of the case study method in terms of the systematisation and generalisation of the knowledge produced on social innovation at the micro-analytical level. In particular this concerned the local emergence of innovations within organisations.

At the methodological level, the purpose of building the relational database was to allow the transformation of qualitative data on social innovation into quantifiable data in one information system, in order to facilitate the structuring and management of a large volume of data and the creation of multiple data sets. The systematic and formal organisation of data allows for rigorous multidimensional and comparative statistical analyses and, therefore, enhances the generalisability of results. The implementation of such an approach at CRISES calls for a more in-depth conceptual examination, if not a re-conceptualisation, of social innovation in order to expand the scope of study to new objects. The transition to a meso-level of analysis would allow social innovation phenomena to be studied that are in the process of emerging or spreading, particularly in the form of clusters, alongside their institutionalisation in the context of differentiated governance regimes. Finally, the expansion of analysis to the macro-level would make it possible to explore social innovation systems, be they regional, sectoral or national and, thereby, the impact of innovations on the social transformations of the Québec model of development.

To conclude, three epistemological issues raised by the development of the CRISES Database on Social Innovations should be mentioned. These relate to the *nature, validity* and *interpretation* of data. The case studies included in the database so far are mainly based on qualitative research methods that take into account the (inter)subjective interpretation of the phenomena under study (Anadón and Guillemette, 2007). This is reflected in the dominance of interviews as a way of learning about the point of view of key actors. To deal with this issue, the proposed database is designed to allow for a transition to a quantitative analysis of data, namely by reducing and formalising the information. Yet, how can it be ensured that their intended meaning does not get lost in the process? On the other hand, the creation of a database of case studies raises the question of the triple interpretation of data: that of the interviewees who provided the information to the researchers conducting the case studies; that of the researchers who collected, organised, analysed and published the data; and the interpretation of the team of researchers who re-conceptualised and organised the information from the case studies for the creation of the database. Given these multiple interpretations, what reading can be given of the results of the comparative analyses generated by the database? Finally, faced with these multiple levels of interpretation, how can the codification of normative evaluations be prevented, in other words, those comprising value judgments rather than facts?

Nonetheless, the case studies all have a common focus: social innovation. Moreover, the three to four data collection templates used in the various research programmes at CRISES through time share many common concepts and dimensions of analysis. The case studies concerned observations that were relatively limited in time (thirty years) and space (Québec). A number of contextual (institutional, demographic, sociopolitical, etc.) variables are, therefore, common to many of them. In short, the many case studies produced by CRISES constitute a source of knowledge and information that has been underutilised to date. Aside from representing a unique opportunity for research of its kind, the project to create a relational database requires formalising a conceptual framework of social innovation to advance the theoretical analysis underlying its work.

To create a quantitative approach and a relational database is a novel way to research social innovation. It is a new way of gathering data in order to develop theories about the generation, emergence and life cycle of social innovations. Should other researchers in the world opt for a similar conceptual framework and relational database model, international comparison would be possible; this would represent a completely innovative way to research social innovation.

Acknowledgements

We wish to acknowledge the especially valuable contribution of David Longtin, who wrote the first draft of this chapter resulting from a collaborative research process. We thank the reviewers for their constructive comments on an earlier version of this text.

Notes

1. Examples include the Welfare Innovations at the Local Level in Favour of Cohesion (WILCO) and TRANsformative Social Innovation Theory (TRANSIT) projects, both of which make extensive use of case studies. See http://sire search.eu/social-innovation/research-projects [Accessed 23 September 2014].
2. Idiographic studies aim at understanding what is a particular activity or individual, in a given context and at a given moment, whereas nomographic studies aim to establish general causal laws of phenomena (Smith, Harré and Langenhove, 1995).
3. The work of formalisation must comply with the main methodological principles, which are the relevance and the operationalisation principle (Flory and Laforest, 2005; Meier, 2006).
4. CRISES bases its work about social innovation on social movement theories, institutionalism theories (French regulation school, convention economy and sociology) and organisation theories. See Bouchard and Lévesque, 2013.

References

Aglietta (1998) *Accumulation et crises du capitalisme*, Paris: Odile Jacob (First edition 1976).
Anadón, M. and Guillemette, F. (2007) 'La recherche qualitative est-elle nécessairement inductive?', *Recherches qualitatives*, 5: 26–37.
Beauquier, D., Berstel, J. and Chrétienne, P. (1992) *Éléments d'algorithmique*. Paris: Masson.
Bélanger, P.R. and Lévesque, B. (1992) 'La théorie de la régulation, du rapport salarial au rapport de consommation. Un point de vue sociologique', *Cahiers de recherche sociologique*, 17: 17–51.
Bernier, L., Bouchard, M.J. and Lévesque, B. (2002) 'La prise en compte de l'intérêt général au Québec. Nouvelle articulation entre l'intérêt individuel, collectif et général', in Enjolras, B. and von Bergmann-Winberg, M.-L. (eds), *Plural Economy and Socio-Economic Regulation – Économie plurielle et régulation socio-économique*. Brussels: CIRIEC-International.
Biernaki, R. (2012) *Reinventing Evidence in Social Enquiry: Decoding Facts and Variables*. New York: Palgrave Macmillan.
Boltanski, L. and Chiapello, E. (1999) *Le nouvel esprit du capitalisme*. Paris: Gallimard.

Boltanski, L. and Thévenot, L. (1991) *De la justification: Les économies de la grandeur*. Paris: Gallimard.

Bouchard, C. (1999) *Contribution à une politique de l'immatériel. Recherche en sciences humaines et sociales et innovations sociales*. Québec: Conseil québécois de la recherche sociale, Groupe de travail sur l'innovation sociale.

Bouchard, M.J. and Lévesque, B. (2013) 'L'innovation et les transformations sociales, une approche théorique plurielle de l'économie sociale. Le cas du Québec', in Hiez, D. et Lavillunière, E. (eds), *Théorie générale de l'économie sociale et solidaire*. Luxembourg: Larcier.

Boyer, R. (1986) *Théorie de la régulation. Une analyse critique*. Paris: La Découverte.

Caulier-Grice, J., Kahn, L., Mulgan, G., Pulford, L. and Vasconcelos, D. (2010) *Study on Social Innovation*. London: Young Foundation, Social Innovation eXchange (SIX) and Bureau of European Policy Advisors.

Comeau, Y., Boucher, J.L., Malo, M.-C. and Vaillancourt Y. (2001) *Essai de typologie des entreprises de l'économie sociale et solidaire*. Montréal: Cahiers du CRISES, no. ET0117.

Cornforth, C. (2004) 'The Governance of Cooperatives and Mutual Associations: A Paradox Perspective', *Annals of Public and Cooperative Economics*, 75: 11–32.

Crouch, C. and Streeck W. (1996) *Political Economy of Modern Capitalism: Mapping Convergence and Diversity*. London: Sage.

Dees, J.G., Battle Anderson, B. and Wei-Skillern, J. (2004) 'Scaling Social Impact', *Stanford Social Innovation Review*, Spring 2004: 1–4.

Defourny, J. and Nyssens, M. (2013) 'Social Innovation, Social Economy, Social Enterprise: What Can the European Debate Tell Us?', in Moulaert, F., MacCallum, D., Mehmood, A. and Amdouch, A. (eds), *The International Handbook on Social Innovation. Collective Action, Social Learning and Transdisciplinary Research*. Cheltenham, UK and Northampton, MA: Edward Elgar.

Enjolras, B. (2008) *Gouvernance et intérêt général dans les services sociaux et de santé*. Brussels: P.I.E. Peter Lang.

Favreau, L. (1995) *Repenser le mouvement communautaire dans une perspective d'économie solidaire. Une hypothèse de renouvellement de la problématique et de la politique du développement communautaire et de l'économie sociale au Québec*. Montréal: Cahiers du CRISES, no. ET9505.

Favreau, L. and Lévesque B. (1995) *Repenser le développement communautaire et l'économie sociale à la faveur de la crise de l'emploi et de la crise de l'État-providence*. Montréal: Cahiers du CRISES, no. ES9504.

Flory, A. and Laforest, F. (2005) *Les bases de données relationnelles*. Paris: Economica.

Fontan, J.-M., Klein, J.-L. and Tremblay, D.-G. (2008) 'Social Innovation at the Territorial Level: From Path Dependency to Path Building', in Drewe, P., Klein, J.-L. and Hulsbergen, E. (eds), *The Challenge of Social Innovation in Urban Revitalization*. Amsterdam: Techne Press.

Freeman, C. (1991) 'Innovation, Changes of Techno-Economic Paradigm and Biological Analogies in Economics', *Revue Economique*, 42 (2): 211–32.

Gilly, J.-P. and Pecqueur, B. (1995) 'La dimension locale de la régulation', in Boyer, R. and Saillard, Y. (eds), *Théorie de la régulation – l'état des savoirs*. Paris: La Découverte.

Hodgson, D.E. and Briand, L. (2013) 'Controlling the Uncontrollable: Project Management and Illusions of Autonomy in Video Game Development', *Work, Employment and Society*, 27 (2): 308–25.

84   *Marie J. Bouchard, et al.*

Hollingsworth, J.R. and Boyer, R. (1997) *Contemporary Capitalism: The Embeddedness of Institutions.* Cambridge: Cambridge University Press.

Howaldt, J. and Schwarz, M. (2010) *Social Innovation: Concepts, Research Fields and International Trends.* Dortmund (Germany), International monitoring (IMO). See http://www.internationalmonitoring.com/research/trend_studies/social_innovation.html [Accessed 11 September 2013].

Klein, J.-L. and Champagne, C. (eds) (2011) *Initiatives locales et lutte contre la pauvreté et l'exclusion.* Québec: Presses de l'Université du Québec. Collection Innovation sociale.

Klein, J.-L., Fontan, J.-M., Harrisson, D. and Lévesque B. (2013) 'The Québec Model: A Social Innovation System Founded on Cooperation and Consensus Building', in Moulaert, F., MacCallum, D., Mehmood, A. and Amdouch, A. (eds), *The International Handbook on Social Innovation. Collective Action, Social Learning and Transdisciplinary Research.* Cheltenham, UK, and Northampton, MA: Edward Elgar.

Klein, J.-L. and Laville, J.-L. (with the collaboration of Moulaert, F.) (2014) 'Repères introductifs', in Klein, J.-L., Laville, J.-L. and Moulaert, F. (eds), *L'innovation sociale.* Paris: Érès.

Lapointe, P.-A. (2000a) *Participation et démocratie au travail.* Montréal: Cahiers du CRISES, no. ET0014.

Lapointe, P.-A. (2000b) *Partenariat, avec ou sans démocratie.* Montréal: Cahiers du CRISES, no. ET0015.

Laville, J.-L. (ed.) (1994) *L'économie solidaire, une perspective internationale.* Paris: Desclée de Brouwer.

Lévesque, B. (2011) *Innovations sociales et pouvoirs publics: Vers un système québécois d'innovation dédié à l'économie sociale et solidaire. Quelques éléments de problématique.* Montréal: Cahiers du CRISES, no. ET1106.

Lévesque, B., Bourque, G. and Forgues, E. (2001) *La nouvelle sociologie économique. Originalité et tendances nouvelles.* Paris: Desclée de Brouwer.

Lipietz, A. (1989) *Choisir l'audace. Une alternative pour le XXIe siècle.* Paris: Éditions la Découverte.

Lundvall, B.-A. (ed.) (1992) *National Systems of Innovation. Toward a Theory of Innovation and Interactive Learning.* London and New York: Anthem Press.

Mata-Toledo, R.A. and Cushman, P.K. (2002) *Introduction aux bases de données relationnelles.* Paris: Dunod.

McAdam, D. (1982) *Political Process and the Development of Black Insurgency.* Chicago, IL: University of Chicago Press.

McCarthy, J.D. and Zald, M. (1973) *The Trend of Social Movements in America: Professionalization and Resource Mobilization.* Morristown, NJ: General Learning Press.

Meier, A. (2006) *Introduction pratique aux bases de données relationnelles (Deuxième édition).* Paris: Springer-Verlag France.

Melucci, A. (1985) 'The Symbolic Challenge of Contemporary Movements', *Social Research,* 52 (4): 789–816.

Mulgan, G., Tucker, S., Ali, R. and Sanders, B. (2007) *Social Innovation: What It Is, Why It Matters and How It Can Be Accelerated.* Oxford: Skoll Centre for Social Entrepreneurship.

Nelson, R. (1993) *National Innovation Systems. A Comparative Analysis.* Oxford: Oxford University Press.

Nelson, R. and Winter, S. (1982) *An Evolutionary Theory of Economic Change.* Cambridge, MA: Harvard University Press.

Nelson, R. and Winter, S. (2002) 'Evolutionary Theorizing in Economics', *Journal of Economic Perspectives*, 16 (2): 23–46.

Nicholls, A. and Murdock, A. (2012) *Social Innovation: Blurring Boundaries to Reconfigure Markets.* Basingstoke: Palgrave Macmillan.

North, D.C. (1990) *Institutions, Institutional Change and Economic Performance.* Cambridge: Cambridge University Press.

Porter, M.E. (1990) *The Competitive Advantage of Nations.* New York: The Free Press.

Schumpeter, J.-A. (1932) 'Entwicklung' (with translation into English 'Development'), http://www.schumpeter.info/ [Accessed 3 November 2014].

Scott, W.R. (1995) *Institutions and organizations.* Thousand Oaks, CA: Sage.

Sinton, D.F. (1978) 'The Inherent Structure of Information As a Constraint to Analysis: Mapped Thematic Data As a Case Study', in Dutton, G. (ed.), *Harvard Papers on Geographic Information Systems.* Reading, MA: Addison-Wesley.

Smith, J.A., Harré, R. and Van Langenhove, L. (1995) 'Idiography and the Case Study', in Smith, J.A., Harré, R. and Van Langenhove, L. (eds), *Rethinking Psychology.* London: Sage.

Strange, S. (1996) 'L'avenir du capitalisme mondial. La diversité peut-elle persister indéfiniment?' in Crouch, C. and Streeck, W. (eds), *Les capitalismes en Europe.* Paris: La Découverte.

Tardif, C. (2005) *Complémentarité, convergence et transversalité: La conceptualisation de l'innovation sociale du CRISES.* Montréal: Cahiers du CRISES, no. ET0513.

Tilly, C. (1976) *From Mobilization to Revolution.* Reading, MA: Addison-Wesley.

Tilly, C. (1986) *The Contentious French.* Cambridge, MA: Harvard University Press.

Touraine, A. (1997) *Le retour de l'acteur. Essai de sociologie.* Paris: Librairie générale française.

Vienney, C. (1994) *L'économie sociale.* Paris: La Découverte.

White, D., Mercier, C., Dorvil, H. and Juteau, L. (1992) 'Les pratiques de concertation en santé mentale: Trois modèles', *Nouvelles Pratiques Sociales*, 5 (1): 77–93.

Xuong, N.H. (1992) *Mathématiques discrètes et informatique.* Paris: Masson.

Yin, R.K. (1994) *Case Study Research. Design and Methods.* Thousand Oaks, CA: Sage.

Young, D.R. (1983) *If Not for Profit, for What?* Lexington, MA: D. C. Heath and Company.

This page intentionally left blank

Part II
Blurring Boundaries and Reconfiguring Relations

This page intentionally left blank

4

Social Innovation: Redesigning the Welfare Diamond

Jane Jenson

Introduction

Decades of neoliberal economics and politics have resulted in major shifts in much of the world in the ways that policy and research communities now understand, shape and work to organise relations between civil society and the state and within civil society itself. Over the last fifteen years, as neoliberalism clearly revealed its limits, these communities began to deploy a range of new or reworked concepts to address ongoing challenges. Social innovation is one. Social cohesion, social inclusion and social investment are three other examples.

This chapter argues that one major contribution that the quasi-concept of social innovation has made to the world of the 'socials' is to provide a novel way to reconfigure market relations in support of social policy initiatives. This is, perhaps, not surprising since so much of the thinking about social innovation – as well as its practices – starts with reference to the work of Joseph Schumpeter (1983 [1934]). As an economist, and as the subtitle of his seminal work said, Schumpeter was most interested in 'profits, capital, credit, interest and the business cycle', the stuff of markets, in other words. Nonetheless, in his discussions of the creative destruction associated with innovation, Schumpeter was careful to consider social as well as economic and institutional factors. Nor does a gesture to Schumpeter mean that discussion of social innovation and markets has to focus narrowly. One overview of the meanings of social innovation – and examples of its practices – that draws on Schumpeter includes the following: new products, new services, new processes, new markets, new platforms, new organisational forms and new business models (Caulier-Grice *et al.*, 2012, pp. 24–5). The examples mentioned place a clear emphasis on market-making and market-shaping activities, whether by private, public or non-profit actors.

Diagnoses of social challenges and social policy agendas have been significantly influenced by such understandings of social innovation. Much that is termed 'social innovation' or promoted by the social innovation community involves innovating in markets and with market actors to generate new well-being, even in areas usually seen as outside of the market. For example, sometimes services previously provided by governments are outsourced to not-for-profit actors such as non-governmental organisations (NGOs) that operate as market actors. Such reconfigurations also often, however, involve explicitly exposing and developing a reliance on non-market dimensions (such as community engagement and public policy) in the processes of market-making, as well as engaging social entrepreneurs in service provision. Social innovation, thus, may involve altering the very goals of markets, turning them towards purposes such as social inclusion and social development, for example, as well as repositioning the profit principle in markets for goods and services or developing a new agenda for business (Nicholls and Murdock, 2012, pp. 2–3 and passim; Osberg and Schmidpeter, 2013).

This market-expanding effect is not the only focus that a study of social innovation may have, of course. The social innovation community may also be concerned, for example, with remaking public policy instruments (see Evers *et al.*, 2014) or with local community and grassroots efforts to remake urban space, with or without support from local government authorities (Moulaert *et al.*, 2010).

The goal of this chapter however is to examine some of the ways that social policy makers use social innovation and social entrepreneurship to offer an alternative vision of market relations and, thereby, are engaged in redesigning the 'welfare diamond'. It does so via a review of initiatives, policies and programmes developed and deployed over the last twenty years, primarily within the borders of the European Union at supranational, national and local levels. It also considers key international actors, such as the Organisation for Economic Cooperation and Development (OECD) as well as national and local-level actors, both private and public. In doing so it provides one account of the blurred boundaries of governance.

New social risks and the welfare diamond

Social innovation is a 'quasi-concept' frequently characterised as having multiple definitions and meanings (Osberg and Schmidpeter, 2013; European Commission, 2013). As such, it is an idea with '... some reputable intellectual basis ... able to operate in both academia and policy domains' (McNeill, 2006, p. 335). A quasi-concept benefits from relying on academics' research but is simultaneously indeterminate enough to make it adaptable to a variety of situations and flexible enough to follow the twists and turns of policy and ideology that everyday politics sometimes makes necessary.[1] Thus, as Bouchard puts it (2012, p. 50, emphasis added), social innovations may serve a variety of purposes: '… social innovations are about challenging the way responsibilities are shared between the public and the private sectors, how the social and economic dimensions are considered independently from one another in public policies, *or* how the global economy is distanced from local communities'.

In recent years social innovation has been deployed alongside other 'socials', all of which are quasi-concepts.[2] Each has been developed in the search for ways of reordering state–society relations in the face of new social risks and new politics. Analytically, this reordering can be described as a reconfiguration of the 'welfare diamond', and in the case of the social innovation initiatives considered here, in particular the market corner of that diamond.

The welfare diamond provides a metaphor for the mixed sources of well-being experienced by everyone.[3] Each corner of the diamond is a potential source of well-being and provides instruments for risk-sharing. For the majority of people, by far their major source of well-being is the *market*, both because of what is earned by themselves or by someone in their family, such as a spouse or a parent and because so much needed for well-being is purchased in markets (Esping-Andersen *et al.*, 2002, p. 11). But welfare is also derived from non-market benefits and services provided within the *family*. Access to welfare also comes from *states* or other public authorities, via public services that do not require the payment of full market prices as well as by income transfers. The fourth source is the *community*, whose volunteers and less than fully marketised exchanges generate welfare by providing a range of services and support, some of which are publicly financed and some of which are privately supported. These four sources of well-being can be represented in the shape of a diamond.

This conceptualisation of a welfare diamond should not be confused with notions of 'sectors' of activity, usually termed the 'private', 'public' and 'third or not-for-profit' sectors. The basis of that typology is the *status of the actor*, whether a private firm, a not-for-profit organisation or a public agency. The welfare diamond, in contrast, distinguishes activity by its *location*. Thus, for example, both a public agency and a not-for-profit association may engage in market activity by charging a fee for products or services, albeit perhaps without seeking a profit. A private firm may be active in the state's portion of the welfare diamond, contracting to buy or sell a product or service. Similarly, the state may shape other parts of the diamond. Nicholls (2012, pp. 230–33), for example, describes in more detail the role of public policy and foundations in building social entrepreneurship and market-making, while Sørensen and Torfing (this volume) describe the co-constitution of innovation by public, private and third-sector social innovators. According to our analytic terminology, they are describing the generation of new activities in the market or community corners of the welfare diamond.

Jurisdictions make their own choices about the content of the welfare diamond and, therefore, about the relationships across the diamond.[4] It is, in fact, the intersecting relational spaces that are often the most interesting to analyse. It is important to look, for example, at how marketised relations are imported into publicly financed social services or the ways that labour markets are structured by the activities of community-based agencies (from the social economy, for example), as well as by the demand of firms.

If each jurisdiction makes choices about the welfare diamond, it also uses a variety of public and private instruments to achieve their goals. For example, even if the labour market is relied on as a primary source of income, many jurisdictions are reluctant to allow markets to distribute access to all goods and services (such as health care, post-secondary education or housing) and rely on actors in the state, family and community corners of the diamond to make a contribution to well-being. While all countries assume that parents have primary responsibility for ensuring the well-being of their children, some countries leave parents on their own to purchase what they can afford in the private market while others provide or subsidise low-cost or free services (childcare and housing, for example) and ensure that parents have adequate income to meet the needs of their children (whether via family allowances or other income supplements). While all countries assume that the community is the place that volunteerism will be located, some rely almost exclusively on voluntary workers, while others maintain and oversee not-for-profit groups that provide good wages and working conditions.

The economic environment around the world has changed over the last thirty years, with significant consequences for the capacity of all corners of the welfare diamond to contribute to well-being (Hall and Lamont, 2013, especially Part I). One significant development is that inequality is on the rise virtually everywhere.[5] Another is that even having a job is not always a reliable source of adequate income. There are many people who are 'working poor', while the labour market fails to absorb vast numbers of work-seekers (Fraser, Gutierrez and Peña-Casas, 2011). The Global South is both experiencing phenomenal development in some places (with the attendant environmental and social challenges) and still facing deep poverty and hunger. Some of this is, in turn, partly but never exclusively related to socio-demographic changes, including ageing societies virtually everywhere around the world, and increases in lone-parent families (ILO, 2011). Global population flows, whether from the Global South northward or within the European Union from poorer to richer member states (whether from east to west or north to south), are also creating new wealth for some and precariousness, poverty and even misery for others (Dustmann and Frattini, 2011). Historically marginalised groups facing prejudice – Aboriginal peoples in many countries and Roma almost everywhere they live – find their lives increasingly difficult (UN, 2009; European Commission, 2011a).

Many of these changes can be summarised under the label of 'new social risks' (Bonoli and Natali, 2012). The structure of these new risks challenges previous configurations of the welfare diamond and associated social policy programmes, practices and ideas about the proper and possible balance of spaces for markets, states, families and communities. In effect, the market corner of the welfare diamond is being exhorted by social policy communities to expand, by recognising the contributions of – and contributing towards – the social economy and social entrepreneurship more generally. But often practices of social innovation also include reworking both the responsibilities of the community corner of the diamond and aligning it in ground-breaking ways with respect to the market. As it does so, social innovation's status as a quasi-concept is very clear. Numerous ways of understanding it co-exist as markets are re-imagined.

Redesigning social and labour market policies by promoting social innovations

The new social risks have provoked a variety of policy responses, and these often result in blurred boundaries. Many call for social innovators to address new social risks by expanding markets as well as by shifting relationships among markets, the community and state.[6] This blurring of boundaries can happen in two ways. In some cases, while states and other public authorities continue to finance interventions to address risk, they are much less willing to design policy that involves them directly in delivery. Instead, they may turn to other actors operating in the market sector of the welfare diamond to form partnerships or to deliver the service according to a contract with public authorities. The second way that the market corner of the welfare diamond is bolstered is by supporting social enterprises of many types, because they are seen as more capable of meeting current needs than either the state or private sector firms. Several policy areas illustrate this direction of change. However, labour markets are probably the key domain in which market-building with the support of social policy has occurred.

The drivers behind policy interest in social innovation within labour markets rests on the recognition that it is no longer possible to count on traditional firms and labour markets to provide an adequate supply of jobs and to match supply to demand for workers. After 1945, the labour market appeared to operate more smoothly, seeming to create an adequate supply of jobs and absorbing most (male) jobseekers. Public policy makers could confine their market-shaping role to regulations about hiring and working conditions, as well as unemployment insurance for those without a job for a short while. The market also provided an expanding array of goods and services. Now and for the last few decades, however, growing needs for many kinds of new services as well as job creation and job-matching, as labour markets have tightened, have become major preoccupations within social policy communities. The previous seemingly smooth operation of the labour market and of service provision can no longer be assumed. This is due to the combined effects of technological change, which has reduced demand for workers in many firms and industries, and the new social risks generated by large-scale social trends such as increased inequality, social exclusion, ageing populations and demographic change. In addition, austerity-driven public policies have brought cutbacks in public-sector employment, a major source of jobs in the post-1945 years. Faced with these challenges, policy makers have turned to fostering and supporting market actors such as social enterprises and a social economy that they hope can simultaneously achieve three objectives: to help to train and prepare workers touched by the social risks to enter paid employment (supply) and to increase the labour market's need for workers (demand) by expanding and better organising markets for goods and services (supply) that the traditional firm in the private sector does not adequately offer. This third contribution is often associated with 'green' products or welfare services, but many types of services might be provided in these new markets.

Policy makers concerned with the levels and rates of employment in contemporary societies have seen social enterprises as job creators as well as 'work integration enterprises' (Evers *et al.*, 2014, pp. 15–16). Initiatives often coming from the community sector of the welfare diamond may seek to shape either – and sometimes both – the supply and demand structures of labour markets, increasingly with the support of public authorities. On the supply side, and usually as part of an agenda around social inclusion, social enterprises can work to enable young people, women, immigrants and the long-term unemployed to enter the labour market. Such efforts rely on a variety of legal forms and can be seen as 'new expressions of organized civil society' (Vidal, 2005, p. 807). These enterprises can be an instrument for the achievement of the 'activa-tion' commitment of European social and economic policy (Evers and Guillemard, 2012, Chapter 7). On the demand side, social enterprises – and the social economy more generally – are often tasked with filling gaps in services that do not attract investment by traditional private-sector firms. These new service providers meet growing societal needs and, in the process, create employment. In this context, social innovation can address existing gaps in the market corner of the welfare diamond and, particularly, its failure adequately to provide work, income and inclusion as well as products and services. In these ways, social innovation can also invoke other quasi-concepts, such as social inclusion or social cohesion.

Some examples serve to illustrate various perspectives on social and labour market policy. The OECD has long been concerned with pro-moting higher employment rates but has also increasingly become cognisant of market imperfections (Mahon and McBride, 2008). It has been actively constructing an analysis of how to address social chal-lenges around employment by relying on social innovation (Noya, 2011). Since its 2005 edition, the OECD's *Oslo Manual* has recognised a social dimension to innovation. While its *Innovation Strategy* still primarily focuses on standard approaches and measures of innovation, social innovation has received some attention when 'global and social challenges' are raised, while social enterprises have been discussed as an instrument of response to such challenges (OECD, 2010a: 182ff; 2010b: Chapter 5). Deployment of the quasi-concept is, in other words, an alternative way of doing entrepreneurship, management and finance. This can be interpreted as a call for greater interaction across the market and community corners of the welfare diamond – perhaps including a blurring of boundary distinctions.

This turn to social innovation is evident in the OECD's efforts to foster development of labour markets and its analysis of the failure of these markets to provide sufficient well-being for all. An analysis of policy documents and initiatives shows that, while there is a range of ideas about social innovation, one strategy in which the OECD has invested significantly, as part of its concern with the levels and conditions of employment, involves emphasising community-based actions to ensure greater inclusion via local partnerships that innovate in economic governance and employment creation.[7] For example, the OECD's Local Economic and Employment Development (LEED) programme has as its mission to contribute to the creation of more and better jobs via innovative policy as well as effective implementation and coordinated strategies.[8]

In 2000, the programme launched its Forum on Social Innovations, framed explicitly around the notion of improving well-being,[9] and developed an officially legitimated definition of social innovation that extended that of the *Oslo Manual*.[10] In this definition, social innovation involves 'conceptual, process or product change, organisational change and changes in financing, and new relationships with stakeholders and territories'. The value added by social innovations is that they can, according to the Forum on Social Innovations, both innovate in services and help in 'identifying and implementing new labour market integration processes, new competencies, new jobs, and new forms of participation, as diverse elements that each contribute to improving the position of individuals in the workforce'. Concretely, this has supported the promotion of social entrepreneurship and social economy organisations, by identifying and celebrating their potential for job creation.[11] LEED provides expert teams of advisors to jurisdictions seeking to put such innovations into place.

Of course the OECD is not alone in seeing social entrepreneurs and their market behaviour as significant within the wider economy. The European Union has also been moving in this direction particularly since the 2008 economic crisis. The European Union launched its Social Business Initiative (SBI) in 2011 (European Commission, 2011b). Initially, the potential for 'social business' was broadly cast to include all types of firms from multinationals to social enterprises.[12] Quickly, however, the SBI narrowed down[13] to focus only on social entrepreneurs and their businesses, valued because 'social enterprises seek to serve the community's interest (social, societal, environmental objectives) rather than profit maximisation. They often have an innovative nature, through the goods or services they offer, and through the organisation or production methods they resort to ...'.[14] The promise of social innovations and social enterprise was incorporated into the European Union's *Europe 2020* strategy.[15] Moreover, a series of high-profile interventions have signalled that the European Union shares the views of those who see a greater role for social enterprises in achieving its targets for social inclusion and poverty reduction via their potential for job creation and new innovative services. It contributes to encouraging and supporting such new market actors via actions such as the 2014 conference on 'Empowering social entrepreneurs for innovation, inclusive growth and jobs'. At that event, workshops focused on the 'potential of social enterprises for job creation and green economy' as well as on the ways that the European Union could use its structural funds to support and foster social enterprises.[16] Leverage for jobs, social inclusion and green initiatives were all identified as necessary because they are inadequately addressed by traditional firms.

Nor is it only international or supranational organisations that engage in behaviour meant to structure labour markets, both on the supply and demand sides. The major cross-national study of social cohesion and innovation reported in Evers *et al.* (2014) documented that 'work integration enterprises' were the most common innovation in local welfare systems. These kinds of businesses exist at the blurry boundary between market and community, often difficult to distinguish from the kinds of community groups, third-sector providers and associations that engage in social development projects, frequently at the local level (Moulaert *et al.*, 2010).

Social policy communities' enthusiasm for the market participation of social entrepreneurs and the social economy has had to go beyond cheer-leading and publicising best practices, of course. The reconfiguration of the welfare diamond has necessitated attention to how social innovations will be financed. This need has resulted in blurring of boundaries between public and private governance as public funds flow into the market corner of the welfare diamond to finance, in whole or in part, services that are no longer public services in the classic meaning of the term, that is provided by public employees at no cost (or little cost) to users. 'Many if not most of the SIs [social innovations] we dealt with rely on a multiplicity of resources and their combination; the mix may vary and state financing may often be the most important component, but in most cases there is a degree of (financial) co-responsibility of other organizations from the civil society or the business sector' (Evers *et al.*, 2014, p. 22). In other words, local, regional, national or European public authorities were actively using their available funds to foster local innovations in labour markets and for services. They were engaged in market-making and in blurring traditional boundaries between public and other forms of services.

Developments in childcare services provide another good example of this blurring, which has intensified as the 'social investment perspective' has taken over more and more of social policy discourse.[17] Where the social investment perspective has been implemented, new public spending has been made and services have been expanded. And indeed, these social investment interventions continued even during the first five years of the economic crisis (Kvist, 2013). However, much of this growth has been achieved via reliance on social enterprises, considered to be most innovative.

The social investment perspective on modernising social policy[18] diagnoses the challenges facing families with children and prescribes strategies to increase parental employment as well as to provide services focussed on the human capital of children in order to 'break the intergenerational cycle of disadvantage'.[19] The social policy analysis underpinning the social investment perspective rests on two main themes (Esping-Andersen *et al.*, 2002; Jenson, 2012). The first is that it is better for children that their parents are employed than that the family is workless. Following from this perspective, lone mothers and underemployed mothers are a prime target for integration into the labour force and, therefore, as clients of the work integration enterprises described above. The second theme is that the emerging knowledge-based economy requires significant investment in human capital and that this must begin with the youngest children and early childhood education. This focus is examined here.

Childcare services have expanded significantly across Europe, with stable or greater public financing of childcare services between 1998 and 2009 in every European country except Luxembourg (OECD, 2014, PF3.1). Nonetheless, while spending increased or remained at least stable, many jurisdictions reduced or limited their own direct service provision and provided incentives to social enterprises to organise services. Thus, public funding has gone to non-public actors to develop services needed to implement the social investment perspective.

For example, Sweden is a country often identified as an early adopter of the social investment perspective (Esping-Andersen *et al.*, 2002). In the 1980s it began to innovate in forms of service provision in the name of 'choice' (Blomqvist, 2004).[20] With respect to services for children, this involved reducing the dominant position of the municipal childcare centre, which had been virtually the only form of service provision used when the system expanded from the 1960s.[21] In the 1980s, Sweden turned to parental and personnel cooperatives to broaden the variety of childcare (Duane-Richard and Mahon, 2001). By the 1990s, the range of providers widened again. Changes to legislation at the time meant that most municipalities would continue to provide services directly, but they would also be responsible for overseeing the conditions and quality of non-municipal services and non-public providers, both commercial and non-profit (OECD, 2005, p. 96).

Permission to establish private pre-schools (as childcare centres are called in Sweden) that would receive public funding similar to that of municipal centres was instituted in 1984. The form of private provision that inspired this social innovation was the parental cooperative. Since that time, reliance on publicly funded pre-school provided by institutions other than the municipal childcare centre has expanded significantly. A market in childcare grew slowly but steadily.[22] By 2006, across Sweden the number of children attending a private preschool was 17%; the parental cooperative remained the most usual form (Korpi, 2007, p. 55). However, the share of service provided by private pre-schools ranged from 0% to 47%, depending on the municipality. The higher share was concentrated in urban areas and better-off neighbourhoods (Blomqvist, 2004, p. 150).

The United Kingdom, after 1997, was a convert to the social investment perspective (Dobrowolsky and Jenson, 2005). The pattern of social innovations in the childcare domain has differed from that of Sweden, however, because the United Kingdom has historically been one of the European countries that relied most on private forms of financing services as well as for providing them (OECD, 2005, p. 93). The 1998 National Childcare Strategy extended an entitlement to free part-time provision for three- and four-year-olds. Funding for childcare provision was increased, and there was recognition of the need to expand the number of spaces available, via both public provision and private and voluntary sectors and via social enterprises. The new funds could be used to finance state, private and not-for-profit providers, and there was an emphasis on cross-sector planning and cooperation. While local authorities in England were 'expected to develop, plan and coordinate childcare and early years services', there was a specific emphasis on working with partners across sectors, 'including local community representatives, Jobcentre Plus, schools, health agencies, NGOs and commercial private childcare providers' (OECD, 2005, p. 99). Several incentives provided support for the development of the childcare market via social enterprises such as worker or parent cooperatives, service cooperatives, community nurseries, and so on (SEL, 2002). Lyon and Fernandez (2012, p. 4) found that in 2009, '73% of the 15,600 full day care nurseries in the UK [were] in the private sector, 15% in the voluntary sector and 12% in the public sector'. Other research suggested that 'within the private childcare sector, there are many small businesses with a well-developed social ethic and purpose' (Capacity, 2008, p. 4).

These two examples reflect the recognition that social entrepreneurs hoping to operate social enterprises may have difficulty obtaining adequate financing. In addition to the transfer of public funds described for both Sweden and Britain, other institutions, particularly banks, can be tapped to finance social innovations in these policy domains. For example, a stakeholder for EU consultations on these issues is the *Fédération européenne des banques éthiques et alternatives* (FEBEA – European Federation of Ethical and Alternative Banks), a network of banks, savings and loan cooperatives, investment companies and foundations, sharing information about their innovations in financial instruments.[23] Cooperatives and other forms of alternative banking have a long history, often arising in the late 19th century to meet the needs of local communities without access to services or groups, such as farmers, whose pooling of risk was complicated. Now the form is often used to provide 'socially responsible investing' (an overview is given in Geobey *et al.*, 2012). Such rejigging of the market relations of investment managers – whether in banks or in other firms – is one way of growing the funding for social innovation. Among other things, they may provide help to social entrepreneurs with their business plans. For example, *Babies and Bosses* (OECD, 2005, p. 23) pointed to a problem in the British childcare system. Providers would '... too often close down after start-up funds run out, as business plans were based on unrealistic expectations about demand or over-optimistic cost assumptions'. Advice from a banking institution knowledgeable about social enterprises and the social economy could be of great help.

All these strategies are responses to the recognition that, in many situations, traditional market practices and institutions have proven themselves inadequate to the task of financing social innovation while public funding is one of the possible sources of finance for the enterprises working within the market corner of the welfare diamond.

Conclusion

This chapter has argued that social policy communities across Europe have participated in the reconfiguration of the welfare diamond. They have faced a set of challenges laid down by the appearance of new social risks among which are rising poverty rates, changing family norms and lone-parenthood, an inadequate supply of jobs and problems of labour market integration. Seeking to improve social inclusion and social cohesion, social policy communities have adopted

strategies for prompting, promoting and supporting social innovations in the market. They have turned to social entrepreneurs to alter
patterns of demand and supply in labour markets. The hope is to
improve labour supply by funding and promoting social enterprises
engaged in training and retraining the hard-to-employ, those excluded
from the labour market or those without the necessary skills. Social
policy communities have also sought to increase demand for workers
by supporting the creation of many types of social enterprises that
provide, often in the welfare and environmental sectors, for needs
that go unmet or services that are not equally accessible when only
commercial firms are active in their provision. They have also turned
to social entrepreneurs to provide the key services identified by the
social investment perspective for modern social policy. These are not
only employment services but also childcare that serves the double
function of enabling parental labour market participation and, even
more importantly from this perspective, adequate investments in
human capital from the pre-school years onwards via accessible and
high-quality early education and care.

   Social innovations, especially social entrepreneurship and quasi-
markets, are now and increasingly presented as positive ways to do social
interventions, avoiding the limits of both 'big business' driven by profit-
seeking and 'big government' driven by the practices and controls of
Weberian-style public administrations. Thus, as the claims increasingly
go, effective social investments will be more likely, at least to be identified and first implemented, if they are left to these market-making
and market-modelled innovators. A range of mechanisms and policy
instruments have been deployed across different jurisdictions, but
many share the characteristic that they allow the market corner of the
welfare diamond to expand by becoming more active in the provision
of services. One key way that this move has been undertaken – usually
at the local level – is by providing public funds for provision of what
might have been or used to be public services. Thus, community-based
social entrepreneurs have increasingly provided employment integration services or immigration integration services which in the past – if
provided – were usually public. Similarly, as childcare services have
increased significantly in number and the amount of public spending
on them has risen concomitantly, the dominant position of public provision has given way to a multitude of market-based actors often operating as social enterprises in many countries. Such changes constitute
significant change in the relations between state and civil society and
within civil society itself.

Notes

1. Linguists focus on these same dimensions. They recognise quasi-concepts' polysemy and describe such concepts as those which are not yet stabilised or are in the process of being destabilised (Bartsch, 2002, p. 50). For a more elaborate presentation of social innovation as a quasi-concept, see European Commission (2013).

2. In this group are other useful notions such as social cohesion (Jenson, 2010a; Bernard, 1999), social investment (Jenson, 2010b), social inclusion (Levitas, 2005) and social capital (McNeill, 2006).

3. The notion of welfare diamond presented here is clearly an extension of Gøsta Esping-Andersen's popular 'welfare triangle', which identifies the state, market and family as the three sources of well-being. I believe that it is a mistake and misleading to try, as he did, to subsume the welfare-generating community sector under the family corner of the triangle and to restrict the production of welfare to 'markets (purchased welfare), families (the reciprocity of kin) and government (solidarity)' (Esping-Andersen, *et al.*, 2002, p. 4). Hence I propose a welfare mix with four corners that make a diamond. For this representation, see also Evers, Pijl and Ungerson (1994) as well as Evers and Guillemard (2012).

4. The recognition that there is no single form led, among other conceptual exercises, to the large literature on welfare regimes (e.g., Esping-Andersen *et al.*, 2002) and welfare mix (e.g., Evers and Guillemard, 2012). For a recent review of the results of such choices in local welfare systems, see Evers, Ewert and Brandsen (2014).

5. The OECD has been tracking mounting inequalities both in the OECD world and in the Global South for almost a decade. See, for example, OECD (2011, p. 22).

6. For one recent discussion of such examples, see Nicholls and Murdock (2012, especially Chapters 3, 5, 6).

7. It is interesting to note than an early precursor was Piore and Sabel's *Second Industrial Divide* (1984), which argued that innovation for the late 20th century could come not from firms organised around the social relations of Fordism but from those harking back to the 19th century's personalised social relations of craft production. A decade later, Charles Sabel led the team assessing the potential for social innovation of the Irish Government's experimental 'creation of urban and rural area-based partnerships to address issues of social exclusion in a more flexible, decentralised and participative way' (OECD, 1996, p. 5). This assessment of partnerships with various civil society groups as well as local authorities concentrated in disadvantaged areas was quickly followed by a number of OECD studies of the innovation potential of local partnerships for local development (OECD, 2001).

8. See http://www.oecd.org/cfe/leed/buildingmoreandbetterjobs.htm [Accessed 22 August 2014].

9. For this Forum, 'Social innovation deals with improving the welfare of individuals and community through employment, consumption or participation, its expressed purpose being therefore to provide solutions for individual and community problems'. http://www.oecd.org/cfe/leed/socialinnovation [Accessed 22 August 2014].

10. This definition received the imprimatur of the LEED Directing Committee (Noya, 2011). It is now consistently used as the OECD's definition of social innovation, sometimes with the claim that it is the first definition generated by an intergovernmental organisation and one of the first ever (OECD, 2010b, p. 196).

11. See the activities listed at http://www.oecd.org/employment/leed/leedforumonsocialinnovations.htm#Activities [Accessed 22 August 2014].

12. http://ec.europa.eu/internal_market/social_business/index_en.htm [Accessed 30 September 2013]. This was intended to be a broad initiative. Other targets were multinationals and SMEs, including their involvement with environmental protection and acceptance of corporate responsibility. See the press release at http://europa.eu/rapid/press-release_IP-11-1238_en.htm?locale=en [Accessed 22 August 2014].

13. A Google search (22 August 2014) on 'social business initiative' led to a web page titled 'social entrepreneurship'. The MNC and SME were nowhere to be found.

14. http://ec.europa.eu/internal_market/social_business/index_en.htm. This attention to social business with innovative potential is not to be confused with *Innovation Union* (http://ec.europa.eu/research/innovation-union/index_en.cfm) which focuses on technological innovation and whose new 'innovation indicator' has nothing 'social' about it. See http://europa.eu/rapid/press-release_IP-13-831_en.htm [All accessed 22 August 2014].

15. Given that social businesses, according to the European Union's conceptualisation, may contribute to smart, sustainable or inclusive growth, 'their key aim is to effect social and economic transformation that contributes to the objectives of the Europe 2020 Strategy' (European Commission, nd [2012], no page).

16. See the conference report at http://ec.europa.eu/internal_market/conferences/2014/0116-social-entrepreneurs/workshops/index_en.htm [Accessed 22 August 2014].

17. Sometimes this approach to social policy is termed the 'social investment state', following Giddens' (1998, Chapter 4) original formulation (e.g., Cantillon, 2011). I prefer the label 'social investment perspective' (Dobrowolsky and Jenson, 2005; Jenson 2010b) precisely because, as is argued here, more than the state corner of the welfare diamond and more than public authorities are involved in its promotion and implementation.

18. The social investment perspective should not be confused with the notion of 'social investments', one that has a long history and another meaning.

19. The European Union committed itself explicitly to the social investment perspective in 2012 and thus provided a succinct summary of the principles that had been in circulation for more than 15 years. See http://ec.europa.eu/social/main.jsp?catId=1060&langId=en, consulted 22 August 2014. See also Kvist (2013, pp. 91–2).

20. Similar innovations to incite the mobilisation of non-public providers were developed in the health and education domains (Blomqvist, 2004).

21. Family daycare providers were also part of the system, but they provided very little of the service (OECD, 2005).

22. The pace of growth was affected by the ongoing debates in Sweden over how to treat commercial childcare providers. The centre-right governments

tended to want to allow them to receive public funds from both the central and municipal governments as any non-profit alternative form of care would, while the Swedish Social Democrats wanted to reserve public funding for non-profits. Korpi (2007) reviews these debates in detail.
23. http://www.ethicalbankingeurope.com/febea/legal/febea [Accessed 22 August 2014].

References

Bartsch, R. (2002) 'Generating Polysemy: Metaphor and Metonymy', in Dirven, R. and Pörings, R., *Metaphor and Metonymy in Comparison and Contrast*. Berlin: Walter de Gruyter, pp. 49–74.
Bernard, P. (1999) 'La cohésion sociale: Critique dialectique d'un quasi-concept', *Lien social et Politiques*, 41: 47–59.
Blomqvist, P. (2004) 'The Choice Revolution: Privatization of Swedish Welfare Services in the 1990s', *Social Policy & Administration*, 38 (2): 139–55.
Bonoli, G. and Natali, D. (eds) (2012) *The Politics of the New Welfare State*. Oxford: Oxford University Press.
Bouchard, M.J. (2012) 'Social Innovation, an Analytical Grid for Understanding the Social Economy: The Example of the Québec Housing Sector', *Service Business*, 6: 47–59.
Cantillon, B. (2011) 'The Paradox of the Social Investment State: Growth, Employment and Poverty in the Lisbon Era', *Journal of European Social Policy*, 21 (5): 432–49.
Capacity (2008) *Social Enterprise: A childcare solution for London?* Available at http://www.capacityltd.org.uk/docs/Social_Enterprise_Report.pdf [Accessed 22 October 2014].
Caulier-Grice, J., Davies, A., Patrick, R. and Norman, W. (2012) *Defining Social Innovation*. A deliverable of the project: 'The theoretical, empirical and policy foundations for building social innovation in Europe' (TEPSIE), Brussels: European Commission.
Dobrowolsky, A. and Jenson, J. (2005) 'Social Investment Perspectives and Practices: A Decade in British Politics', in Powell, M., Bauld, L. and Clarke, K. (eds), *Social Policy Review*, 17. Bristol: Policy Press at the University of Bristol.
Duane-Richard, A. and Mahon, R. (2001) 'Sweden: Models in Crisis', in Jenson, J. and Sineau, M. (eds), *Who Cares? Women's Work, Childcare, and Welfare State Redesigns*. Toronto: University of Toronto Press.
Dustmann, C. and Frattini, T. (2011) 'Immigration. The European Experience'. Centro Studi Luca d'Agliano Development Studies Working Paper No. 326. Available at SSRN: http://ssrn.com/abstract=2023575 [Accessed 27 November 2014.]
Esping-Andersen, G., Gallie, D., Hemerijck, A. and Myles, J. (2002) *Why We Need a New Welfare State*. Oxford: Oxford University Press.
European Commission (2011a) *An EU Framework for National Roma Integration Strategies up to 2020*, COM(2011) 173 final.
European Commission (2011b) (nd) The Social Business Initiative. Promoting Social Investment Funds. Staff Working Paper. Brussels: DG Internal Market and Services.
European Commission (2012) (nd) *The Social Business Initiative of the European Commission*. Brussels: European Commission.

European Commission (2013) *Social Innovation Research in the European Union. Approaches, Findings and Future Directions. Policy Review*. Brussels: European Commission.

Evers, A. and Guillemard, A-M. (eds) (2012) *Social Policy and Citizenship*. Oxford: Oxford University Press.

Evers, A., Ewert, B. And Brandsen, T. (eds) (2014) *Social Innovations for Social Cohesion. Transnational Patterns and Approaches from 20 European Cities.* Available at http://www.wilcoproject.eu/downloads/WILCO-project-eReader. pdf [Accessed 3 November 2014].

Evers, A., Pilj, M. and Ungerson, C. (eds) (1994) *Payments for Care. A Comparative Overview*. Aldershot: Avebury.

Fraser, N., Gutiérrez, R. and Peña-Casas, R. (eds) (2011) *Working Poverty in Europe: A Comparative Approach*. Work and Welfare in Europe Series. Basingstoke: Palgrave Macmillan.

Geobey, A., Westley, F. and Weber, O. (2012) 'Enabling Social Innovation through Developmental Social Finance', *Journal of Social Entrepreneurship*, 3 (2): 151–65.

Giddens, A. (1998) *The Third Way. The Renewal of Social Democracy*. Cambridge: Polity Press.

Hall, P.A. and Lamont, M. (eds) (2013) *Social Resilience in the Neoliberal Era*. New York: Cambridge University Press.

ILO [International Labour Organization] (2011) *A Social Protection Floor for a Fair and Inclusive Globalization*. Geneva: ILO.

Jenson, J. (2010a) *Defining and Measuring Social Cohesion*. London & Geneva: Commonwealth Secretariat & UNRISD.

Jenson, J. (2010b) 'Diffusing Ideas after Neo-liberalism: The Social Investment Perspective in Europe and Latin America', *Global Social Policy*, 10 (1): 59–84.

Jenson, J. (2012) 'A New Politics for the Social Investment Perspective: Objectives, Instruments and Areas of Intervention in Welfare Regimes', in Bonoli, G. and Natali, D. (eds), *The Politics of the New Welfare State*. Oxford: Oxford University Press, pp. 21–44.

Korpi, B.M. (2007) *The Politics of Pre-School: Intentions and Decisions Underlying the Emergence and Growth of the Swedish Pre-School*. 3rd Edition. Stockholm: Ministry of Education.

Kvist, J. (2013) 'The Post-Crisis European Social Model: Developing or Dismantling Social Investments?' *Journal of International and Comparative Social Policy*, 29 (1): 91–107.

Levitas, R. (2005) *The Inclusive Society? Social Exclusion and New Labour*. Basingstoke, Hampshire: Palgrave Macmillan.

Lyon, F. and Fernandez, H. (2012) Scaling Up Social Enterprise: Strategies Taken from Early Years Providers. Working paper 79. Birmingham: Third Sector Research Centre.

Mahon, R. and McBride, S. (2008) *The OECD and Transnational Governance*. Vancouver: University of British Columbia Press.

McNeill, D. (2006) 'The Diffusion of Ideas in Development Theory and Policy', *Global Social Policy*, 6 (3): 334–54.

Moulaert, F., Martinelli, F., Swyngedouw, E. and González, S. (eds) (2010) *Can Neighbourhoods Save the City? Community Development and Social Innovation*. Milton Park: Routledge.

Nicholls, A. (2012) 'Postscript: The Legitimacy of Social Entrepreneurship; Reflexive Isomorphism in a Pre-paradigmatic Field', in Gidron, B. and Hasenfeld, Y. (eds), *Social Enterprises. An Organizational Perspective*. Basingstoke, Hampshire: Palgrave Macmillan, pp. 222–53.

Nicholls, A. and Murdock, A. (eds) (2012) *Social Innovation: Blurring Boundaries to Reconfigure Markets*. Basingstoke: Palgrave Macmillan.

Noya, A. (2011) 'Presentation', at the International Conference on *Challenge Social Innovation. Innovating Innovation by Research*. Vienna, 19–21 September.

OECD (1996) *Local Partnerships and Social Innovation. Ireland*. Paris: OECD.

OECD (2001) *Local Partnerships for Better Governance*. Paris: OECD.

OECD (2005) *Babies and Bosses – Reconciling Work and Family Life. Volume 4. Canada, Finland, Sweden and the United Kingdom*. Paris: OECD.

OECD (2008) *Growing Unequal*. Paris: OECD.

OECD (2010a) *The OECD Innovation Strategy. Getting a Head Start on Tomorrow*. Paris: OECD.

OECD (2010b) *SMEs, Entrepreneurship and Innovation*. Paris: OECD.

OECD (2011) *Divided We Stand*. Paris: OECD.

OECD (2014) *OECD Family Database*. Paris: OECD. Available at www.oecd.org/social/family/database [Accessed 7 November 2014].

Osberg, T. and Schmidpeter, R. (eds) (2013) *Social Innovation. Solutions for a Sustainable Future*. Berlin: Springer.

Piore, M. and Sabel, C. (1984) *The Second Industrial Divide. Possibilities for Prosperity*. NYC: Basic Books.

Schumpeter, J. (1983) [1934] *The Theory of Economic Development. An Inquiry into Profits, Capital, Credit, Interest and the Business Cycle*. New Brunswick, NJ: Transaction.

SEL (Social Enterprise London) (2002) *Social Enterprise Guide to Childcare*. London: SEL.

Vidal, I. (2005) 'Social Enterprise and Social Inclusion: Social Enterprises in the Sphere of Work Integration', *International Journal of Public Administration*, 28 (9–10): 807–25.

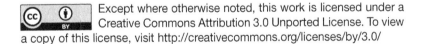

5
Social Innovation for Social Cohesion

Adalbert Evers and Benjamin Ewert

Introduction

In light of the major challenges facing societies and political and social systems in Europe, there is an increasing focus on micro-scale social innovations. But what can such innovations contribute? How can they best be understood? And how can a positive interaction between these forms of social innovation and public policies for reform be ensured? The EU-funded international research project, 'Welfare Innovations at the Local Level in Favour of Cohesion' (WILCO) aimed to explore how social innovations can help political actors as well as organisations and movements from civil society in finding better coping strategies with respect to social inclusion. The project analysed both specific social innovations and the ways in which they are taken up by established local welfare systems. This remit implied studying both sides of the social innovation phenomenon: first the projects that represent social innovation; second, the developments that have been set in train within established welfare systems as a consequence.

This chapter, however, focuses on the former of these aspects only: the nature of social innovation itself. It is based on case studies involving seventy-five social innovations[1] in twenty cities and ten countries across Europe.[2] The chapter describes and analyses the approaches and instruments used in these local projects, which all have a strong innovative dimension. By doing this, the aim is to bridge the gap between social innovation debates, on the one hand, and wider discussions about public policy and welfare system reform on the other.

The phenomenon of social innovation (and its various promoters, agents of change and social entrepreneurs) is seen as distinct from social movements that theorise new 'utopias' as solutions to social problems.

The effects of social innovation typically work 'in the here and now' in the places in which they are operating, but they also contain wider messages concerning values, hopes and assumptions. Social innovations are practical devices, but they can also act as larger symbols of hopes and aspirations. Other actors, such as the political-administrative system, can then engage with and react to social innovation in various ways. They can borrow successful instruments, adapting them to their own administrative and policy frameworks. But equally, these other actors may also feel challenged by the underlying hopes and aspirations of the innovators themselves. There is, then, a significant difference, as well as significant room for variation, between *making use* of social innovations, their methods and instruments, and actually learning from them and the background of aspirations and convictions that motivates them.

The analysis of the social innovations included in the WILCO research aims to facilitate such a broader concept of policy learning that goes beyond making (greater) use of some instruments and devices alone.

This chapter, first, outlines definitions and methods used in the WILCO research into social innovation. It then presents a number of approaches and instruments that public policy could use and learn from and, finally, a series of questions are raised about learning and change in welfare systems and related public policies.

Definitions and methodology

For the purposes of the WILCO project, social innovation was defined in terms of both products and processes, namely new ideas translated into practical approaches that were also new in the context where they appeared. However, the problem with defining social innovation resides less in innovation and more in the meaning of 'social'. Studying the current literature on conceptualising and defining *social* innovation, it is clear that 'social' is mainly equated with 'improvement' (Phills, 2008), finding a better answer to basic social needs and improving social relations (Moulaert, 2010), amongst other 'good things'.

However, while most analyses apply this broad consensus on the positive definition of the social aspect of social innovation (see BEPA, 2010, and Mulgan, 2006), the values, actions and outcomes of social innovations will, in fact, be widely contested. By definition, innovations differ from prevailing routines, forms of thinking and acting. It is possible that they may become a mainstream practice, but this is never the case at the outset. They can be linked with a diverse range of goals and come to take on different meanings over time. Just as important as the initial goals of social innovation are the wider political concepts and institutional systems in which they become embedded (see e.g., Osborne and Brown, 2011): how the social and economic environment reacts to them in terms of the better strategies and solutions that they advance. Hence, social innovations are, over the course of their development, marked by a high degree of risk and uncertainty.

For these reasons, the definition used here seeks to avoid objectivising what is 'social' or 'better', since this is a normative issue, subject to widespread debate and an evolving area of study that remains subject to a great deal of uncertainty. The simple criterion was applied: *social innovations are those that, at any given moment, raise the hope and expectations of progress towards something 'better' (a more socially sustainable/democratic/effective society).* Whether or not these hopes and expectations come to fruition is harder to ascertain, depending on the values and strategies of the observer and the impact of the social innovation, which can often only be fully understood in retrospect.

Since the dynamics of social innovation were examined as part of the project, only projects that had progressed past the initial start-up stage were selected for analysis. Each innovation that was selected involved a practical project that had been realised. This project could take the form of an organisation or an organisational subunit with new services that clearly differed from the services already on offer in the field. It could also include legislative measures or interventions such as a new economic transfer, tax or resource arrangement. Innovations could be manifested in a local network rather than a single organisational unit, or they could be experimental models and units found in plural forms in a local setting (e.g., new family centres). So, within the WILCO project, 'social innovation' may refer not only to a large project but also to a cluster of smaller, similar projects. One requirement was that in each of the twenty cities under scrutiny, a minimum of three and a maximum of six innovations had to be featured and analysed by each team. The actual number of cases chosen in a city depended largely on the complexity of the respective cases.

When selecting case studies, each team had to include three policy fields (child care, employment and housing) and three target groups (single mothers, young people and migrants) that had been agreed by the WILCO project team. For the purposes of comparison, every innovation had to cover a specific field. However, this was challenging since, in practice, innovations can cut across several fields and groups at once. Therefore, as a general guideline, it was agreed to make sure that all fields and groups were at least somehow covered when selecting innovations. As well as reviewing documents and programmes, interviews formed another key source when analysing social innovations. The number of interviews carried out was linked to the number of innovations selected. On average more than three interviews were conducted for each case.

The main aim of the WILCO research was to look at common international innovatory trends that were manifesting themselves despite otherwise diverging national trajectories. The project was not concerned with whether innovations make a difference to a particular type of national welfare culture or regime (liberal, conservative or social democratic) or, indeed, to its form of governance (such as corporatist). It was concerned with the differences across shared patterns of welfare and governance in the European region. Two elements can be seen as widely shared across welfare regimes:

• The commonalities of post-war welfarism (Wagner, 1994), such as standardisation and the search for uniform regulations in welfare institutions, which corresponds to the minor role of participative elements and civil society in welfare systems and democratic decision-making; and
• The influence of new public management, neoliberal economic policy and associated managerial concepts, with their desire to rationalise welfare agencies and cut costs, both using concepts of governance that originated in the business sector.

Interestingly, the social innovations that were recommended by local experts to WILCO interviewers as 'socially useful' and 'promising' were consistently characterised by their difference from the practices, services and regulations that are part of the two welfare traditions mentioned above.

When it came to singling out these differences, this also showed that quite a number of the characteristic patterns of these social innovations relied on something that is shared in positive terms – with each other and in relation to the context in which they have developed. This demonstrates the existence and impact of a third element: of cultural and social aspirations and social movements that have developed since the 1970s and continue to develop today. All European countries have, in some form or another, gone through phases when cultural and social movements have revitalised elements of self-organisation and created new forms of social solidarity. These range from the social movements of the early 1970s and the democratic revolutions in Central and Eastern

Europe, through to a new wave of movements linked with the issues of economic growth, the environment, sustainability and participation as they have emerged at the beginning of the new century (Evers, 2009).

Moreover, the first field visits and the later process of selecting innovations confirmed a difference between the sample and the kinds of social innovations that have typically been portrayed in the mainstream literature. The latter usually looks at social innovations with a focus on social service innovations (see, e.g., Mulgan, 2006; BEPA, 2010; Osborne and Brown, 2011). What was discovered during the first city surveys and international meetings of the WILCO teams, however, was that innovations touch on more than services and the organisation of service provision. Changes in rules and regulations (e.g., concerning access to financial benefits), in governance (new forms of democratic participation, how decisions on priorities in welfare are taken, and so on) and in modes of working and financing are all equally important fields for social innovation.

The central task and mandate of the WILCO research project was to look at the impact of social innovations on local welfare *systems*, that is, the pluralism of the 'welfare mix' or mixed economy of welfare as it is constituted by contributions and actors from the state/public authorities, the market sector, the third sector of various associations and the community sector, including families and various informal networks (see Evers and Wintersberger, 1990, and Jenson in this book). For this reason, the findings are presented with an eye to the constitutive elements of welfare systems and not along the lines of *separate* policy fields.

This factor also had an impact on the research concept used here and the dimensions of innovation that were explored, as shown in Table 5.1. Organising the findings into various dimensions should mean that they can be integrated not only into current debates within the community of researchers on welfare and social policy, on urbanism and local policy, but also on public policy research more generally.

When analysing the case studies of innovation it was the aim to find out whether there are recurring features that give them a distinctive profile. It has already been said that together they represent forms of acting and thinking that can be defined first of all in disruptive terms – breaking with the traditions of both 'industrial welfare' and the more recent wave of managerial and neoliberal reforms. However, these innovations can also be defined in more creative terms. Recurring features of them point to a style of doing things, a shared culture and perspective of thinking and acting across national borders that brings about positive change. Table 5.1 sketches out the types of innovation found in

Table 5.1 Five dimensions of recurring innovative features

Dimension	Recurring innovative features
Innovations in services and how they address users	Investing in capabilities Approaches that avoid stigmatisation Bridging the gap between professional services and people's lives Developing personalised support packages
Innovations in regulations and rights	Creating flexible forms of ad hoc support that meet newly emerging risks 'Social contracts' with individuals and groups
Innovations in governance	Fostering units and types of organisation that operate in a more embedded and networked way Giving a voice in the public domain to new concerns and groups Building issue-related coalitions and partnerships
Innovations in methods of working and financing	Various working collectives Professionalism that combines previously fragmented knowledge Short-term and time-limited funding: combining resources from different stakeholders
Innovations that concern the whole of (local) welfare systems	Reaching out to all sectors of local welfare systems Aiming for less standardisation, more diversity and more localisation in welfare arrangements Upgrading the community component in mixed welfare systems Integrating economic and social logics Integrating welfare and urban politics

Source: Authors' compilation.

the cases that will be explained and illustrated further in this chapter. Some of the cases of innovation illustrated only one of the dimensions or merely one of the sub-categories listed in the table. Others were interesting with respect to several of the five dimensions, in different ways and to different degrees.

The innovative dimensions and hallmarks synthesised in the table above do not represent a kind of social or political programme. Rather, they represent a loose assemblage of elements of a kind of 'cultural turn' in dealing with issues of welfare and, more specifically, with social inclusion. Different political actors and parties may take up the concerns and aspirations of a social innovation and direct it towards different uses and ends. Therefore, the real impacts and meanings of the categories listed in the table may only become clear over time, according to the way the wider social and policy context integrates them in its discourses and actions (Schmidt, 2010). For example, linking social and economic concerns or striving for more flexibility and personalisation can end up with quite different meanings and implications. This point about the importance of (discursive) contexts and the different faces of mainstreaming innovations will be discussed later in the chapter. Each category is now discussed in turn.

Innovations in services and how they address users

The majority of the social innovations that were chosen for inclusion in the study were service innovations. Since services are generally organised along less closed and standardised lines than – for example – pensions systems, it is little wonder that they have provided more ground for small-scale innovations. Four features characterise the differences between social innovations and service systems as these have developed in tandem with the main post-war welfare traditions and the more recent trend towards managerialism in public and private services. These features play a role not only in the specific field of social inclusion policy but also more generally across the field of personalised social services.

Investing in capabilities
The characteristic of 'investing in capabilities' was found in most of the social innovations in this study. These services were less about filling gaps in provision and were more oriented towards establishing the kind of relationships that reduce the dependency of users by opening up new opportunities for them or enhancing their skills. This aspect was linked with the 'activation' and 'empowerment' rhetoric familiar in the debate on public welfare. Different discourses on these subjects produced service innovations that aimed to strengthen capabilities in various ways. A telling example in this respect was the project called 'Her Second Chance' from Varazdin, Croatia, which aimed to support women and mothers who encountered special difficulties in acquiring skills, seeking to enhance their employability and self-esteem in a way that led them back to paid work (Evers *et al.*, 2014, p. 53).

Approaches that avoid stigmatisation
Most of the occupational and social integration programmes provided as part of 'workfare' policies (unemployment policy that links benefits

to active engagement with the job market: Handler, 2004) employed strict targeting that clearly indicated who was 'in' and 'out', along with detailed rules and requirements governing the process of admissions and integration. Thus, being entitled or forced to take part in a special programme for the long-term unemployed was linked with various forms of categorising, classification and control. This carried a high risk of stigmatisation. By contrast, many of the innovations that addressed issues such as occupational and social integration took a looser and more open approach that did not impose admission requirements on (potential) users and did not prescribe in detail how re-integration should proceed and which stages it should include. While personal help and advice played an important role, the whole approach was less top-down and less prescriptive. An illustrative example was the Family Office in Münster, Germany (Evers *et al.*, 2014, p. 143), which provided support in a way that was open to all – even though some families would need it much more than others.

Bridging the gap between professional services and people's lives

Cultural and ethnic diversity and the problems of poverty and social exclusion have increased in the age of large-scale migration, unemployment and growing inequality. This makes it increasingly difficult for services and professionals to reach the groups that might need their help most, often because the services offered are simply not known about, are too hard to understand or are not taken up due to a lack of trust. As such, bridging the gap between professional services and real people's lives has become ever more challenging. One example from the sample that related to this problem was 'Neighbourhood Mothers' from Berlin, Germany (Evers *et al.*, 2014, p. 124). This project engaged as mentors women from Turkish families who were well connected and trusted in their communities but who were – after a short special training course – also experienced in dealing with welfare administrators and the services and entitlements that they could offer.

Developing personalised support packages

While public administration and welfare bureaucracies have, during the course of their development, sought to differentiate between groups and their needs, specialisation has made it hard to address the complex and sometimes unique needs of clients within a highly segmented welfare system. Bundling existing support measures tends to be complicated and discouraging. However, among the selection of innovations that were studied here, there were a number of organisations that provided service-offerings that allowed access to otherwise separate, siloed, forms of support. Various schemes included in the study operated with personal advisers, care- and case-managers and various forms of 'one-stop entry-points'. A good example of this was in Nantes, France (Evers *et al.*, 2014, p. 96), where a scheme offered joint assessments of the needs of families in terms of linking access to jobs and day care, something that was especially important for single-parent families.

Innovations in regulations and rights

Creating flexible forms of ad hoc support that meet newly emerging risks

Increasingly, patterns of working and living are changing and becoming less continuous, and the zones of transition between life situations and life stages are becoming more complicated (Bovenberg, 2008). Traditional services cannot always cope with these complexities. This may mean being out of school but not yet in a job or on the track back to employment but without access to somewhere to live. Often this coincides with other acute problems that may require immediate help. What some have called 'new social risks' (Bonoli, 2005) cannot be dealt with using the manual of standard risks that typically shape the range of social services and transfer-systems of post-war welfare states. Innovative ways of offering a quick fix, often provisionally, may well be the critical missing link when it comes to providing living and working arrangements that keep people 'in the game'. Quite a number of the social innovations studied in the WILCO project involved establishing this kind of short-term, time-limited, *ad hoc* support. One telling example was the 'Welfare Foundation Ambrosiano' in Milan, Italy (Evers *et al.*, 2014, p. 182), that aimed to support individuals and families with a quick supply of credit who were temporarily in need for various reasons (redundancy, illness, and so on), regardless of their previous or current type of employment contract and country of origin.

'Social contracts' with individuals and groups

Traditionally, most public welfare services have the status of rights that are unconditional insofar as they usually simply require a set of material preconditions to be fulfilled. A new tendency in welfare arrangements, particularly in the field of workfare, has been for clients to enter a form of contractual relationship where the preconditions for support concern their future behaviour. These types of contractual relationship involve the clients taking exclusive responsibility for themselves.

Among the set of innovations studied here, there were also other types of contracts, that defined the notion of 'giving something back for what one gets from society': more broadly, people got access to some goods and services once they committed to doing something for others in the form of volunteer work or providing clearly defined personal support for vulnerable people in the community. One example of this phenomenon was 'Time for a Roof', an inter-generational home-share service in Nantes, France (Evers *et al.*, 2014, p. 93), that offered cheap accommodation to students who entered into an inter-generational co-habitation arrangement.

Innovations in governance

The social innovations that were studied all represented a combination of new social 'products' and new social 'processes', the latter term referring to the internal organisation of decision-making and interaction with the environment, the public, various stakeholders, social partners and political and administrative authorities. Many social innovations that sought to develop new kinds of services also had a novel governance dimension. However, for some innovations, influencing and changing the system of governance was found to be their core focus. This was the case, for example, in Bern, Switzerland (Evers *et al.*, 2014, p. 355), where new integration guidelines that became mandatory for public stakeholders were worked out in a cooperative process by a group of administrators, experts and representatives of local NGOs.

Fostering units and types of organisation that operate in a more embedded and networked way

Traditional service organisations and systems focus very much on their respective special tasks, effectively functioning in silos (Boyle *et al.*, 2010). This limited degree of cooperation and sharing also applies, however, in those parts of the service landscape that have been shaped by managerial reforms. Social innovations, by contrast, are characterised by bringing together what is usually separate, whether this is ideas, concerns or practices. Since the social innovations that were studied have a highly localised character, they were much more embedded than organisations that were part of a hierarchical system, whether in business or in centralised welfare administrations. A good example of an unconventional form of networking was the 'Neighbourhood Stores for Education, Research, and Talent Development' in Amsterdam, the Netherlands (Evers *et al.*, 2014, p. 208), where teachers and students from universities cooperated with activists in a community development programme that linked governmental, not-for-profit and business organisations together.

Giving a voice in the public domain to new concerns and groups

Innovation also means addressing issues, concerns and related forms of self-organisation in a way that is more up-to-date in terms of emerging challenges and pressures. Conventional methods of presenting and organising concerns are often no longer effective (Westall, 2011). When it came to women's concerns, both the 'MaMa Foundation' in Warsaw, Poland, and the 'RODA' initiative, Zagreb (Evers *et al.*, 2014, p. 246; p. 37) had overcome the traditional restrictions placed on women in a labour market designed for men. They highlighted other concerns that had previously been seen simply as private issues, exposing local systems that, both under socialism and post-socialism, displayed little interest in the manifold challenges of childcare, and then raising awareness of new ways of working and family life on the public policy agenda. These, and other, innovative projects and initiatives had been eager to discover new ways of organising debates, deliberation processes and publicity in order to set agendas and establish a new consensus on priorities. A related project from the Western context was the 'Maggio 12 Initiative' in Milan, Italy (Evers *et al.*, 2014, p. 187). This project aimed to bring together concerned citizens, experts, politicians, professionals and administrators as part of an organised consultation process on a new agenda in the field of children and childhood.

Building issue-related coalitions and partnerships

Coalitions, partnerships and alliances can be seen as denser forms of networking that are often concerned with raising awareness of a particular issue. Establishing these kinds of partnerships, which are both unified and plural, can be seen as an important and innovative aspect of policy making, fostering participating in governance. As well as examples from the field of urban housing and neighbourhood regeneration, the 'Foundation Ambrosiano' in Milan, Italy (Evers *et al.*, 2014, p. 182), provided a good example of bringing together stakeholders from quite diverse social and political arenas and binding them into a coherent alliance.

Innovations in methods of working and financing

When innovation means dealing differently with a given challenge or pressure, this often needs to involve a way of accepting and living with worsening material conditions. This tends to increase the imbalance between ambitions on the one hand and conditions and means on the other hand. Innovative projects and organisations with precarious funding may then be marked even more by those negative trends to be observed in today's labour markets, such as time-limited working contracts that offer no job security. This may be counterbalanced by the fact that people working in innovative projects and earning their money there may enjoy an atmosphere of creativity and cooperation and more 'positive' stress than the negative type that comes from hierarchies and lack of appreciation. Trust-based relationships may cause many contributors to participate for short periods and accept short-term contracts, secure in the knowledge that a new contract is a possibility once circumstances allow. Innovative elements such as building trust, cooperation and unwritten rules of respect are part of the working climate. However, they can hardly be seen as an adequate antidote to low levels of job security. Making them part of the working conditions in innovative projects is, therefore, essential but not sufficient.

Various working collectives

Models for individual engagement in social innovation projects were typically much more diverse than in the public or business sector, since they included not only various forms of (casual) paid employment but also many forms of voluntary and civic contributions. The latter ranged from short-term activism to regular, unpaid, volunteering over the long term or from hands-on volunteer work to regular contributions in the form of civic engagement on a board of management. Various working fields were taking shape that linked paid work, volunteering and civic engagement. It was remarkable how blurred the boundaries were becoming between those who operated inside organisations and those that were considered as 'co-producers'. An illustrative example, which is representative of many other similar instances, was an initiative named 'Bimbo Chiama Bimbo' (Child Calls Child) in Brescia, Italy (Evers *et al.*, 2014, p. 164). This project offered various forms of support for households with children through collaboration with neighbourhood and municipality stakeholders. For the organisational network and the profile of its activities, both professional and lay contributions were indispensable. About 400 volunteers were active in addition to full-time staff within the core organisation and supporters from other cooperating local organisations.

Professionalism that combines previously fragmented knowledge

The kind of professional found in many innovative projects and initiatives typically had to manage tasks that often fell outside the limits of traditional professions and the divisions of labour that these imply. Professionals working within social innovations may have to learn to converse with various kinds of users, clients, co-citizens and volunteers: they were sometimes specialists, entrepreneurs and managers simultaneously. Many of them needed both technical and social knowledge. This kind of 're-professionalisation' process may, for example, involve co-operators that were professionals by training but worked simultaneously as community organisers and mediators. The social innovation based in Lille, France (Evers *et al.*, 2014, p. 73), that supported those renovating their own houses called 'Companion Builders' (Les Compagnons Bâtisseurs) is a good example here. It managed, trained and supervised activities that were mostly confined to the margins and not seen as part of the professional field of architecture.

Short-term and time-limited funding: Combining resources from different stakeholders

Many, if not the majority, of the social innovations that were studied were based on combining multiple sources of funding. The mix varied and often state financing remained the most important component, but usually there was a degree of (financial) co-responsibility on the part of other organisations from civil society or the business sector. Furthermore, funding arrangements were very often precarious and time-limited. Here, once again, innovative elements were combined with difficulties that would ideally be reduced or prevented completely. An interesting example of such possibilities and limitations can be found in the social innovation 'Job Explorers' in Berlin, Germany (Evers *et al.*, 2014, p. 119), an initiative that matched money from the local Chambers of Industry and Commerce with the local labour market office through programmes that built links between schools, their young apprentices and local employers.

Innovations that concern the whole of (local) welfare systems

The WILCO project sought to examine the possible contributions of social innovation in terms of changes and developments in local welfare *systems*. It was understood that this label meant that more was being addressed than just local welfare-*state* institutions. Referring to a welfare system usually means including – in addition to the local welfare state and municipal welfare – welfare-related activities and responsibilities from the third sector, the market sector and the spheres of community and family. The cases of social innovations that were examined demonstrated the mutual relationships that exist between all of these four components of a (local) welfare system – (local) state, business sector, third sector organisations and the, often informal, networks of community and family life.

Reaching out to all sectors of local welfare systems

Even though there was considerable variation in the level and impact of state funding and support for the social innovations that were studied, overall it could be stated that these initiatives were concerned with establishing links with all sectors and that the organisations involved thereby often took on a hybrid character. It could be argued that most social innovations would have liked to receive more state and municipal support, but equally it can also be assumed that they would not have wished to be incorporated into the public sector. It can be suggested, therefore, that social innovations could best be captured by concepts of welfare that were based on a deliberate mixing and pluralism among actors, resources and responsibilities. Needless to say, the share of state-public welfare contributions of various kinds of third-sector organisations, ranging from associations to social enterprises, from NGOs to community networks and, finally, the level of corporate social responsibility was a matter that involved some controversy and conflict. Such conflicts not only concerned ideas and finances but also power.

Aiming for less standardisation, more diversity and more localisation in welfare arrangements

Innovation became difficult, if not impossible, wherever the right to act, organise or provide differently was denied. This could be the case in both large private-sector business organisations, which were managed centrally, and in certain market sectors that were controlled by private sector oligopolies. This means that those who wanted a more important role for social innovation would have to secure a degree of decentralisation, diversity, difference and, moreover, the possibility of unconventional mergers between elements that were usually separate. What is more, supporting innovation meant opting for arrangements that allowed for a new balance between guaranteed universality and diversity in localised arrangements. A good example of what is involved in combining and balancing concerns with universalism and diversity could be found in those municipalities that had worked to secure the right to develop their own options for occupational integration strategies, such as the 'Optionskommune' in Münster,

Germany (Evers *et al.*, 2014, p. 137). This is an example of one of many municipalities in Germany that had opted for local responsibility rather than being part of an integrated centralised service system.

Upgrading the community component in mixed welfare systems

Given that the community sphere was often subsumed within the third sector of voluntary associations in society, excluding family relationships and informal neighbourhood-communities, it was all the more important to see that a major aspect of many social innovations was developing innovative forms of community. A good example of combining the public and community spheres and sharing the responsibility for care between these two was the 'Children Cafés' in Lille, France, which opened up the tasks and concerns of family life to the community. Another example was from Amsterdam (the Netherlands), where a housing corporation decided to support community organisations ('Neighbourhood Management Companies') in their housing as it was being reconstructed (Evers *et al.*, 2014, p. 80; p. 203). It should certainly be noted that many social innovations were, in various ways, challenging traditional interpretations of welfare, in which community, building on a shared sense of duty, was seen as a rather parochial element to be gradually substituted by more state-public, professionalised and completely voluntary elements.

Integrating economic and social logics

In contrast to the previous point, the integration of social and economic logics is much better established as a concern in the debates on the profile of future welfare systems. The creeping economisation of all spheres of life, and an increasingly productivist attitude that evaluates all social actions and relationships primarily with respect to their quantifiable economic effect, is just one side of the coin. The other side can be found in the debate on the welfare state as a 'social investment state' (Morel *et al.*, 2012) that advocates modernising public welfare through an approach that stresses the positive economic effects of social policy interventions in education, family support, and occupational and social integration. In urban regeneration, those social innovations that sought to combine the active participation of people as co-producers and co-decision-makers with public and private investment could be seen as part of this perspective on social investment as a means of societal development.

Integrating welfare and urban politics

Policy fields that are usually excluded from the welfare system, such as environmental policy or cultural activities, played an important role in socially innovative developments. The two examples of innovations in the sample that were linked with the urban gardening movement, the 'Gardens of Life' from Varazdin, Croatia, and the 'Princesses Gardens' from Berlin, Germany (Evers *et al.*, 2014, p. 57; p. 116), showed the role of this urban element in environmental politics. This led to the important policy field of spatial planning and development – whether on the level of regions, cities or neighbourhoods. The innovative element here consisted of linking urban transformation and social intervention, something quite new in local politics, based on combining knowledge and professionals from a range of fields (architects, economists, educators and social workers). A good example was the 'Omradesprogrammet' which aimed to regenerate several districts in Malmö, Sweden (Evers *et al.*, 2014, p. 338), using the cooperation of 'resource groups' in fields such as city development, the elderly, young people, culture and recreation and the labour market and economic growth. It is no coincidence that the collection of social innovations considered in this study was in large part located at the intersection of welfare and urban development. Traditionally, local and urban politics have been less prominent in the system of public policy making. This may change, as Barber (2013) has argued. He asserted that cities, and the mayors who run them, are the primary incubators of the cultural, social and political innovations that shape our lives, offering in many ways the best new forces of good governance.

Conclusion

This chapter has presented some of the research findings of the WILCO project regarding recurring patterns in the approaches and instruments of localised social innovation. This has been done in a way that suggests that such patterns may well become useful tools within established welfare systems themselves. Public welfare policies could do more than just use social innovations – they could learn from them. To conceive a form of interplay between social innovation and welfare politics that could grow and develop, broader issues such as the impact of given welfare discourses (Schmidt, 2010) are very important – that is, the way in which key actors and the public understand the nature and tasks of welfare policies and what this means for the place occupied by social innovation. However, so far there is a considerable gap between the established perceptions of social change by 'welfare reform' and thinking in terms of social change by social innovation. So far the latter has hardly found yet a place in welfare discourses. When it comes to bridging the gap between welfare politics and social innovation, four points are of particular importance.

First of all, it should be taken into account that many social policy textbooks have a narrow focus on just state policies, debates and decisions on reforms within state institutions, whereby societal actors are brought in through their role within social movements and pressure groups that try to influence the nature of state decisions on welfare – in other words by protest, negotiation and deliberation. However, when it comes to welfare provision (i.e., socio-economic contributions), organised societal actors often get little attention in mainstream textbooks. It is usual to find the state, the market and the family cited as the three pillars of welfare provision (e.g., Esping-Andersen, 2002). Civil society and the third sector, which contribute to new and innovative welfare arrangements not only through participation in the decision-making process but also by creating and preserving all kind of social services, are typically not mentioned. There is, therefore, a need to learn more about the history of welfare as *a history of social innovations* – a feature of a civil society. There has always been an important role for many social movements and organisations in inventing and creating welfare arrangements of their own – mutual organisations in the field of social security, co-operatives as early social enterprises and voluntary associations that have run all kind of services. This rich history of a social economy of invention, innovation and creation throughout Europe (Evers and Laville, 2004) was not simply a forerunner of the 'real thing' in the form of state-based social security and service system; rather, it entailed a voluntary, not-for-profit and community sector that has, right up until the present day, included an important role for social innovation. Therefore, when discussing potential links between social innovation and welfare, welfare systems and welfare mixes (Evers and Wintersberger, 1990; Evers and Guillemard, 2012; Jenson, 2012 and in this volume) that encompass this third sector should be seen as the framework of reference and not just state action alone.

Second, strategies that want to give more space for social innovation have to *rethink the balance between equality and diversity*. In various ways, historical welfare policies have sought to ensure greater equality in society. It is generally agreed that all people should have access to the same institutions and facilities, whether in health, social support services or education. Standards should be guaranteed in both urban and rural areas, and the same quality and procedural standards should ensure that this is always the case. This idea of equal provision was primarily linked with hierarchical systems of decision-making and administration.

However, uniform and centralised school and health systems, as well as centrally regulated workfare services and the attitudes of their professionals typically allow little space for social innovation. The latter needs, by definition, institutional space to do things differently; it often builds on the specificity of local contexts and traditions, something that is frequently viewed with mistrust from a conventional welfare perspective, as well as by system managers. How can the need for standardised and uniform regulations be balanced with the space to experiment with something new and different? To what degree should – for example – different and new forms of schooling and education be allowed to grow and receive state support? How can innovation and diversity be combined with reliability and equality? These are questions that the community of welfare researchers is only just beginning to reflect on (see, e.g., Anttonen *et al.*, 2012).

Third, dealing with social innovation calls for *a new balance between change by comprehensive reforms and a policy of democratic experimentalism* (Sabel, 2012). Much policy making has traditionally been guided by the concept of building comprehensive institutions and regulations top-down. To be effective, therefore, socially innovative concepts either have to make it to the top of political and professional elites that design far-reaching reforms or have to find a niche at the margins. However, there has always been a second tradition in policy making that has gained in influence over the last decade, especially at the local level: initiating change and paving the way for reform through time-limited programmes that take up an innovation, support it for a limited timespan, evaluate the results and then decide on whether to roll out the reform in a longer-term and more far-reaching design. Among the social innovations that have been studied, many have formed part of such programmes: trying out new methods of urban regeneration, family support, or occupational and social integration. A great many social innovations may become mainstreamed in this way. However, not all programmes succeed, different schemes reflect different concepts and priorities, and changes often remain incomplete. But does this diversity and incompleteness not in some ways reflect the needs of society better than the dream of an ultimate 'grand design'? A metaphor may be found in the history of urban planning and its often rather frightening attempts to construct completely new cities by following a single design logic throughout.

All that has been argued before points finally to the need for *thinking of the current politics of welfare reform and policies for social innovation together, even if they mostly do not go together well.* Each of the overarching discourses on the future economic and societal priorities that currently coexist in our societies attributes different meanings, roles and incentives to social innovation. How credible is, then, a policy discourse that promises an effective alliance between support for innovations and their intentions and the established priorities in modernising societies? At a time of economic turmoil and crisis – with widespread calls for the further slimming-down of the welfare state, particularly in welfare benefits and services that can be seen as consumptive and protective rather than productive (expenses for social protection, elderly care, etc.) – a focus on social innovation and its support by public authorities may well be a difficult proposition. The combined effects of less labour market regulation, rising levels of in-work poverty, the increased difficulty of being employed, less old age security, and so on probably cause more social disintegration than could ever be addressed by socially innovative services that try to empower people and communities. When it comes to social cohesion, there is a need to think about the net-balance of the current scaling-back of basic welfare systems and regulations of protection, on the one hand, and the diversity of attempts to innovate services and local networks, on the other. How do EU policies for economic and welfare modernisation (European Commission, 2010) and the planned special programmes for stimulating social innovation (European Commission, 2013) go together? To avoid the rather cynical conclusion that local social innovation essentially represents – in light of the massive structural problems that welfare democracies are suffering – a 'mission impossible', it is crucial to think about the links and tensions between policies for welfare reform and policies for upscaling social innovation. Are social policy researchers and social innovation researchers prepared for that?

Notes

1. All cases of social innovations are available as an e-book, edited by Adalbert Evers, Benjamin Ewert and Taco Brandsen (Evers *et al.*, 2014).
2. The sample included the following cities: Zagreb and Varazdin (Croatia), Nantes and Lille (France), Berlin and Münster (Germany), Milan and Brescia (Italy), Warsaw and Plock (Poland), Barcelona and Pamplona (Spain), Stockholm and Malmö (Sweden), Berne and Geneva (Switzerland), Amsterdam and Nijmegen (the Netherlands) and Birmingham and Dover (United Kingdom).

References

Anttonen, A., Häikiö, L. and Stefánsson, K. (2012) *Welfare State, Universalism and Diversity*. Cheltenham: Edward Elgar.

Barber, B. (2013) *If Mayors Ruled the World. Dysfunctional Nations, Rising Cities.* Yale, CT: Yale University Press.

BEPA (2010) *Empowering People, Driving Change. Social Innovation in the European Union.* Brussels: Bureau of European Policy Advisors and European Commission.

Bonoli, G. (2005) 'The Politics of the New Social Policies: Providing Coverage against New Social Risks in Mature Welfare States', *Policy & Politics*, 33 (3): 431–49.

Bovenberg, A. L. (2008) 'The Life-Course Perspective and Social Policy. An Overview of the Issues', *CESifo Economic Studies*, 54 (4): 593–641.

Boyle, D., Coote, A., Sherwood, C. and Slay, J. (2010) *Right Here, Right Now. Taking Co-production into the Mainstream.* London: New Economics Foundation.

European Commission (2010) *EUROPE 2020. A Strategy for Smart, Sustainable and Inclusive Growth.* Brussels: European Commission.

European Commission (2013) *Guide to Social Innovation.* Brussels: European Commission.

Esping-Andersen, G. (2002) *Why We Need a New Welfare State.* New York: Oxford University Press.

Evers, A. (2009) 'Civicness and Civility: Their Meanings for Social Services', *Voluntas*, 20 (3): 239–59.

Evers, A., Ewert, B. And Brandsen, T. (eds) (2014): *Social Innovations for Social Cohesion. Transnational Patterns and Approaches from 20 European Cities.* Available at http://www.wilcoproject.eu/downloads/WILCO-project-eReader. pdf [Accessed 3 November 2014].

Evers, A. and Guillemard, A.M. (2012) 'Reconfiguring Welfare and Reshaping Citizenship', in Evers, A. and Guillemard, A.M. (eds), *Social Policy and Citizenship.* New York: Oxford University Press, pp. 359–88.

Evers, A. and Laville, J.-L. (2004) *The Third Sector in Europe.* Cheltenham: Edward Elgar.

Evers, A. and Wintersberger, H. (eds) (1990) *Shifts in the Welfare Mix – Their Impact on Work, Social Services and Welfare Policies.* Frankfurt/Boulder: Campus/Westview.

Jenson, J. (2012) 'Redesigning Citizenship Regimes after Neoliberalism: Moving towards Social Investment', in Morel, N., Pailier, B. and Palme, J. (eds), *Towards a Social Investment Welfare State? Ideas, Policies and Challenges.* Bristol: Policy Press, pp. 61–90.

Handler, J.F. (2004) *Social Citizenship and Workfare in the United States and Western Europe. The Paradox of Inclusion.* Cambridge: Cambridge University Press.

Morel, N., Pailier, B. and Palme, J. (eds) (2012) *Towards a Social Investment Welfare State? Ideas, Policies and Challenges.* Bristol: Policy Press.

Moulaert, F. (2010) 'Social Innovation and Community Development. Concepts, Theories and Challenges', in Moulaert, F., Martinelli, F., Swygedouw, E. and González, S. (eds), *Can Neigbourhoods Save the City?* London and New York: Routledge, pp. 4–16.

Mulgan, G. (2006) 'The Process of Social Innovation', *Innovations*, 1 (2): 145–62.

Osborne, St. P. and Brown, L. (2011) 'Innovation, Public Policy and Public Services Delivery in the UK: The Word that Would Be King?', *Public Administration*, 89 (4): 1335–50.

Phills, J. (2008) 'Rediscovering Social Innovation', *Stanford Social Innovation Review*, 6 (4): 36–43.

Sabel, C. (2012) 'Dewey, Democracy, and Democratic Experimentalism', *Contemporary Pragmatism*, 9 (2): 35–55.

Schmidt, V. A. (2010) 'Taking Ideas and Discourse Seriously: Explaining Change through Discursive Institutionalism As the Fourth "New Institutionalism"', *European Political Science Review*, 2 (1): 1–25.

Wagner, P. (1994) *A Sociology of Modernity: Liberty and Discipline*. London: Routledge.

Westall, A. (2011) *Revisiting Associative Democracy*. (e-book) Available at: http://www.lwbooks.co.uk/ebooks/RevisitingAssociativeDemocracy.pdf [Accessed 3 November 2014].

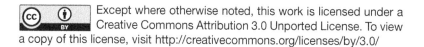

6

Collaborative Services in Informal Settlements: Social Innovation in a Pacified Favela in Rio de Janeiro

Carla Cipolla, Patricia Melo and Ezio Manzini

Introduction

Informal settlements, such as favelas (slums), are complex social ecosystems, characterised by their lack of basic services and by their particular social ties. Favelas in Rio de Janeiro are undergoing rapid changes, and new organisations and relationships are beginning to appear. This is largely as a result of the Rio de Janeiro government's policy of 'pacification' – a strategy to occupy the favelas formerly controlled by drug dealers, aimed at extending citizens' rights (and duties) in these areas (Fleury, 2012).

This chapter discusses these transformations, considering in particular if and how new services are emerging. This discussion is based on one significant case study – Light Recicla. Light Recicla, in Favela Santa Marta, Rio de Janeiro, is a service operated by the city's energy company that seeks to reduce the electricity bills of local residents by exchanging recyclable materials for energy credits, helping them to adjust to the new reality brought by pacification.

Under the framework of the pacification strategy, commercial companies and favela residents are establishing new relationships. Light Recicla aims to define a new mode of collaboration between the energy company, Light, and its customers that addresses this new set of social relations. Light's initiative is considered in this chapter as an example that highlights specific issues related to social innovation, particularly in terms of new social relations. The focus here is on social innovation 'as new ideas (products, services and models) that simultaneously meet social needs and create new social relationships or collaborations' (Murray *et al.*, 2010, p. 3). In the context of the emergence of new market-based relations within the pacification process, the Light

Recicla service is examined as a type of service that meets the demands of informal settlements via new, hybrid and collaborative services. It is also argued that the effectiveness of these new types of services is based on specific socio-cultural qualities.

In analysing informal settlements, this chapter draws on the work of the DESIS[1] Thematic Cluster,[2] 'Formal, Informal, Collaborative (IFC)', which sets out a typology of actions based on two main issues:

- Underserved communities. Informal settlements are complex social ecosystems, characterised by their lack of basic services (which has led to them being described as 'underserved' communities) and by the (relative) density of specific forms of social ties – from traditional ones, such as those of family, clan and village, to new ones that have emerged in the particular context of informal settlements, including those imposed by criminal gangs.
- Informal settlements in transformation. Driven by different factors, several informal settlements have recently entered a phase of rapid change (Echeverri and Orsini, 2011). In this changing environment, new organisations and forms of relationships, both inside the settlements and between them and the rest of the city, are appearing. In some places, such as Brazil, the starting point of this transformation has been the set of actions known as 'pacification' – the effects of which are still being evaluated (Fleury, 2012).

The working hypothesis presented in this chapter is aligned with a planning approach that, although not new, has only been widely adopted in the last decade.[3] This hypothesis can be summarised in the following way:

- informal settlements can and must be improved;
- these improvements must make best possible use of existing physical and social resources;
- they should be enhanced by a set of local projects (at different scales) promoted and coordinated within a broader framework; and
- these local projects should be driven by and, in turn generate, social innovation.

Therefore, in the context of this chapter, pacification is not only seen as a public security project but also as a public policy enabling a myriad of projects to flourish, either in the favelas or in the neighbouring areas. The focus here is on one such project.

To explore the development of new services in informal settlements, this chapter draws on a conceptual framework formulated in previous research, in which the notions of *collaborative services* and *experiential* versus *relational* interactions were developed.

The first notion came to light when research on design for social innovation (Manzini, 2007) identified types of service interactions that have been called *collaborative services* in social innovation cases (Manzini, 2008). The term 'collaborative' emerged from the fact that the qualities of interpersonal interactions were far removed from those of a *delivery* approach to services in which participants, including frontline employees (representing the organisation) and clients/users, have predefined roles (i.e., employees are active; clients are passive). These social innovations deconstructed the delivery approach to services, creating new collaborations and transforming all participants into active co-producers of commonly recognised benefits. They also gave rise to a special form of interpersonal interaction in services known as *relational services* (Cipolla and Manzini, 2009; Cipolla, 2012), where participants needed not only to be operationally active and collaborative, but also intentioned and willing to relate to, and interact with, one another in an intensely interpersonal way.

Based on Buber's (1996; 2006) theoretical framework, these findings led to the definition of *experiential* versus *relational* services as polarities by which to identify the interpersonal qualities of services (Cipolla, 2004). Those relating to clearly designed roles and procedures for service actors, which predefine the range of possibilities for interpersonal encounters, are *experiential*, and those that increase the possibilities for (or even favour) unexpected interpersonal encounters, whether intentionally or otherwise, are *relational*.

On this basis, this chapter assumes two further working hypotheses. Given that informal settlements are underserved, it is proposed that:

- services in which all the people involved actively participate in achieving the final result are more likely to be successfully implemented in informal settlements than traditional delivery services; and
- collaboration can be both 'vertical' between service provider and service users/co-producers, and 'horizontal' between service users/co-producers themselves.

This chapter presents the possibility of building on existing and new social ties to create a new generation of services – *collaborative services* – able to involve resident communities in solving concrete problems of everyday life and in promoting the evolution of the existing mesh of social ties towards more open, flexible and transparent social networks. It does so with reference to a 'pacified' favela in Rio de Janeiro, and aims to understand better the features and socio-cultural qualities of a service recently introduced there. To address this objective, this chapter focuses on the following questions:

- What is the nature of the collaborations between service users and service provider and between service users themselves? How collaborative is the service overall?
- What are the features of core service encounters, the character of interpersonal interactions in the service and the interpersonal qualities of the service?
- What is the relationship between effectiveness and socio-cultural qualities, and what is the role played by social-cultural qualities in achieving the outcomes desired by the promoters and the users/ co-producers?

Field research was carried out on a service developed by the Electricity Company of Rio de Janeiro in pacified favelas, called 'Light Recicla'. Investigations were undertaken in all five favelas where the service was installed (Santa Marta, Rocinha, Chácara do Céu, Babilônia e Chapéu Mangueira and Cruzada S. Sebastião), while in-depth research was carried out in the Santa Marta favela, which was the first one to be pacified. To achieve the research objectives,[4] a single case study in Santa Marta was completed. The qualitative research, carried out between March and August 2013, included:

- desk research, that examined news reports, reviews and official communication, including company reports;
- semi-structured interviews, which included talking to the company representative responsible for developing and implementing the project, and to those involved in the core service encounter (clients and agents); and
- observational research with direct observation of the service in its 'natural' setting (with particular focus on the characteristics of the service encounters), that included taking photographs (when allowed).

The Light Recicla project

Light Recicla was designed to support people living in pacified favelas in Rio de Janeiro who were in the process of obtaining legal access

Figure 6.1   A Light Recicla collection point
Source: Photograph © Patricia Melo.

to energy. Light Recicla was designed as a complex service resulting from the combination of two services: delivery of electricity and collection of recyclable materials. The parent company – Light – itself managed the delivery of electricity. Meanwhile, a Light partner operated the collection of recyclable materials. Electricity was delivered in the standard way except for the payment system: citizens were requested to bring recyclable materials to dedicated collection points, where the value of these materials was converted into credits towards a discount in their next electricity bill.

Customers played an active role in the Light Recicla service: they collected the rubbish, washed it, separated it and brought it to the Collection Point, where the rubbish was weighed and the appropriate discount calculated and recorded in the system to appear on the next bill. Every consumer had a card with a user number that was used to record the discount. To participate in the project the user just needed to bring an energy bill to the Collection Point and to sign in. On the same day they could obtain a project card and could start bringing their rubbish to recycle, getting credits in their next monthly bill. Through the Light

Figure 6.2   Recyclable materials separated at a Light Recicla collection point
Source: Photograph © Patricia Melo.

Recicla service, the company got paid for the energy it provided (even though the bills were paid in a way that was far from conventional).

Background to the project

Before the pacification process, heavily armed drug dealers dominated the favelas, making it difficult for the energy company to get access to the area and control how people were using the service. This resulted in only a few people paying their energy bills, creating a lose-lose situation: the energy company was losing because the energy it was providing was not being paid for and the favela residents were losing because

Figure 6.3   Light Recicla service process
Source: Drawn by the authors.

the service they were receiving was low quality. Moreover, since they were not paying for the service, they could not complain about any problems they encountered.

When the government permanently occupied the favelas with special police units that sought to establish a close and friendly relationship with locals, the energy company, Light, was able to offer services in a formal and legal way. This chapter will not discuss the pros and cons of the pacification model – rather it is assumed here that, as a result, the favelas are now more accessible and, as far as electricity delivery and consumption is concerned, this process brought about many changes in the consumer–provider relationship. This greater openness allowed Light to renew the power grid in favelas, to put new light meters in houses and to charge for electricity consumption in these communities. As a consequence of this formalisation of energy delivery, it was possible for people in the favelas to have a better quality energy service.

In turn, consumers were expected to start paying their bills regularly. However, in practice, this proved difficult. The cost of electricity was a new expense added to consumers' monthly budgets and, since they had no additional income, many found the payments a huge problem. An additional, related problem was that since they were not used to paying energy bills, consumers often had no concept of responsible consumption or of using energy in a way that they could ultimately afford.

Electricity theft was, therefore, a considerable problem for energy suppliers and providers. Aware of these issues, Light decided to try a different approach in pacified favelas, one based on dialogue and collaboration rather than punishing consumers.

Light's approach to tackling this problem through the Light Recicla project was aligned with research in the energy provision field that increasingly focussed on rethinking the relationship between energy suppliers/providers and users/customers. For example, on the basis of sixteen months of ethnographic fieldwork stretching over fifteen years in countries such as Zanzibar, Winther (2012) proposed that electricity theft is a *relational* issue. Her research aimed to show:

> The merits of applying a grounded, socio-technical and relational analysis for understanding and addressing electricity theft in particular, and for realising sustainable energy systems in general. (p. 111)

Citing a previous study, she described how:

> Conventional, top-down approaches to the problem tend to centre on either technical innovations such as smarter meters; managerial methods, for example, inspection, control and audits; or system changes, typically through privatisation of public energy companies. [However,] Experience shows that, taken alone, neither of these methods provides blueprint solutions to the problem. Broader and more contextually sensitive approaches are called for (Winther, 2012, p. 112).

Design process

Dialogue between Light and favela residents developed into a concrete project – Light Recicla – via an open exchange of experiences and ideas. Once the pacification process started, Light sent some of its employees into the communities to talk about how the company was going to formalise the electricity delivering process. In these visits the company started a dialogue with members of the community in order to make the transition from an informal to formal situation easier. One of the points raised was the amount of rubbish in favelas, much of which was recyclable.

This observation led the Light team to focus on a previous experience in the State of Ceará (Brazil) – developed by an electricity company called COELCE – where people exchanged recyclable materials for credits towards their electricity bill. This scheme was introduced to reduce waste in some areas of the state, using the reduction in energy bills as an incentive. Light Recicla was inspired by the Ceará project, but with a shift in focus from an environmental gain to a social gain. It was, therefore, an adaptation with a different focus, in a different context. Light's team realised that, if the Ceará project could be adapted to the pacified favelas in Rio de Janeiro, it would have a big impact given the new social demands brought by pacification. Waste, a huge problem in these areas, could become the solution that helped people pay their bills just as they were starting to gain legal access to an energy service. Thus, the project was also able to meet the demand for *contextually sensitive approaches* (Winther, 2012) in relationships with consumers, constituting a marked change to conventional company strategy.

Project stakeholders and their motivations

The main stakeholders in the project included the energy company, Light, energy users – the residents of the favela, and a range of other companies that acted as partners in the project.

Light believed that the best way to introduce a formal service in the previously informal settlement was to adopt a strategy that avoided being punitive and that embraced a more dialogical form of interaction. The company also believed that by building a good relationship with its customers, it would be able to reduce energy theft and bad debt overall, which would lead ultimately to a better economic result. An additional motivation for Light was that it was obliged by the terms of its contract with ANEEL (the National Electricity Agency in Brazil) to dedicate at least 0.5% of its net operating revenues each year to actions that aimed to combat electricity waste. Light Recicla helped fulfil this requirement. It also enhanced the brand value of Light, as it is could be presented as a project focussed on social benefit, enhancing the company's image within the pacification process.

Users' motivations within the project were of different kinds. Economic motivations were the most apparent – collecting recyclable materials in exchange for a reduction in their electricity bills. This was particularly true for users who were able to integrate the collection of recyclable materials into their own everyday work: for example, owners of local bars, food kiosk workers and janitors. These groups could collect large quantities of recyclables, allowing them to have large discounts or even offset their entire energy bill. However, deeper observation indicated that some domestic users considered the economic gains from the exchange too low and, therefore, engaged with the project because of the socio-cultural value of doing something good for themselves and for their community. In other words, some domestic users valued the environmental benefits brought by the project beyond the discount in their own bills, and this motivation appeared to be a meaningful driver for their active participation.

To operate the project, Light promoted a partnership with other companies: 3E Engenharia, which provided the ICT system through which the credits were recorded and managed the infrastructure of the collection points; Doe Seu Lixo, which received the waste from customers and took it to be recycled, while also managing the employees involved; and the Coopama, which was responsible for the collection and recycling of cooking oil. These companies were technically and economically involved in the project. The local government also cooperated with Light, granting the space and legal conditions for the project to function and recognising its potential benefit to the success of pacification.

Findings and discussion

The Light Recicla project has garnered some notable successes. In 2011, in its first year of operation, Light reported that Light Recicla gave an average discount per month of 22 reals per user (£5.79; Light, 2011, p. 82). The report noted that in 2012, the average discount per month was 40 reals per user (£10.52), an increase of almost 82% compared to 2011, and the project had 1715 registered customers (Light, 2012, p. 36).

According to the company, Light Recicla had 4,898 registered customers by June 2013, about 60% of whom were active – meaning they were collecting recyclable materials regularly. Light had granted Light Recicla's customers a total of 183,891.17 reals (£48,373.77) of credit against electricity bills. On average, between January and May 2013, 160,115.87 kg per month of material and 458.3 litres of cooking oil was collected across all collection points. Light reported that the company aimed to increase the number of beneficiary communities and users benefitting from the project.

In terms of the framework outlined above, research undertaken as part of this case study showed that Light Recicla could be considered a collaborative service, at least regarding the collection of recyclable material. It included both vertical and horizontal collaboration.

Vertical collaboration took place between service users (favela inhabitants) and the service provider (Light). This collaboration was a required condition for the collection of recyclable materials. Therefore, this component was necessarily a co-produced service: a service in which results could be achieved only if people actively participated and were motivated to engage in the service. Light Recicla aimed to open up a new relationship between the energy company and its users. The company–customer relationship in the favelas had historically been difficult and had led to distrust by both parties. The power company faced default and electricity theft, whilst customers were afraid of being overcharged, believing companies were benefitting to their detriment. Such feelings were particularly strong during the transition process, where users had no real idea of the value of their monthly consumption since it had not been formalised before. Despite residents being wary of their monthly bills, many users reported that Light Recicla was helping to build a more positive image of the company. Besides that, the company was also promoting consumer education concerning energy usage.

Horizontal collaboration is a form of collaboration between service users themselves. In the Light Recicla project, this kind of collaboration was not foreseen. Nevertheless, observation undertaken as part of this research showed that it was starting to take place in spontaneous, self-organised initiatives, when neighbours and family members helped each other. It could occur without payment or – as in one case observed – by payment. In this case, a user called Benedito, who owned a bar near the collection point, observed that other users were not motivated to separate, clean and take their recyclable materials to the collection points. He started to collect other citizens' recyclables in exchange for half the value obtained in credits, developing a small business that increased his monthly income while helping others to lower their bills.

Moving on to consider the types of interactions or service encounters within the project, this research has shown that the Light Recicla service was conceived and implemented in such a way that personal interactions tended to happen following predefined procedures (in Buber´s language, it was a collaborative service based on experiential interactions: 1996; 2006). Nevertheless, in practice, relational interactions appeared too. They were created in two main kinds of service encounter:

- encounters between service users and service frontline employees at the collection point, where the formalised interactions (in exchanging waste for electricity credits) were often surrounded by conversations of a more personal character. Here the frontline employees became personally involved with the users, despite the fact that they were not locals. Users brought their complaints to the frontline employees, since they represented the human face of the company; and
- encounters between peers, aimed at mutual help in collecting waste and delivering the material to the collection points, where some form of relational interactions were always needed. One of the users said he brought the waste of 'the grandmother of his girlfriend', who had time to clean up and organise the waste, but was not easily able to bring it to the collection point. In the case of Benedito and his small business, the social ties between him and his peers enabled his activity, as it was based also on trust. He prepared and delivered the recyclable materials of other users and discounts were credited to their accounts. Only later, and informally, by presenting the ticket showing the registered discount obtained, was he paid half the overall discount in cash for his contribution.

Finally, the relationship between effectiveness and socio-cultural qualities was considered. Both service provider and service users had a clear economic motivation for taking part in the Light Recicla project and its success was mainly based on its practical effectiveness. The reduction of defaults on energy bills in the favelas can be considered an objective measure of effectiveness for both the company and its consumers. People in these areas were gradually required to act like any other citizen in Rio de Janeiro, where citizenship presupposes rights, but also duties. As regards electricity, regular bill payment also required an adequate connection to the power grid, which increased both the quality and safety of provision. With this in mind, it was reported by a company representative that the default rate fell to as little as 2% in the communities where the Light Recicla service was running.

This research suggests that the socio-cultural qualities expressed in the way the Light Recicla service was designed played an important role in making the service effective, although in different ways. These qualities can be summarised as follows:

- *Openness*: the service was based on an agreement in which different roles and procedures were clearly defined and could be easily communicated.
- *Transparency*: the whole service, and in particular the transaction of 'credits-for-recyclables', was visible and immediate, being directly related to the way service touch points were designed. The key items were the devices that weighed the recyclables, calculated their value, sent the information to the administration and printed, immediately, a receipt indicating the credit/discount obtained by the user. This is a key point since users in the favelas were typically wary of public service providers.
- *Dignity*: the service dealt with waste, but it was designed and managed to be clean, hospitable and friendly. This was clearly manifested in the nature of the service touch points and collection points, where staff were very well presented and efficient.
- *Collaboration*: the service introduced a complex idea of collaboration: formalised, vertical collaboration with the company, based on the previous three socio-cultural qualities, and more flexible, freer and more informal, horizontal collaboration on a personal–local scale.

Conclusion

The service analysed here was conceived as a collaborative service, based on vertical collaboration between service deliverers and service users/co-producers. In turn, this vertical collaboration, and the enabling systems on which it was based, enabled the users/co-producers to establish forms of horizontal collaboration with micro-businesses and/or mutual help activities through both experiential and relational interactions. The viability of the service was based on two main characteristics:

- a blend of vertical and horizontal collaboration, top-down and bottom-up initiatives, experiential and relational interactions. This blend was crucial to give the service the necessary transparency – through clear norms and procedures proposed by a legitimate, trustworthy authority – and embedded it in the local social fabric through horizontal collaboration and relational interaction; and
- a double link between its effectiveness and the socio-cultural qualities it generated, such as openness, transparency, dignity and collaboration. These qualities were fundamental for the success of the whole service. In turn, in practical terms, its success demonstrated and spread these qualities, that were essential in the situation facing the favelas.

The service was based on vertical, experiential interactions that, in turn, enabled horizontal, self-organised (often relational) ones. It can be defined as a hybrid collaborative service based on three pillars:

- structural features in terms of economic gains, effectiveness and the friendliness of its functioning;
- recognition of the positive meanings it conveyed and the socio-cultural qualities that gave sense to active citizen participation; and
- the potential to enrich vertical collaboration with horizontal peer-to-peer cooperation.

Given these empirical observations on a hybrid collaborative service model in an informal setting, the following lines of future research emerge. First, is this format viable in different contexts and application fields and, if so, with what limits? Second, can it contribute to improving the service levels in these settlements, because such services can be cheaper and/or more appropriate to their particular characteristics? Finally, can it contribute to creating a new kind of public space (and therefore open these settlements to other residents of the city)?

Notes

1. DESIS – Design for Social Innovation for Sustainability – is a network of design labs based in design schools (or in other design-oriented universities) promoting social innovation towards sustainability. DESIS Labs are teams of professors, researchers and students who orient their didactic and research activities towards starting and/or facilitating social innovation processes.
2. Thematic Clusters are initiatives promoted by groups of DESIS Labs that have found a theme of common interest, and agreed to align and systemise their ongoing, programmed activities, with the aim of creating the most favourable conditions to conceive and enhance, locally and/or internationally, new and stronger outcomes. More about IFC thematic cluster on: <http://www.desis-ifc.org> [Accessed 1 August 2013].
3. A well-known example in the United Kingdom of use of this approach in the design field has been promoted by the British Design Council in two projects: Design of the Time 2007 (Dott07) and Design of the Time Cornwall. These projects, addressing the social and economic dynamisation of regions in difficulty, have been pursued through a series of local projects emerging from careful attention to local demands and existing social capital (in terms of existing associations and enterprises already active on those topics). In Rio de Janeiro, an example of this approach – not related strictly to the design field – is given in 'pacification': 'The strategy of pacification encompasses a first moment of military occupation, a second moment of installing a permanent police unity in the territory and a third one that aims to establish a dialogue among social actors in the territory and convey their demands to a policy network' (Fleury, 2012, p. 198).
4. 'A single case, meeting all of the conditions for testing the theory, can confirm, challenge, or extend the theory. The single case can then be used to determine whether a theory's propositions are correct or whether some alternative set of explanations might be more relevant' (Yin, 2013, p. 47).

References

Buber, M. (1996) *I and Thou* (W. Kaufmann, Trans.). New York: Simon and Schuster-Touchstone (Original work published 1921).

Buber, M. (2006) *Between Man and Man* (R. Gregor-Smith, Trans.). New York: Routledge Classics (Original work published 1947).

Cipolla, C. (2004) 'Tourist or Guest: Designing Tourism Experiences or Hospitality Relations?' *Design Philosophy Papers*, 2 (2): 103–13.

Cipolla, C. (2012) 'Solutions for Relational Services', in Miettinen, S. and Valtonen, A. (Org.), *Service Design with Theory. Discussions on Change, Value and Methods*. Rovaniemi: LUP – Lapland University Press.

Cipolla, C. and Manzini, E. (2009) 'Relational Services', *Knowledge, Technology & Policy*, 22: 45–50.

Echeverri, A. and Orsini, F.M. (2011) 'Informalidad y Urbanismo Social en Medellín', *Sostenible?* 12.

Fleury, S. (2012) 'Militarização do social como estratégia de integração – o caso da UPP do Santa Marta', *Sociologias*, 14 (30): 194–222.

Light (2011) Relatório de Sustentabilidade de 2011 [Sustainability Report 2011]. <http://www.relatoriolight.com.br/> [Accessed 1 August 2013].

Light (2012) Relatório de Sustentabilidade de 2012 [Sustainability Report 2012]. <http://www.relatoriolight.com.br/> [Accessed 1 August 2013].

Manzini, E. (2007) 'Design Research for Sustainable Social Innovation', in Michel, R. (ed.), *Design Research Now*. Basel: Birkhauser Verlag, pp. 233–45.

Manzini. E. (2008) 'Collaborative Organisations and Enabling Solutions. Social Innovation and Design for Sustainability', in Jegou, F. and Manzini, E. (eds), *Collaborative Services. Social Innovation and Design for Sustainability*. Milan: Edizioni Polidesign, pp. 29–41.

Murray, R., Caulier-Grice, J. and Mulgan, G. (2010) *The Open Book of Social Innovation*. London: The Young Foundation.

Winther, T. (2012) 'Electricity Theft As a Relational Issue: A Comparative Look at Zanzibar, Tanzania, and the Sunderban Islands, India', *Energy for Sustainable Development*, 16: 111–19.

Yin, R. (2013) *Case Study Research. Design and Methods*. California: Sage.

Part III
Producing Social Innovation through New Forms of Collaboration

This page intentionally left blank

7

Enhancing Public Innovation through Collaboration, Leadership and New Public Governance

Eva Sørensen and Jacob Torfing

Introduction

Innovation aiming to develop and implement new public policies, services and organisational designs is frequently praised as an intelligent alternative to across-the-board cuts in times of shrinking budgets. It is also seen as a promising tool for breaking policy deadlocks and adjusting welfare services and delivery systems to new and changing demands (Bason, 2010). At the same time, there is growing evidence that multi-actor collaboration in networks, partnerships and inter-organisational teams can spur public innovation (Sørensen and Torfing, 2011; Ansell and Torfing, 2014). The involvement of different public and private actors in public innovation processes may improve the understanding of the problem or challenge at hand, bring forth new ideas and proposals, and build joint ownership of new and bold solutions (Hartley, Sørensen and Torfing, 2013). It may also ensure that the needs of users, citizens and civil society organisations are fully taken into account (Bason, 2010).

Public innovation continues to be driven largely by the managers and employees of particular public agencies (FTF, 2013). The 'silo trap' often prevents collaboration across public agencies, and professionally trained public employees' reliance on their own expertise tends to prevent them from tapping into the knowledge and ideas of lay actors (Eggers and O'Leary, 2009). Nevertheless, there seems to be significant growth in collaborative forms of innovation that cut across the institutional and organisational boundaries within the public sector and that also, frequently, involve a host of private actors equipped with relevant innovation 'assets'. A recent study from North America compared the semi-finalists in the competition for the Innovations in American

Government Awards from 1990 to 1994 with all the 2010 applications and found that the proportion of innovation projects based on external, inter-organisational collaboration had increased from 28% to 65%, and the proportion of innovation projects based on intra-organisational collaboration within the US government had increased from 21% to 58% (Borins, 2014). Indeed, the enhancement of collaborative innovation has become a key aspiration of public organisations in many Western countries (HM Government, 2010; Sunstein, 2012). National campaign organisations such as MindLab, Nesta and the Government Innovators Network tend to recommend collaboration as a strategy for enhancing public innovation.

Despite the inherent risks and frequent failures of public innovation projects, the innovation agenda is rapidly gaining momentum in the public sector. Such efforts to develop and implement new and bold ideas in government often bring together a plethora of public and private actors. However, the recent attempt to turn collaborative innovation into a permanent, systematic and pervasive focus of public agencies remains poorly institutionalised. Hence, unless a more precise and sophisticated understanding of the concepts of 'innovation' and 'collaboration' is developed, there is a risk that both terms are reduced to buzzwords and gain little traction with key stakeholders. Moreover, in reality, collaborative and innovative processes are difficult to trigger and sustain in the public sector without proper innovation management and a supportive cultural and institutional environment. So, in order to realise fully the opportunities offered by collaborative innovation, there is a need for further reflection on the role of public sector leaders and managers and for a transformation of the entire system of public governance.

This chapter aims to spur collaborative innovation in the public sector by clarifying the basic terms of debate and by exploring how new forms of innovation management and new forms of public governance can enhance collaborative innovation. To this end, it defines the basic notions of innovation and public innovation and discusses the relationship between public innovation and social innovation in order to understand better the purposes of different forms of innovation. The chapter then seeks to clarify the notion of collaboration and pinpoint why, how and under which conditions collaboration enhances public innovation. Next, it offers some theoretical and practical reflections about how public sector leaders and managers can advance collaborative innovation. Finally, the chapter argues that the enhancement of collaborative forms of social innovation calls for a transformation of the entire system of public governance that shifts the balance from New Public Management towards New Public Governance (Osborne, 2006, 2010; Ansell and Torfing, 2014).

Innovation, public innovation and social innovation

Developing a new and promising idea through a heuristic process based on intuition, brainstorming and a pragmatic recombination of old and new elements is a manifestation of creativity, but creativity only becomes innovation when a new idea is implemented and makes a difference (Mulgan and Albury, 2003). As such, innovation is defined here as the development and practical realisation of new and creative ideas in order to produce some added value (Hartley, 2005). Innovation may or may not be successful in terms of added value. Nevertheless, it tends to be driven by the ambition to outperform existing products or practices and generate solutions that are better than the status quo.

Innovation involves change, but not all forms of change qualify as innovation. Only step-changes that disrupt existing practices and common wisdom in a particular area are innovations (Sørensen and Torfing, 2011). The disruptive character of innovation means that it is very different from continuous improvement that aims to enhance the quality of public services through marginal adjustments (Hartley, 2011; Osborne and Brown, 2005). Step-changes can be small and incremental and merely change the form and content of particular products and practices, or they can be large and radical and transform both the goals and operational logic of an entire system of commodity or service production or a whole regulatory regime. However, step-changes always involve some degree of discontinuous change and that is precisely the essence of innovation: to develop and implement new and creative solutions that somehow break with the past.

Innovative solutions can be either the result of the invention of something entirely new or the result of the imitation of innovative solutions from elsewhere through a process of adoption and adaptation. Hence, it is not the source of innovation but the local context that determines whether something is an innovation or not (Roberts and King, 1996).

Since Marx and Schumpeter, innovation has been regarded as a key driver of economic growth and a necessary condition for ensuring the competitiveness and profitability of private firms (Hagedoorn, 1996). Market competition forces private enterprises to develop and successfully adopt innovative products, production methods and marketing strategies in order to stay in business. The role of individual entrepreneurs – or, in larger firms, well-organised research and development departments – is to produce a sufficient amount of innovation to build sustainable competitive advantage and to beat rivals in the market place. For a long time innovation was perceived as driven by the intense competition found in private markets. As a result, innovation was not considered relevant and necessary in the public sector, in which competition is replaced by hierarchical command and control (Hartley, Sørensen and Torfing, 2013). Public innovation was considered an oxymoron as innovation was assumed to be incompatible with institutional inertia and the bureaucratic 'red tape' of the public sector. Hence, despite the fact that policy problems seem to drive ongoing policy reforms (Pollitt and Bouckaert, 2004) and that small teams of professionally trained public employees tend to respond to emerging problems by creating innovative solutions (Swan, Scarbrough and Robertson, 2002), it has been a persistent myth that the public sector – due to the lack of competition and the absence of a profit motive – is much less innovative than the market-based private sector (Borins, 2001; Moore and Hartley, 2008; Hartley, Sørensen and Torfing, 2013). As such, the interest in public innovation as a tool for improvement in the public sector is a recent one, dating back to the 'Reinventing Government' movement in the early 1990s (Osborne and Gaebler, 1992).

The idea that innovation is more relevant to the private than the public sector is inherently problematic because it underestimates the ability of the public sector to innovate and exaggerates the innovative capacity of the private sector. First, it fails to recognise that political and professional ambitions, policy problems and changing demands often replace competition as a trigger of innovation in the public sector (Rittel and Webber, 1973; Polsby, 1984; Koch and Hauknes, 2005). Second, it forgets that, although competition incentivises private firms to innovate, it does not provide a method for innovation in and of itself (Hartley, Sørensen and Torfing, 2013). Hence, when private firms of a certain size seek to respond to competitive pressures by innovating their products and production systems, they tend to face many of the same barriers as public organisations because they are also organised as bureaucracies with hierarchical command structures, an internal division of labour, cultural boundaries between different professions, rule-governed behaviour and a tendency towards institutional isolation that means that innovation is often produced in-house by research and development departments or through separate 'skunk works' outside of the main firm (Halvorsen *et al.*, 2005).

The public sector also has some sector-specific barriers due to the fact that it is politically governed, lacks economic incentives and produces regulations and services that are extremely complex and often based on legal rights and entitlements. However, these specific barriers are partly offset by sector-specific drivers in terms of the large public budgets that make it possible to absorb the costs of failures; well-educated and professionally trained staff who possess relevant competencies; relatively easy access to scientific knowledge from public universities and research institutions; favourable conditions for getting inputs from citizens and users who are often directly involved in the production of public services; and the absence of competition between public agencies, giving the possibility of interagency learning, policy transfer and innovation diffusion (Rashman and Hartley, 2002; Halvorsen *et al.*, 2005).

With these drivers in mind, it comes as no surprise that the public sector is far more dynamic and innovative than its reputation suggests. Contrary to classical public administration theory – from Max Weber, to Anthony Downs and Charles Lindblom – the public sector seems to create a lot of innovation (Borins, 2001; Hartley, Sørensen and Torfing, 2013). This becomes clear when we compare the public sector in today's advanced industrial economies with that of thirty years ago. Within that short time span, new policy areas such as preventative care, active employment policy and climate change mitigation have emerged. A whole range of innovative services have been developed, such as online education, neighbourhood renewal programmes based on the empowerment of local citizens, training of chronically ill patients to master the management of their own illness and the possibility of serving prison sentences at home with an electronic tag. Public organisations have been transformed by the introduction of systems of strategic management, performance-related wage systems and quasi-markets. Innovations in service delivery processes have seen the creation of one-stop service agencies, public–private partnerships and digital services. Finally, the role and position of the public sector has been subject to innovation due to the recent emphasis on active citizenship, co-production and volunteering that shifts the balance from state to society by giving citizens and civil society organisations a much more active role in relation to the public sector and the provision of welfare services (Bovaird and Löffler, 2012).

Historical studies of the development of social policies (Ehrenreich, 1985; Dean, 1991) confirm that the public sector has always produced a considerable amount of policy and service innovation. However, it is only recently that researchers and policy makers have begun to talk about public innovation and discuss how it can be stimulated in response to globalisation, fiscal and demographic pressures and the rising service expectations of citizens and private companies. In the last decade, public innovation has moved up the public sector agenda in many countries in Europe, America and the Asia-Pacific region, but it seems that the action still falls short of broader aims and aspirations. The rhetoric about how public innovation can help to get 'more with less' has become stronger, but public innovation as a tool for changing policies and services remains underexplored and underexploited and is far from constituting a permanent, systematic or pervasive endeavour in the public sector.

The notion of social innovation has played an important role in the recent expansion of the public innovation agenda. When, in the 1980s, innovation was first discussed in relation to the public sector, the focus was primarily on how the public sector could contribute to innovation and growth in the private sector through scientific research, knowledge transfer, technology policy and participation in national innovation systems that brought together relevant public and private actors to stimulate the growth of clusters and networks (Porter, 1985; Lundvall, 1992). The public sector was merely seen as a 'midwife' for innovation and growth in the private sector.

The Reinventing Government movement (Osborne and Gaebler, 1992) – that emerged in the United States at the beginning of the 1990s and later came to be associated with the advancement of New Public Management in Europe (see Hood, 1991) – changed the focus. This was based on the premise that a combination of public entrepreneurship, strategic leadership, performance management, contracting out and increased user orientation would help the public sector to become more dynamic and innovative in order to increase its efficiency and enhance user satisfaction. Although the attempt to make the public sector more efficient would eventually make it possible to reduce public expenditure, cut taxes and stimulate private sector growth, the purpose of the innovative public sector reforms proposed by the Reinventing Government movement and the supporters of New Public Management was, primarily, to improve the public sector rather than the private sector.

The attempt to improve the public sector and make it more efficient could be supported by new technologies. Hence, whereas the public sector was initially seen as a driver of competitiveness in the private sector, private sector innovation – in terms of new computer technologies – was increasingly seen as a driver of public sector improvement. As such, an expanding stream of research from the 1980s onwards focussed on the conditions for introducing and exploiting new technologies into the public sector (Perry and Danzinger, 1980; Perry and Kraemer, 1980; Kraemer and Perry, 1989; Perry et al., 1993).

Whereas both the Reinventing Government movement and the attempt to spur technological innovation in the public sector focussed on a combination of organisational and process innovation, the recent emphasis on social innovation has shifted the innovation agenda in the direction of service and policy innovation. Social innovation emerged as a concept in British and French debates in the 1960s and 1970s but was only recently embraced by the European Commission, which described it as 'innovations that are both social in their ends and in their means' (European Commission, 2010). The scholarly definition of social innovation varies, but one of the authoritative sources defined it as 'innovative activities and services that are motivated by the goal of meeting a social need and that are predominantly developed and diffused through organisations whose primary purpose are social' (Mulgan *et al.*, 2007, p. 8). There are two important novelties in this definition of social innovation. First, the purpose of innovating is not merely to make the public sector more efficient but rather to develop new programmes and services that aim to meet unmet social needs. Second, innovation is not created merely by actors and processes internal to the public sector but involves deliberative attempts to tap into the creativity of charities, associations and social entrepreneurs in order to find new ways of meeting pressing social needs.

The notion of 'social innovation' has not caught on to the same extent in all Western countries, and the discourse on social innovation appears to be stronger in the Anglo-Saxon countries than in continental Europe, despite the attempts of the European Commission to promote social innovation as an important response to the economic and social crisis in Europe (European Commission, 2010; 2013a; 2013b; BEPA, 2010). However, the underlying idea that public innovation should both seek to make the public sector more efficient by reforming administrative processes and organisational designs and serve a social purpose by fostering new and better policies and services is shared by policy makers, public managers and public employees in many European countries (European Commission, 2013b). As such, the key question is no longer whether the public sector should aim to spur innovation in policy, services and organisational designs in order to enhance the production of social and public value but, rather, how this can be done.

The case for collaborative innovation

It is often assumed that innovation in the private sector is generated by forward-looking business leaders, risk-taking entrepreneurs and creative inventors (Schumpeter, 1976; Drucker, 1985; Knight, 2005). However, the truth is that most innovations in private enterprises are created either by large R&D departments or by strategic alliances with other firms (Teece, 1992; Nambisan, 2008). Nevertheless, the myth about the individual innovation 'heroes' that allegedly drive innovation in the private sector has inspired the public sector to look for its own innovators (Doig and Hargrove, 1987). Some highlighted the role of elected politicians in bringing new ideas to the table in order to gain support from the voters (Polsby, 1984). The Reinventing Government movement celebrated the entrepreneurial spirit of public managers engaged in strategic management as well as private contractors who were competing for tenders in newly created quasi-markets (Osborne and Gaebler, 1992). More recently, there has been a growing interest in employee-driven and user-driven innovation in the public sector (LO, 2008; Bogers, Afuah and Bastian, 2010).

This search for public innovation heroes fails to recognise that innovation is seldom the result of the efforts of a single actor (Csikszentmihalyi, 1996). In fact, it is often in the meeting between different public and/or private actors that new ideas are developed, processes of mutual learning are accelerated, and joint ownership of new and bold solutions is built.

Research suggests that multi-actor collaboration strengthens and improves all phases in the innovation process (Roberts and Bradley, 1991; Roberts and King, 1996; Hartley, 2005; Nambisan, 2008; Eggers and Singh, 2009; Sørensen and Torfing, 2011). The first phase – *generating understanding of problems and challenges* – is improved when the experiences and knowledge of different public and private actors are taken into account. Hence, the experiences of particular user groups can fundamentally change the way that problems in public service delivery systems are perceived and can prevent public actors from wasting money, time and energy on solving the 'wrong' problem.

Meanwhile, *the development of new ideas* (the next stage in the process) is strengthened when actors with different perspectives and opinions are brought together. Inter-organisational exchange and the involvement of lay actors may bring forth new ideas that the lead agency would never have thought about. For example, collaboration between the chief of the fire and rescue department and the leader of municipal eldercare services in Greve Municipality in Denmark fostered an innovative solution to the deaths by fires caused by elderly people falling asleep while smoking in bed: when elderly people applied for municipal care, the social worker who visited the elderly person to assess their needs would from now on be accompanied by a fire and rescue worker who would give advice about fire safety. This innovative solution led to a drastic decline in the number of elderly deaths by fire.

The selection and testing of the most promising solutions is enriched if actors with different backgrounds and concerns participate in the negotiation of gains and risks as well as in the real-life testing of new solutions. As such, patients participating in trials and experiments provide invaluable insights that help to adapt innovative solutions before they are rolled out in the entire public sector.

Meanwhile, *implementation of innovative solutions* is promoted when the relevant actors coordinate their actions and have joint ownership of the new solution. Exchange and pooling resources in the implementation phase helps to avoid overlaps and create synergies, and broad participation by different actors, including employees and user groups, fosters a common understanding of the motives for adopting an innovative solution, which in turn will often help to reduce implementation resistance.

Last but not least, *the diffusion of successful innovations* is enhanced by collaboration because the participants will act as ambassadors and disseminate information concerning both the content and the advantages of the innovative practices. As such, it is well established that innovation diffusion is propelled by collaboration in inter-organisational networks (Rogers, 1995).

Bommert (2010) captured the core of the argument for collaborative innovation when he claimed that collaborative innovation is the only innovation method that ensures that the possession of relevant innovation assets such as creative ideas, courage, venture capital and implementation capacity – rather than organisational and institutional boundaries – determine who contributes to the production of public innovation. Both competitive markets and hierarchical forms of government tend to create innovation processes that are trapped within the narrow confines of a single organisation. As a consequence, they fail to reap the fruits of collaboration with relevant actors who can provide important inputs to the innovation process.

The literature on social innovation also tends to emphasise the collaborative aspect of innovation processes. It is frequently asserted that end users, vulnerable groups and community organisations in particular should participate in initiating, designing and implementing innovative policies and services, because their input to the innovation process is critical to its success (Von Hippel, 2005; 2007; European Commission, 2013a). However, this chapter argues that collaborative innovation should not privilege a specific group of actors but aim to include all the relevant actors who can somehow contribute to the different phases of public innovation processes. End users, disadvantaged citizens and civil society organisations may prove to be important for creating innovative solutions that enhance social justice, but experts, private firms, consultancy houses, interest groups, politicians, and so on may also provide insights, ideas and resources that spur the creation of innovative solutions in the public sector.

The notion of collaborative innovation resonates well with the growing interest in 'collaborative governance' through networks, partnerships and inter-organisational communities of practice (Agranoff, 2007; Ansell and Gash, 2008; O'Leary and Bingham, 2009). 'Governance' is defined as the formal and informal processes through which society and the economy are steered and problems are solved in accordance with common objectives (Torfing *et al.*, 2012). However, it is not always clear how 'collaboration' is conceptualised.

One approach is to distinguish between cooperation, coordination and collaboration (Keast, Brown and Mandell, 2007). Cooperation involves the exchange of relevant information and knowledge across organisational and sectoral boundaries, while coordination involves conscious efforts to create synergies and prevent overlaps in public regulation and service delivery. Collaboration, meanwhile, is based on a sustained interaction through which a plethora of actors aim to find common solutions to shared problems. Nevertheless, collaboration involves more than sustained interagency communication and more than pragmatic attempts to escape the silo trap by pooling resources and facilitating joint action. Collaboration is based on a mutual commitment of two or more actors to work together towards a common end that can only be reached through the transformation of materials, ideas and/or social relations (Roberts and Bradley, 1991). In collaborative processes social and political actors work on a shared problem in order to find mutually acceptable ways to conceptualise and solve them. In the course of interaction the actors may not only transform their shared objective in terms of a particular policy, service, process or organisational design. They may also change their roles and identities and the logic of appropriate action that guides their actions (March and Olsen, 1995; Engeström, 2008).

Collaboration is sometimes associated with deliberation that fosters 'unanimous consent' (Straus, 2002). However, reaching a total consensus can be extremely demanding in terms of time and resources. It is also detrimental to innovation because problematising conventional wisdom is an important driver of innovation and because total consensus is often achieved by getting everybody to agree on the lowest common denominator. As a method, this favours incremental adjustments rather than more discontinuous change and disruptive innovation (Gorman, 2013). In contrast to the predominant view that consensus is obtained through deliberation in a power-free space of communicative reason governed by the force of the better argument that leaves no space for dissent (Habermas, 1987), this chapter follows Gray (1989) in defining collaboration as involving the constructive management of differences in order to find joint solutions to shared problems. People collaborate because they are different and expect that their different experiences and perspectives will provide a more complex and nuanced understanding of the world, challenge and disturb tacit knowledge, and produce new and creative ideas through passionate debates based on joint aspirations, constructive contestation and mutual respect.

Collaboration breaks down if the participants develop antagonistic relationships with each other, but if the differences between the actors are managed in a constructive way, they will be able to reach agreement about the content and character of the innovative solution that they aim to realise (Gray, 1989; Mouffe, 2005). The agreement will be provisional, contested and involve compromise, but a majority of the actors will rally behind it, despite their potential reservations and concerns (Norval, 2007). The advantage of this way of conceptualising collaboration – as a conflict-ridden attempt to find joint solutions to shared problems through provisional and disputed agreements – is that it makes room for the differences and passions that fuel the processes of creativity and innovation.

Rethinking public leadership in the face of collaborative innovation

The attempt to enhance collaborative innovation in the public sector requires the development of a new kind of public leadership and management. In the last few decades public leaders and managers have been trained and encouraged to focus on inputs – in terms of the use of different public resources – and outputs – in terms of the performance of their staff and department (Osborne, 2006). However, this limited focus on resource consumption and performance can neither help drive innovation nor initiate and orchestrate collaborative processes.

Leading and managing innovation requires the ability to manage 'emergence' in the sense of the future development and realisation of new and creative solutions that break with and, perhaps, outperform existing practices. To manage emergence, it is not enough to recruit, instruct and correct public employees through what is commonly referred to as 'transactional leadership', nor is it sufficient to inspire, motivate and incentivise staff through what has been referred to as 'transformational leadership' (Parry and Bryman, 2006). Transactional and transformational leadership continue to be important to ensure an efficient implementation of predefined goals through well-described bureaucratic practices, but they have limited value when it comes to rethinking goals and practices and changing the way that problems and challenges are reframed and new practices are designed, tested and adjusted. Rather, the promotion of public innovation requires a combination of 'adaptive' and 'pragmatic' leadership.

Adaptive leadership aims to determine which public activities to maintain and which to adapt and transform. It then seeks to develop new practices by crafting and testing prototypes and by aligning people across an organisation in order to ensure effective execution and to facilitate the integration of new activities with old ones (Heifetz, Linsky and Grashow, 2009). *Pragmatic leadership* aims to transform the culture of public organisations in ways that enhance double loop learning and use existing tools to solve problems by changing established practices – including transformative learning that develops new metaphors and narratives that help frame what is difficult to comprehend, expand knowledge and toolboxes and change identities and roles (Argyris and Schön, 1978; Mezirow *et al.*, 2000).

Leading and managing collaboration, meanwhile, also poses a huge challenge to public leaders and managers who in the last decades have been told to focus on the performance of the staff, agency or department that they are in charge of (Christensen and Lægreid, 2006). In the 1980s many people thought that the public sector was in need of more charismatic and visionary leadership that was capable of redefining public sector objectives, inspiring the workforce and turning around ossified and run-down public organisations. In hindsight it can be seen that this kind of 'change leadership' was only relevant for executive managers, who often failed to connect to the rest of their organisation and its external stakeholders and failed to generate sustainable and long-lasting transformation of public organisations (Parry and Bryman, 2006). The efforts of public leaders and managers to enhance public innovation through multi-actor collaboration call for a new type of leadership and management that is more 'distributive', 'horizontal', 'collaborative' and 'integrative'.

Distributive leadership encourages public leaders and managers to lead others in ways that enable them to lead themselves (Pearce and Conger, 2003; Parry and Bryman, 2006). In order to spur collaboration, leaders and managers at different levels of an organisation must distribute and disperse leadership functions within their organisation by facilitating the empowerment of their employees and the creation of self-managing projects, teams and networks (Wart, 2013). People who possess the competences and knowledge to develop and implement new and bold solutions need support from sponsors and champions at the executive level, but most of all, they need decentralised day-to-day leadership within their organisation. For example, they need project and team leaders and network managers who can help them to focus their attention, search for new ideas and test the most promising ones in the course of daily operations. Middle managers must find ways of recruiting, training and empowering employees who can exercise innovation leadership, even though they do not have a formal leadership role. In addition, they must support and coach those employees who take on dispersed leadership functions and act as innovation managers in concrete innovation projects. The ultimate goal of distributive leadership is to facilitate self-regulation.

Horizontal leadership aims to support and enhance interactive and collaborative processes among peers. Horizontal leadership of projects, teams and networks enables different professions to engage in creative problem solving, based on dialogue and collaboration (Denis, Langley and Sergi, 2012). However, horizontal leadership can also help to facilitate collaboration with, and between, private actors such as service users, citizens, NGOs and private firms that can bring new ideas to the innovation process. To illustrate, some Danish municipalities have begun to recruit and train local 'playmakers' – public employees who are given the task of initiating and supporting cooperation between public and private actors – in order to spur the development of new and better public solutions. Public facilitators dedicated to stimulating horizontal interaction between public and private actors are likely to play an important role in opening up the public sector to new ideas. Unfortunately, public authorities are not always committed to collaboration with private actors because they think that it is too complicated and time-consuming and because they do not think that collaboration will generate inputs that match the ideas of the trained professionals in the public sector. This is confirmed in a Danish survey that showed that, although a majority of the public managers who responded claimed that they made efforts to involve users and citizens in collaborative innovation, they also stated that they seldom used the inputs and ideas from users and citizens when designing new and innovative solutions (FTF, 2013). Horizontal leadership is sometimes referred to as *collaborative leadership*. The task of collaborative leadership is to design appropriate institutional arenas for collaborative governance and facilitate collaborative processes by emphasising the mutual interdependence of public and private actors, building trust, developing a shared understanding of the overall mission and encouraging the production of intermediate outcomes (Ansell and Gash, 2008; Archer and Cameron, 2008). A crucial challenge for collaborative leadership is to drive the process onwards from problem definition, direction setting and policy development to decision-making and implementation. Making bold decisions and implementing them in practice is the *sine qua non* for innovation but often presents a challenge to leaders of collaboration since the choice of one solution over another may give rise to conflicts and antagonism. This makes conflict mediation a key part of collaborative leadership (Gray, 1989; Ansell and Gash, 2008).

Integrative leadership also focuses on collaboration in horizontal arenas. As such, the key ambition of integrative public leadership is to bring diverse groups and organisations together in semi-permanent ways, and typically across sector boundaries, to solve complex problems by developing a new set of solutions that help to achieve common goals (Crosby and Bryson, 2010). According to Crosby and Bryson (2010), the research on integrative public leadership has shown that leaders are most likely to have success with creating cross-sector collaboration in turbulent environments and when separate efforts by several actors from different sectors have failed. Their research indicated that successful leaders aimed to form an initial agreement about a problem and sought to design the collaborative process in ways that involved the creation of boundary objects, experiences and groups. They drew on the competences of the collaborators, were responsive to key stakeholders and made a point of avoiding imposed solutions. Integrative leaders ensured that trust-building activities were continuous and that the structure of collaboration was flexible and open to new actors, as well as for leader succession. Integrative leaders were prepared to commit time and energy to mitigate power imbalances and deal with shocks, and they managed to reframe conflicts and disputes in ways that had appeal across sectors. Finally, such leaders focused on building accountability systems that track inputs, processes and outcomes and on developing methods for gathering, interpreting and using data in processes of creative problem solving. Nevertheless, Crosby and Bryson cautioned not to exaggerate the impact of integrative leadership by insisting that 'the normal expectation ought to be that success will be very difficult to achieve in cross-sector collaborations, regardless of leadership effectiveness' (Crosby and Bryson, 2010, p. 227).

The challenge of integrative leadership is to design and govern institutional arenas for collaborative governance while mobilising the knowledge, resources and energies of relevant actors and to facilitate self-regulated processes of collaboration based on the recognition of a mutual interdependency among public and private actors. According to recent theories of 'governance networks' (Jessop, 2002; Kooiman, 2003; Meuleman, 2008), this challenge can be met by the exercise of '*meta-governance*'. Meta-governance is defined as the 'governance of governance' and can be seen as an attempt to influence collaborative governance processes without reverting to traditional forms of command and control – it is exercised by means of creating and framing interactive arenas and facilitating and managing processes of multi-actor collaboration (Sørensen and Torfing, 2009). The tools of meta-governance are network design, goal and framework steering, process management and direct participation in interactive arenas.

In order to enhance collaborative innovation, these abstract ideas about leadership and management need to be translated into more concrete recommendations. In order to do so, this chapter proposes that the barriers to collaborative innovation in the public sector can be mitigated or overcome by public leaders and managers who assume the role of 'conveners', 'facilitators' and 'catalysts' (Straus, 2002; Crosby and Bryson, 2010; Morse, 2010; Page, 2010; Ansell and Gash, 2012).

The role of the *convener* is to bring together relevant actors and spur interaction and the exchange of information, views and ideas. Tasks for conveners include:

- Selecting teams of innovators by identifying people with relevant innovation assets in terms of knowledge, practical experience, creative ideas, resources, formal power and so on, and motivating them to participate in the innovation process;
- Clarifying the roles of different actors and drawing up a process map that delineates who participates, when and how in the different phases of the innovation process;
- Encouraging interaction and exchange between participating actors by stimulating the recognition of their mutual dependence on each other's resources;

- Securing political support for the search for innovative solutions and protecting the integrity of the collaborative arena; and
- Giving direction to the joint search for innovative solutions and aligning the goals and expectations of the actors.

The role of the *facilitator* is to get the actors to collaborate by constructively managing their differences and engaging in processes of mutual learning that bring them beyond the common denominator. Facilitators can:

- Lower the transaction costs of collaborating by arranging good and effective meetings, ensuring smooth communication and activating those actors who are not contributing as much as they could by motivating and empowering them;
- Enhance and sustain trust between actors by creating opportunities for informal social interaction, encouraging the development of common rules and procedures for interaction and triggering a virtuous cycle of trust-creation through a unilateral display of trust in the other actors;
- Develop a common frame of understanding by creating a common knowledge base through knowledge exchange and joint fact finding missions and developing a common language based on jointly accepted definitions of key terms and ideas;
- Resolve or mediate conflicts so that they become constructive rather than destructive and ensure that irresolvable conflicts are de-personalised and conceived as joint puzzles rather than road blocks; and
- Remove obstacles to collaboration by securing support from the executive leaders in the participating organisations and negotiating how the costs and gains of innovative solutions are distributed among the actors.

The role of the *catalyst* is to create appropriate disturbances that bring the actors out of their comfort zone and force them to think creatively and develop and implement new and bold solutions. As such, the catalyst can:

- Construct a sense of urgency either by referring to the presence of a 'burning platform' in the sense of a situation that demands immediate and radical change due to dire circumstances or by demonstrating the presence of a 'window of opportunity' that creates a unique chance to change established practices;
- Prevent tunnel vision by encouraging actors to change their perspectives where necessary, including new and different actors in the team, or bringing new and inspiring knowledge into play;

- Create open and creative search processes by changing the venue for meetings and the way that actors interact and collaborate when they are together;
- Facilitate the management and negotiation of the risks associated with innovative solutions and coordinate implementation processes to enhance synergy and avoid overlap; and
- Ensure that participating actors assume the role of 'ambassadors' and use their strong and weak ties to diffuse explicit and tacit knowledge about the innovative solution.

The deliberate attempt of public leaders and managers to convene the relevant actors, facilitate collaboration and co-creation and catalyse the development and realisation of innovative ideas needs to be supplemented with persistent attempts to build a strong 'innovation culture' in public organisations (Dobni, 2008). Creating an innovation culture involves recruiting and nurturing creative talent, enhancing diversity and mobility, and encouraging staff members to use their professional knowledge to generate and test new ideas. It also involves challenging a zero-error culture, the detailed rules and regulations and demotivating performance measurement systems that prevent innovation (Ansell and Torfing, 2014). Finally, it involves attempts to create flatter and more flexible organisations with clear mission objectives and strong leadership to breach administrative silos and create more borderless organisations with flexible and permeable boundaries. What is called for is a cultural revolution in the public sector that requires a complete rethinking of the way that the public sector is organised, governed and led in terms of its relation to society. In short, there is a need to transform governance in order to enhance innovation.

Transforming governance

The public sector has traditionally been organised as a Weberian bureaucracy, but the mounting critique of public bureaucracies for being too ineffective and inefficient (Downs, 1967) stimulated the adoption of governance reforms inspired by the concept of New Public Management (Hood, 1991; Osborne and Gaebler, 1992). According to this school of thought, the performance of the public sector could be enhanced if some public services were privatised or contracted out and the remaining public service organisations were subjected to competitive pressures from private contractors who were operating in new quasi-markets, or from the creation of internal markets in the public sector. In the market-driven public sector, service users were re-cast as 'customers' and given the right to choose freely between competing public and private service providers. In order to be able to deal with these competitive pressures, New Public Management thinking asserted that the public sector should import a number of strategic management tools from the private sector, such as contract steering of private providers and special purpose agencies, fixed budget frames with internal flexibility and management by objectives, performance measurement and performance-based pay systems.

New Public Management has not been systematically implemented in all countries, but most Western democracies have been influenced by at least some of its core ideas (Pollitt and Bouckaert, 2004). The total effects of New Public Management are difficult, if not impossible, to assess. However, while the public sector in some countries has benefitted from a stronger emphasis on policy goals, evaluation and public leadership, there are also critical reports about increasing fragmentation, growing distrust and the excessive costs and distorting effects of performance measurement (Dent, Chandler and Barry, 2004; Christensen and Lægreid, 2007).

Most importantly, however, New Public Management does not seem to have fulfilled its promise of enhancing public innovation (Ansell and Torfing, 2014). Contrary to expectations, performance management has tended to create a zero-error culture that prevents innovation; competition has tended to prevent the exchange of new ideas that are treated as business secrets; and free consumer choice has turned citizens into demanding and complaining users who do not feel part of the solution (Hartley, Sørensen and Torfing, 2013). New Public Management may have succeeded in spurring public innovation through a combination of an increased focus on results, competitive tendering and procurement and an emphasis on public entrepreneurship, but it has failed to stimulate collaboration across organisational and sectoral boundaries.

Consequently, the enhancement of collaborative innovation in the public sector requires a shift from New Public Management to what is increasingly referred to as New Public Governance (Osborne, 2006; 2010; Torfing and Triantafillou, 2013; Morgan and Cook, 2014). The contrast between the two paradigmatic ways of governing the public sector and their relation to the external environment is shown in Table 7.1.

The comparison of these two conceptual paradigms brings out the defining features of New Public Governance. These features tend to enhance and sustain collaborative innovation. Trust-based management resting on co-leadership, mutual feedback and empowerment tends to enhance the motivation of public employees to help solve

Table 7.1 Comparison of New Public Management and New Public Governance

New Public Management	New Public Governance
Self-interested public employees must be subjected to tight monitoring and control	Self-interest is combined with a strong public service motivation that calls for trust-based management
The problem is the public monopoly over service production that makes services too poor and too expensive	The problem is the growing complexity and wickedness of the problems and challenges that are facing public service production
The solution is to enhance competition through privatisation and contracting out	The solution is public–private collaboration through networks and partnerships
Intra-organisational management should focus on resources and performance	Inter-organisational leadership should focus on processes and results
Citizens are customers with free service choice	Citizens are co-producers and co-creators of welfare services
The goal is the enhancement of efficiency through rationalisation based on LEAN technologies that aim to cut slack	The goal is the enhancement of efficiency, effectiveness and quality through resource mobilisation and innovation

Source: Authors' compilation.

social problems, and creates a space for collaboration that can produce innovative solutions (Nyhan, 2006). Focusing on complex problems and challenges can stimulate a cross-disciplinary and inter-organisational search for new and bold solutions, and the turn from product- to service-orientation may open the eyes of public administrators to the active and creative role of citizens in co-production (Osborne, Radnor and Nasi, 2013). The emphasis on collaboration rather than competition is bound to enhance the exchange of knowledge, ideas and resources, and to stimulate mutual learning processes and generate support for new and innovative strategies (Sørensen and Torfing, 2011). Collaborative leadership aiming to create effective and constructive processes may help to overcome organisational and professional boundaries and stimulate mutual and transformative learning processes (Wart, 2013). Turning citizens from passive consumers to active citizens enhances co-production and co-creation that can harness the experiences, competencies and energies of end users to renew public services (Bovaird and Loeffler, 2012). Lastly, the transgression of the narrow confines of 'lean-based' rationalisation technologies, that merely aim to cut slack within a given process of service production, opens up opportunities for creative processes that aim to re-cast the systems of public service production – as well as the underlying perception of the problems, goals and causalities – in the search for disruptive innovations that can provide more and better services for less (Radnor and Osborne, 2013).

New Public Governance is likely to stimulate collaborative innovation and, for those seeking to reap the fruits of this potent innovation method, it is encouraging to see that the ideas and practices associated with New Public Governance are gaining momentum in public sectors throughout Europe (Torfing and Triantafillou, 2013) and in North America (Morgan and Cook, 2014). However, just as New Public Management did not replace bureaucratic forms of government, it seems likely that New Public Governance will co-exist with remnants of former public administration paradigms, thus adding a new layer of institutional practice to existing systems. The co-existence of different governing paradigms will no doubt give rise to the formation of hybrid forms of governance with unforeseen and ambiguous effects on the innovative capacity of the public sector (Christensen and Lægreid, 2011). Nevertheless, the more hegemonic the New Public Governance paradigm becomes, the greater the chances that public innovation will flourish and help improve public policies and services in the face of present and future challenges.

Conclusion

This chapter has explained how the notion of social innovation has helped to create a new focus on service and policy innovation in the public sector and has shown how collaboration – defined as the constructive management of difference – can drive public innovation. It has also explored the challenges that collaborative innovation poses to public leadership and management and delineated three important roles for public leaders and managers aiming to enhance collaborative innovation. Finally, it has shown that the further advancement of collaborative innovation is predicated on a shift from New Public Management to New Public Governance.

Despite its importance and promise, the research on collaborative innovation is only in its infancy and further research is needed. Five top priorities for this future research agenda are clear. First, a combination of qualitative case studies and quantitative research is needed in order further to document the causal relationships between multi-actor collaboration and public innovation. Second, research should seek to explain why the involvement of private stakeholders in the implementation phase tends to be stronger and more frequent than participation in the initiation and design phases, and also aim to explore how this imbalance can be corrected. Third, a detailed mapping of the political and institutional barriers and drivers of collaborative innovation is needed, so that the barriers can be removed and the drivers can be further sustained. Fourth, the dilemmas associated with the exercise of innovation management need to be identified. Finally, the political conditions for a transition to New Public Governance must be assessed.

References

Agranoff, R. (2007) *Managing within Networks: Adding Value to Public Organizations.* Washington, D.C.: Georgetown University Press.

Ansell, C. and Gash, A. (2008) 'Collaborative Governance in Theory and Practice', *Journal of Public Administration Research and Theory*, 18 (4): 543–71.

Ansell, C. and Gash, A. (2012) 'Stewards, Mediators and Catalysts: Toward a Model of Collaborative Leadership', *The Innovation Journal*, 17 (1): 1–21.

Ansell, C. and Torfing, J. (eds) (2014) *Public Innovation through Collaboration and Design.* Abingdon: Routledge.

Archer, D. and Cameron, A. (2008) *Collaborative Leadership: How to Succeed in an Interconnected World.* Oxford: Elsevier.

Argyris, C. and Schön, D. (1978) Organizational Learning: A Theory of Action Perspective. Reading, MA: Addison-Wesley.

Bason, C. (2010) *Leading Public Sector Innovation: Co-Creating for a Better Society.* Bristol: Policy Press.

BEPA (2010) *Empowering People, Driving Change. Social Innovation in the European Union.* Brussels: Bureau of European Policy Advisers and European Commission.

Bogers, M., Afuah, A. and Bastian, B. (2010) 'Users As Innovators: A Review, Critique, and Future Research Directions', *Journal of Management*, 36 (4): 857–75.

Bommert, B. (2010) 'Collaborative Innovation in the Public Sector', *International Public Management Review*, 11 (1): 15–33.

Borins, S. (2001) 'Encouraging Innovation in the Public Sector', *Journal of Intellectual Capital*, 2 (3): 310–19.

Borins, S. (2014) *The Persistence of Innovation in Government: A Guide for Public Servants.* Washington, D.C.: IBM Center for the Business of Government.

Bovaird, T. and Loeffler, E. (2012) 'From Engagement to Co-production: How Users and Communities Contribute to Public Services', in V. Pestoff, T. Brandsen and B. Verschuere (eds), *New Public Governance, the Third Sector and Co-production.* London: Routledge, pp. 35–60.

Christensen, T. and Lægreid, P. (eds) (2006) *Autonomy and Regulation: Coping with Agencies in the Modern State.* Cheltenham: Edward Elgar.

Christensen, T. and Lægreid, P. (eds) (2007) *Transcending New Public Management: The Transformation of Public Sector Reforms.* Aldershot: Ashgate.

Christensen, T. and Lægreid, P. (2011) 'Complexity and Hybrid Public Administration: Theoretical and Empirical Challenges', *Public Organization Review*, 11 (4): 407–23.

Crosby, B. and Bryson, J. (2010) 'Integrative Leadership and the Creation and Maintenance of Cross-Sector Collaboration', *Leadership Quarterly*, 21 (2): 211–30.

Csikszentmihalyi, M. (1996) *Creativity: Flow and the Psychology of Discovery and Invention.* New York: Harper Perennial.

Dean, M. (1991) *The Constitution of Poverty.* London: Routledge.

Denis, J.-L., Langley, A. and Sergi, V. (2012) 'Leadership in the Plural', *The Academy of Management Annals*, 6 (1): 211–83.

Dent, M., Chandler, J. and Barry, J. (2004) *Questioning the New Public Management.* Aldershot: Ashgate.

Dobni, C. B. (2008) 'Measuring Innovation Culture in Organizations', *European Journal of Innovation Management*, 11 (4): 539–59.

Doig, J.W. and Hargrove E.L. (1987) *Leadership and Innovation: Entrepreneurs in Government.* Baltimore, MD: Johns Hopkins University Press.

Downs, A. (1967) *Inside Bureaucracy*, Boston, MA: Little, Brown and Company.

Drucker, P.F. (1985) *Innovation and Entrepreneurship: Practices and Principles.* Oxford: Elsevier.

Eggers, W.D. and O'Leary, J. (2009) *If We Can Put a Man on the Moon: Getting Big Things Done in Government.* Harvard, MA: Harvard Business Press.

Eggers, W.D. and Singh, S. (2009) *The Public Innovator's Playbook.* Washington, D.C.: Harvard Kennedy School of Government.

Ehrenreich, J. (1985) *The Altruistic Imagination: A History of Social Work and Social Policy in the U.S.* Ithaca, NY: Cornell University Press.

Engeström, Y. (2008) *From Teams to Knots: Activity Theoretical Studies of Collaboration and Learning at Work.* New York: Cambridge University Press.

European Commission (2010) *This Is European Social Innovation.* Brussels: EU.

European Commission (2013a) *Industrial Innovation: Social Innovation.* Brussels: EU.

European Commission (2013b) *European Public Sector Innovation Scoreboard.* Brussels: EU.

FTF (2013) *Udviklingen i FTF-ledernes erfaring med Innovation.* FTFs Lederpejling no. 8, available at: http://www.ftf.dk/aktuelt/ftf-dokumentation/artikel/leder pejling-nr-8-udviklingen-i-ftf-lederes-erfaring-med-innovation/   [Accessed 31 October 2014.]

Gorman, M. (2013) 'The Psychology of Technological Innovations', in Fiest, G. and Gorman, M. (eds), *Handbook of the Psychology of Science.* New York: Springer, 383–96.

Gray, B. (1989) *Collaborating: Finding Common Ground for Multiparty Problems.* San Francisco, CA: Jossey-Bass.

Habermas, J. (1987) *Theory of Communicative Action.* Vol. 1–2, Boston, MA: Beacon Press.

Hagedoorn, J. (1996) 'Innovation and Entrepreneurship: Schumpeter Revisited', *Industrial and Corporate Change*, 5 (3): 883–96.

Halvorsen, T., Hauknes J., Miles, I. and Røste, R. (2005) *On the Difference between Public and Private Sector Innovation.* Publin Report, D9.

Hartley, J. (2005) 'Innovation in Governance and Public Service: Past and present', *Public Money & Management*, 25 (1): 27–34.

Hartley, J. (2011) 'Public Value through Innovation and Improvement', in J. Benington and M. Moore (eds), *Public value: Theory and Practice.* Basingstoke: Palgrave Macmillan, pp. 171–84.

Hartley, J., Sørensen, E. and Torfing, J. (2013) 'Collaborative Innovation: A Viable Alternative to Market-Competition and Organizational Entrepreneurship?', *Public Administration Review*, 73 (6): 821–30.

Heifetz, R.A., Linsky, M. and Grashow, A. (2009) *The Practice of Adaptive Leadership: Tools and Tactics for Changing your Organization and the World*. Cambridge, MA: Harvard Business Press.

HM Government (2010) *Working Together – Public Services on Your Side*. Norwich: Her Majesty's Stationery Office.

Hood, C. (1991) 'A Public Administration for All Seasons?', *Public Administration*, 69 (1): 1–19.

Jessop, B. (2002) *The Future of the Capitalist State*. Cambridge: Polity Press.

Keast, R., Brown, K. and Mandell, M. (2007) 'Getting the Right Mix; Unpacking Integration Meanings and Strategies', *International Public Management Journal*, 10 (1): 9–33.

Knight, F.H. (2005) *Risk, Certainty and Profit*. New York: Cosimo Inc.

Koch, P. and Hauknes, J. (2005) *On Innovation in the Public Sector – Today and Beyond*. Public report no. 20D.

Kooiman, J. (2003) *Governing As Governance*. London: Sage.

Kraemer, K.L. and Perry, J.L. (1989) 'Innovation and Computing in the Public Sector: A Review of Research', *Knowledge in Society*, 2 (1): 72–87.

LO (2008) *Employee Driven Innovation*. Copenhagen: LO.

Lundvall, B.Å. (ed.) (1992) *National Systems of Innovation: Towards a Theory of Innovation and Interactive Learning*. London: Pinter.

March, J.G. and Olsen, J.P. (1995) *Democratic Governance*. New York: Free Press.

Meuleman, L. (2008) *Public Management and the Metagovernance of Hierarchies, Networks and Markets*. Heidelberg: Physica Verlag.

Mezirow, J. *et al*. (2000) *Learning As Transformation: Critical Perspectives on a Theory in Progress*. San Francisco, CA: Jossey-Bass.

Moore, M. and Hartley, J. (2008) 'Innovations in Government', *Public Management Review*, 10 (1): 3–20.

Morgan, D.F. and Cook, B.J. (eds) (2014) *New Public Governance: A Regime-Centered Perspective*. New York: M.E. Scharpe.

Morse (2010) 'Integrative Public Leadership: Catalyzing Collaboration to Create Public Value', *The Leadership Quarterly*, 21(2): 231–45.

Mouffe, C. (2005) *On the Political*. Abingdon: Routledge.

Mulgan, G. and Albury, D. (2003) *Innovation in the Public Sector*. Strategy Unit, Cabinet Office.

Mulgan, G., Tucker, S., Ali, R. and Sanders, B. (2007) *Social Innovation: What It Is, Why It Matters and How It Can Be Accelerated*. Oxford: Skoll Centre for Social Entrepreneurship.

Nambisan, S. (2008) *Transforming Government through Collaborative Innovation*. Washington, DC: IBM Center for the Business of Government.

Norval, A. J. (2007) *Aversive Democracy*. Cambridge: Cambridge University Press.

Nyhan, R. C. (2006) 'Changing the Paradigm: Trust and Its Role in Public Sector Organizations', *The American Review of Public Administration*, 30 (1): 87–109.

O'Leary, R., and Bingham, L.B. (eds) (2009) *The Collaborative Public Manager*. Washington, DC: Georgetown University Press.

Osborne, D. and Gaebler, T. (1992) *Reinventing Government: How the Entrepreneurial Spirit is Transforming the Public Sector*. Reading, MA: Addison-Wesley.

Osborne, S. (2006) 'The New Public Governance?', *Public Management Review*, 8 (3): 377–88.

Osborne, S. (ed.) (2010) *The New Public Governance?* London: Routledge.

Osborne, S. and Brown, K. (2005) *Managing Change and Innovation in Public Service Organizations*. London: Routledge.

Osborne, S., Radnor, Z. and Nasi, G. (2013) 'A New Theory of Public Service Management? Toward a (Public) Service-Dominant Approach', *The American Review of Public Administration*, 43 (2): 135–58.

Page, S. (2010) 'Integrative Leadership for Collaborative Governance: Civic Engagement in Seattle', *The Leadership Quarterly*, 21 (2): 246–63.

Parry, K.W. and A. Bryman (2006) 'Leadership in Organizations', in S. Clegg, C. Hardy, T. Lawrence and W. Nord (eds), *The Sage Handbook of Organization Studies*. London: Sage (pp. 447–68).

Pearce, C.L. and Conger, J.A. (2003) *Shared Leadership: Reframing the Hows and Whys of Leadership*. London: Sage.

Perry, J.L. and Danzinger, J.N. (1980) 'The Adoptability of Innovations: An Empirical Assessment of Computer Applications in Local Governments', *Administration and Society*, 11 (4): 461–92.

Perry, J.L. and Kraemer, K.L. (1980) 'Chief Executive Support and Innovation Adoption', *Administration and Society*, 12 (2): 158–77.

Perry, J.L., Kraemer, K.L., Dunkle, D. and King, J. (1993) 'Motivations to Innovate in Public Organizations', in B. Bozeman (ed.), *Public Management: The State of the Art*. San Francisco, CA: Jossey-Bass, pp. 294–306.

Pollitt, C. and Bouckaert, G. (2004) *Public Management Reforms*. Oxford: Oxford University Press.

Polsby, N.W. (1984) *Political Innovation in America: The Politics of Policy Initiation*. New Haven, CT: Yale University Press.

Porter, M.E. (1985) *Competitive Advantage of Nations: Creating and Sustaining Superior Performance*. New York: Simon and Schuster.

Radnor, Z. and Osborne, S. (2013) 'Lean: A Failed Theory for Public Services?', *Public Management Review*, 15 (2): 265–87.

Rashman, L. and Hartley, J. (2002) 'Leading and Learning? Knowledge Transfer in the Beacon Council Scheme', *Public Administration*, 80 (2): 523–42.

Rittel, H.W. and Webber, M.M. (1973) 'Dilemmas in a General Theory of Planning', *Policy Sciences*, 4 (2): 155–69.

Roberts, N.C. and Bradley, R.T. (1991) 'Stakeholder Collaboration and Innovation', *Journal of Applied Behavioural Science*, 27 (2): 209–27.

Roberts, N.C. and King, P.J. (1996) *Transforming Public Policy: Dynamics of Policy Entrepreneurship and Innovation*. San Francisco, CA: Jossey-Bass.

Rogers, E.M. (1995) *Diffusion of Innovations*. New York: The Free Press.

Schumpeter, J.A. (1976) *Capitalism, Socialism and Democracy*. Abingdon: Routledge.

Sørensen, E. and Torfing, J. (2009) 'Making Governance Networks Effective and Democratic through Metagovernance', *Public Administration*, 87 (2): 234–58.

Sørensen E. and Torfing, J. (2011) 'Enhancing Collaborative Innovation in the Public Sector', *Administration and Society*, 43 (8): 842–68.

Straus, D. (2002) *How to Make Collaboration Work?* San Francisco, CA: Berrett-Koehler.

Sunstein, C. (2012) 'Regulations.gov: Remaking Public Participation', The Open government Partnership, http://www.whitehouse.gov/blog/2012/02/21/regulationsgov-remaking-public-participation [Accessed 31 October 2014].

Swan, J., Scarbrough, H. and Robertson, M. (2002) 'The Construction of Communities of Practice in the Management of Innovation', *Management Learning*, 33 (4): 477–96.

Teece, D.J. (1992) 'Competition, Cooperation and Innovation', *Journal of Economic Behavior and Organization*, 18 (1): 1–25.

Torfing, J., Peters, B.G., Pierre, J. and Sørensen, E. (2012) *Interactive Governance: Advancing the Paradigm*. Oxford: Oxford University Press.

Torfing, J. and Triantafillou, P. (2013) 'What's in a Name? Grasping New Public Governance As a Political–Administrative System', *International Review of Public Administration*, 18 (2): 9–25.

Von Hippel, E. (2005) *Democratizing Innovation*. Cambridge, MA: MIT Press.

Von Hippel, E. (2007) 'Horizontal Innovation Networks – By and for users', *Industrial and Corporate Change*, 16 (2): 1–23.

Wart, M.V. (2013) 'Lessons from Leadership Theory and Contemporary Challenges of Leaders', *Public Administration Review*, 73 (4): 553–64.

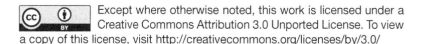

8

Seoul City's Social Innovation Strategy: New Models of Communication to Strengthen Citizen Engagement

Jungwon Kim, Sojung Rim, Sunkyung Han and Ahyoung Park

Introduction

Social innovation is attracting considerable interest from public policy makers all around the world and South Korea is no exception. Since October 2011, when a well-known civil society leader, Wonsoon Park, became mayor, Seoul City has been going through rapid change. Led by the mayor on a mission to bring about change from the ground up, Seoul Metropolitan Government (SMG) has embraced citizen engagement and open dialogue in its policy-making processes.

One of the core mechanisms SMG has used to embed openness in the city's administration and to enable citizen participation is new models of communication, both online and offline. This chapter examines whether and how SMG's multi-channel communication has strengthened citizen engagement in Seoul. It aims to answer the following questions:

- How has SMG's multi-channel communication strategy helped foster citizen engagement?
- Has citizen engagement been strengthened by SMG's multi-channel communication approach and has this supported and sustained social innovation in Seoul?
- What challenges did SMG's use of multi-channel communication to strengthen citizen engagement face?

This chapter draws together information and insights from various reports, academic literature and public data on Seoul City's social innovation and citizen communication agenda. Eleven in-depth interviews were conducted with city officers in key departments to examine the new multi-channel communication tools introduced by SMG. The first part of this chapter introduces the 'social innovation mayor' in Seoul and places his social innovation plans in the South Korean context. Definitions of social innovation and citizen engagement employed within SMG are then provided. This is followed by an overview of SMG's citizen engagement strategy and an introduction to its major communication tools and programmes. The chapter then explores a case study that shows how multi-channel communication tools were employed to solve a specific social problem. The chapter concludes with a discussion of the challenges faced by SMG in using these new communication channels.

The 'Social Innovation Mayor'

When Wonsoon Park took office as the Mayor of Seoul City, many regarded him as the 'social innovation mayor'. While previous mayors had mainly focused on leaving a physical legacy after their mayoral terms, for example, by removing local street vendors and commissioning various landmark construction projects, Mayor Park declared that his legacy for Seoul City would be different. He would not leave behind a 'physical' legacy (Ryu and Kwon, 2014) but rather focus on changing the culture and the relationship between SMG and Seoul City's citizens.

Mayor Park had no previous experience in politics before running as the independent candidate in the mayoral by-election in 2011.[1] Park's election slogan in 2011 was to become 'the mayor who changes the everyday lives of citizens'. He declared, 'citizens are mayors' and encouraged citizen engagement as a principle, underpinning the work of the new city administration. Mayor Park's philosophy and practice of listening to and acting on citizens' concerns was evident from early on in his election campaign. He met and talked with citizens on the street[2] and used various social media tools to communicate and listen to the needs of voters. His election campaign team was able to raise 3.9 billion won (US$ 3.3 million) just three days into his official campaign, fundraising mainly through small donations made online from 5,778 supporters, who were mobilised through Twitter and Facebook (Seok, 2011).

During his first term between 2011 and 2014, Mayor Park led SMG to use many of the communication tools introduced in this chapter and to 'listen until citizens open their hearts'. His core philosophy and strategy during this period aimed at closing the distance between politics and citizens' everyday lives, giving citizens the confidence to voice their concerns and needs (Yoon, 2014). Throughout his term, Mayor Park was committed to making Seoul City a more 'liveable' human-centred city by restoring a sense of local well-being in communities (SMG, 2013d). He also envisioned Seoul City as a 'platform for collaboration and sharing', opening up and sharing the city's underutilised spaces, information and data with its citizens (Park, 2014). Park's vision and action gained support from citizens, especially the young, which led to a landslide victory for the Mayor for his second term.[3]

Many Koreans found Mayor Park's human-centred approach to city planning and design refreshing. South Korea is well known for its remarkable economic growth. In the aftermath of the Korean War, the country transformed itself from one of the poorest in Asia to one of the wealthiest countries in the world.[4] Yet these rapid changes came at a cost. The decades of economic growth came about under authoritarian governments, which encouraged the growth of family-owned business conglomerates, known as 'chaebol', but stifled the vitality and diversity of civil society. The strong focus on materialistic abundance and hypercompetition, as well as rapid urbanisation, contributed to the breakdown of family and community relationships that were previously the safety net of traditional Korean society (Noland, 2014). South Korea has experienced growing income inequality (Oh, 2014). Among OECD countries, it has one of the highest suicide rates and one of the highest average numbers of hours worked annually per worker (OECD, 2014). South Korea also has the unhappiest children in the world (Phillips, 2013). Mayor Park's human-centred approaches were an attempt to restore social capital that was lost or forgotten during the fifty years of relentless economic growth. Cynics may view Park's citizen-focused strategy merely as a vote-winning tactic or a PR stunt. However, by translating the rhetoric into real action and change, new possibilities emerged.

SMG's definitions of social innovation and citizen engagement

The term 'social innovation' has been widely used in many different ways (Kim and Han, 2011). This study follows the definition introduced by The Young Foundation (2012). The main reason for following this definition is that it brings together the perspectives of both social innovation practitioners and academic researchers. As this study is focused on analysing a real case and aims to ensure that the lessons and conclusions are useful for practitioners and municipal administrations, it avoids a definition that is specific to certain academic subjects or fields.

The Young Foundation (2012) defines 'social innovation' as 'new solutions (products, services, models, markets, processes, etc.) that simultaneously meet a social need (more effectively than existing solutions) and lead to new or improved capabilities and relationships and better use of assets and resources. In other words, social innovations are both good for society and enhance society's capacity to act'. Within this definition, The Young Foundation (2012) suggests five core elements that need to be present in social innovation practices. These are: novelty; a focus on moving from ideas to implementation; a focus on meeting a social need; effectiveness; and evidence of enhancing society's capacity to act.

In comparison, SMG's definition of social innovation is much looser. SMG defined social innovation as 'a new way of solving social problems that either have been previously unsolved or have newly emerged' (SMG, 2013d, p. 305). This definition appears to focus on social problems (a deficit-based approach), rather than social needs (a less stigmatising approach) and capabilities (an asset-based approach). However, a study of SMG's practices and approaches (explored in the following sections) indicates that SMG in fact aimed to 'meet a social need' and to 'enhance society's capacity to act' by placing citizen engagement at the heart of SMG's strategy to catalyse social innovation.

SMG has developed new policies and solutions that meet social needs by listening to citizen voices directly through new models of communication. Furthermore, these approaches have forged new collaborations and interactions between citizens, civil servants and policy makers, going beyond usual working processes. In this way, SMG can be said to have enhanced society's capacity to act, empowering 'beneficiaries by creating new roles and relationships, developing assets and capabilities and/or better use of assets and resources' (The Young Foundation, 2012).

In the context of social innovation, citizen engagement is increasingly considered as the critical attribute that allows more diverse actors to be brought into the process of developing and then sustaining new answers to meeting social needs (Davies and Simon, 2013; Brodie *et al.*, 2009). Westley argued that re-engaging populations and ideas that are excluded and disenfranchised from resources can enhance social innovation capacity and add to the resilience of the system in question (Westley, 2008). Citizen engagement is also important in identifying and better understanding social needs and challenges. Citizens have first-hand experience and tacit knowledge that is critical to the social innovation process (Davis *et al.*, 2012).

SMG regarded citizen engagement as one of the core strategies driving social innovation across Seoul. Citizen engagement was used as a mechanism that empowered Seoul citizens to express what they needed, explore how these needs could be met and decide what could be done in response. In this way, SMG was able to understand citizens' needs better, collect unexpected but working solutions, and create opportunities to resolve conflicting issues among different stakeholders (Y. Kim, 2013; T. Kim, 2013).

One way of conceptualising citizen engagement is to use the Spectrum of Public Participation developed by the International Association for Public Participation (IAP2, 2014). This sets out different public participation goals (from the perspective of the state) in order of increasing level of public impact, from 'inform' to 'consult', 'involve', 'collaborate' and finally, 'empower'. Prior to Mayor Park's administration, SMG used citizen engagement activities such as public hearings and citizen surveys to implement new city policies. However, these programmes were limited to the 'informing' and 'consulting' types of engagement. In contrast, many new tools and programmes developed and operated by SMG under Mayor Park's leadership specifically centred around 'involving', 'collaborating with' and 'empowering' citizens in decision-making activities. The next section will explore these tools and programmes together with the principles underpinning SMG's citizen engagement strategy.

Citizen engagement strategy, principles and tools driven by SMG

SMG is a large organisation, consisting of thirty departments and employing roughly 17,000 people (J. Ryu, 2013). The two departments primarily involved in developing and implementing social innovation activities were the Social Innovation Bureau (SIB) and the Public Communication Bureau (PCB) (Y. Kim, 2013; T. Kim, 2013). These two bureaus sat directly under the Mayor's Office, reflecting his determination to embed social innovation and citizen engagement as the core principles of city administration. While the SIB was set up to plan the city's social innovation strategy and support social innovation activities in Seoul, PCB was reorganised to develop ways in which citizens could be better engaged in the city's policy-making process. This chapter focuses primarily on the innovative communication strategy, principles and tools that were developed by the PCB to encourage citizen engagement.

The Mayor was a leading proponent of Seoul City's so-called 'Big Ear Policy', which put listening to citizens' voices at the heart of all the city administration's activities. The objective of these 'listening policies' was to enable citizens to express their own ideas and opinions, and to change the mindset of Seoul City officers to make them regard citizen voices as a valuable input for city policies.

Although the importance of citizen engagement in driving social innovation was recognised by the Mayor, it was difficult to shift the overall culture surrounding Seoul citizens and civil officers to embrace active and productive citizen engagement. Accepting diversity of ideas and viewpoints in the city administration was a new process for citizens as well as for the city government. Civil servants associated citizen voices with pickets, rallies and vigils and viewed them as an obstacle to their work. Citizens themselves had no experience of using other ways to make their voices heard. In the past, the process of receiving ideas and suggestions had been limited to only select groups of experts (J. Ryu, 2013; K. Ryu, 2013).

The Big Ear Policy aimed to build the foundations for initiating and fostering citizen engagement by breaking away from the entrenched culture within SMG. In order to reach the stage where citizens and SMG officers could develop innovative policies together, SMG initially focused on developing a new culture of citizen participation. It created symbols and spaces that reinforced the idea of a 'listening' culture. For instance, a large sculpture, the 'Big Ear', was installed outside the City Hall. When a person spoke into this object, his or her voice was recorded and broadcast live through speakers installed in the basement of the City Hall. Some messages were saved and passed to city officers for consideration. The Big Ear sculpture symbolised the city's commitment to listen to citizens more carefully and was one of many examples of attempts to create a listening culture within the city administration.[5] A diverse range of tools, programmes, events, spaces, artefacts and banners were placed around Seoul to remind citizens of the Big Ear Policy. These were backed up with a series of opportunities for citizens to take part in engagement activities (see Tables 8.1 and 8.2).

To develop communication tools and programmes to implement the Big Ear Policy, the PCB, which was in charge of communication between SMG and Seoul citizens, defined three principles. These principles were set out to ensure that SMG's listening activities encouraged citizen engagement and the creation of policies that better met citizen needs. These three principles were: (1) an appreciation of two-way dialogue between SMG and Seoul citizens (in particular, this suggested a constant exchange of input and feedback between SMG and citizens, rather than seeing communication simply as one-time notifications); (2) making SMG's policy-making processes more transparent and opening up related information to citizens so that citizens could provide constructive input for the city's administration; and (3) sharing SMG's communication media with citizens (H. Kim, 2013; D. Kim, 2013). SMG encouraged citizens to express their opinions via its communication channels (including websites, radio stations, billboards and subway/ bus advertisement spaces), which were previously used exclusively to inform and promote SMG's work to citizens. In 2013, around 30% of these media outlets could be used by citizens to promote their own social activities.[6] There were also increased opportunities for citizens to contribute their own writing, photographs or videos on websites such as WOW Seoul and Seoul Talk Talk.

These three communication principles underpinned the implementation of new communication tools and programmes developed and operated primarily by the PCB. Two types of new communication channels – online and offline – were designed to serve different purposes.

The main goals of the online communication tools were to achieve real-time communication, fast responses and feedback, to reach out to diverse groups of citizens and to open up policy-making processes (see Table 8.1). Several online broadcasting channels showed live SMG meetings and events, and multiple social media tools were used to help engage and listen to citizen voices on a real-time basis (PCB, 2012; PCB, 2013).

Table 8.1 SMG's online communication tools

Name	Description	Features
Hope Seoul (www.seoul.go.kr)	Official SMG website	'Electronic Petition'; SMG public data and meeting minutes; participatory budget programme reports; SMG administration news.
WOW Seoul (wow.seoul.go.kr)	Website showing User Created Content (UCC)	Video and photo sharing platform and webtoon (web+cartoon) services.
Live Seoul (tv.seoul.go.kr)	Online live broadcasting platform	Real-time streaming of SMG meetings and events, e.g., Mayor Park's Seoul Story, *Cheong-Chek* forums. Citizens can add feedback.

(*continued*)

Table 8.1 Continued

Seoul Talk Talk (inews.seoul.go.kr)	Citizen news	News on issues such as welfare, job openings and cultural events. Regularly publishes newsletters in which citizens create content as 'Citizen Reporters'.
Social Media Center (social.seoul.go.kr)	Central location for SMG social-networking tools	Official social media platform integrating forty-four social media accounts run by various SMG departments.
Online Dasan Call Center (120dasan.seoul.go.kr)	Online citizen petition platform	The 120 Dasan Call Center is a 24-hour call centre that Seoul citizens can ask any question related to city life. The Online Dasan Call Centre is the extended online platform providing the same service.
Online Mayor's Office (mayor.seoul.go.kr)	Official website of Seoul city Mayor	Information on the Mayor's activities and core SMG policies, including the Mayor's personal blog, online channel streaming MMOs, the Mayor's daily schedule, and citizen feedback pages linked to various social media accounts.
Ten Million Imagination Oasis (oasis.seoul.go.kr)	Online platform for gathering policy ideas	Seoul citizens can post suggestions for policies. The process starts from ideation to policy adoption and promotes collective intelligence and communication among citizens, experts and public officials.
Seoul Smart Complaint Report App	Mobile application for processing citizen complaints	Citizens can report complaints on public facilities, traffic, environment and many more by using the web and mobile application. Users can upload text complaints with photo and geographic information, and also track SMG's responses to their complaints.
Seoul Safety Keeper App	Mobile application for disaster prevention and notification	Mobile app for reporting disasters such as heavy rain, storms, heavy snowfalls, etc., with photos and geographic information.

Source: Authors' compilation.

Meanwhile, SMG's offline communication activities typically involved discussions with different stakeholders in order to better understand complex issues and build consensus among diverse citizen groups with conflicting opinions. The range of offline communication activities used is summarised in Table 8.2.

Figure 8.1 illustrates the range of online and offline communication tools typically used at different stages of policy making, from problem identification and agenda setting to policy formulation, selection and approval. However, it is important to note that not all communication tools were used chronologically to develop each policy, nor did SMG's policy-making process follow a structured linear path. The early stages of the policy-making process featured SMG's multi-channel communication tools including the *Cheong-Chek* Forum (CCF), *Suk-Ui*, the Mobile Mayoral Office (MMO) and social media platforms. Social media was used continuously throughout the entire process (including implementation and evaluation stages), so that citizens could receive information about ongoing progress and give real-time feedback and comments.

Table 8.2　SMG's offline communication tools

Tools	Description
Cheong-Chek (Policy by Listening) Forum (CCF)	Town hall meeting designed to develop new policies or programmes
Suk-Ui (Deliberation)	Meeting to formulate and approve policies
Honorary Deputy Mayor	Following Mayor Park's slogan, 'The citizens are the Mayor', citizens act as an honorary deputy Mayor for a year
One Day Honorary Mayor	Citizens from a variety of fields become honorary Mayor for a day
Citizen Speakers' Corner	Speech podium located at Seoul City Hall, based on Speakers' Corner at Hyde Park in London
Mobile Mayoral Office (MMO)	The Mayor, SMG directors and managers visit places and listen to citizen voices
Policy Expo	Annual event promoting citizen participation in policy-making processes
Seoul Citizen Hall	Public space located at the basement of the Seoul City Hall

Source: Authors' compilation.

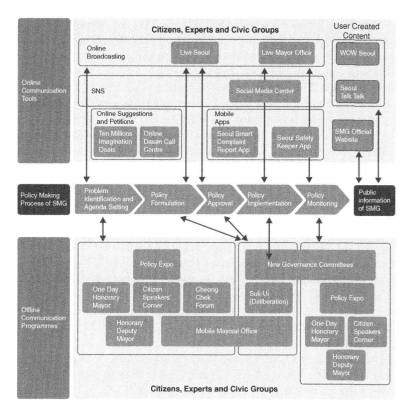

Figure 8.1 Overview of SMG online and offline communication tools and programmes
Source: Drawn by the authors.

Three tools for engagement and communication

This section introduces three major communication tools and programmes used by SMG.

The Social Media Centre (SMC)

SMG started its blog service in 2008, and since then, it has actively used social media tools – such as Twitter, Facebook and MeToday[7] – to communicate with citizens. SMG also set up several websites to inform citizens of the activities it was undertaking. Under the so-called 'SNS administration' communication approach, SMG provided interactive information to citizens in real time and encouraged citizens to add and share content (J. Kim, 2013; SMG, 2013a).

The Social Media Centre (SMC) took on the responsibility of centralising and coordinating information sent by citizens through diverse routes, ensuring quicker and more efficient communication. The SMC automatically gathered all messages received through SMG's forty-four social media accounts.[8] It operated as a centralised system channelling relevant messages to appropriate teams, receiving feedback from those teams and sending feedback to the public through various accounts owned by the relevant teams and the Mayor. With this centralised approach, SMG was able to handle the large volume of citizen messages received through its social media accounts. Mayor Park's personal Twitter and Facebook accounts functioned as the most important direct communication channels between the Mayor and the citizens of Seoul. Between January and October 2012, a total of 29,976 suggestions (an average of 105 suggestions per day) were made to the Mayor through his social media accounts. Using a centralised system significantly reduced message processing time and enabled SMG to handle more citizen suggestions per day. Between November 2012 and March 2013, a total of 18,807 messages were received, and on average 125 messages were processed per day, an increase of twenty messages per day compared with the period January to October 2012 (J. Kim, 2013; SMG, 2013a).

The SMC was particularly useful when unforeseen disasters or emergency situations occurred, as it enabled SMG to send out urgent messages through its many accounts at the same time. For instance, when Seoul's public bus system was affected by strikes, Seoul citizens were informed of alternative routes on a real-time basis (C. Kim, 2012; SMG, 2013c). Citizen comments passed to the SMC covered a broad range of issues, from small problems that could be fixed quickly to long-standing issues requiring innovative solutions. Social media communication was also helpful in gathering citizen feedback on pilot services. For instance, when Seoul City announced new night bus routes through its Facebook account, an instant online debate started, with 3,000 replies and 50,000 'likes' (SMG, 2013c). Citizens' comments were reviewed when nine new night bus routes were changed.

The Cheong-Chek (Policy by Listening) Forum

The *Cheong-Chek* Forum (CCF), a town hall meeting, has become a core part of Seoul City's policy development process (H. Kim, 2013; K. Ryu, 2013; J. Ryu, 2013). *Cheong-Chek* was a new word made by combining two Korean words 'listening' and 'policy'. By engaging with citizens through these forums, SMG aimed to understand local needs, find better ways to handle these issues and understand the views of the main beneficiaries of a policy.

In the past, consultation meetings with citizens had been carried out at the final stages of the policy-making process, where additional comments and suggestions from citizens made little or no difference to the major direction or content of a new policy (K. Ryu, 2013; J. Ryu, 2013). In contrast, CCFs took place at the early stages of the policy-making process and provided a space for citizens to propose and suggest new ideas, giving them more influence in terms of setting the agenda and making decisions. This was an innovative approach for Korean public administration, which had often regarded citizen engagement in a perfunctory manner (K. Ryu, 2013).

After the first forum was held in November 2011, CCFs took place on average once a week. The subjects discussed ranged from the local economy, education, welfare, homelessness and health to other issues that affect the daily lives of citizens. The topics for these forums were determined by reviewing diverse citizen opinions collected from multi-communication channels. After the review, the Attentive Listening Team within the PCB – which was in charge of running the CCFs – selected a subject for discussion and contacted relevant civic groups and experts working in the field. The team held several meetings with different groups to discuss the agenda and format of the CCF and whom to invite.

The CCFs were open to every citizen, but motivating citizens to participate was hard work. The Attentive Listening Team put substantial effort into advertising them through various online communication channels and also directly invited relevant groups of citizens. The entire process was broadcast live through the 'Live Seoul' site, SMG's Twitter account and Facebook page. A CCF usually lasted for 100 minutes and could be run in various formats, such as *World Café* or TED-style presentations followed by a question-and-answer session. The Mayor typically sat with the citizens, listening to their ideas and suggestions and sharing his thoughts at the end of each CCF. When each forum finished, the Attentive Listening Team compiled the suggestions made from the CCF and established an action committee comprised of city officers in relevant departments, representatives from civic groups and other experts. This committee continued to hold official discussions until the suggestions made by citizens were implemented. Usually it took between two months and a year for suggestions to be realised. During this period of time, SMG officers published a progress report every two weeks on the CCF website and shared updates with CCF participants through a text messaging service.

Between November 2011 and November 2012, forty-one CCFs were held, with a total of 5,456 citizens in attendance. The forty-one forums produced 717 citizen suggestions and 538 suggestions (75%) were subsequently implemented. The remaining 166 suggestions were to be included in SMG's long-term plans. The 717 suggestions can be categorised into three groups: development of new programmes (84.1%); improvement of existing systems such as youth employment and homelessness policies (13%); and allocation of new budgets (2.9%).

A key outcome of the CCF after its first year of operation was the creation of new public-citizen governance bodies that aimed to develop and support public policies. One of the biggest tasks was to report on the progress being made while SMG implemented the citizen proposals made at the CCF. This required SMG to set up public–civic groups to gather feedback and to ask these bodies to take some responsibility in implementing citizen ideas. One example of a programme implemented as a result of the CCF is the Seoul Library Network, which was created after discussing new policies supporting libraries in Seoul.

The Mobile Mayoral Office

The Mobile Mayoral Office (MMO) was designed to identify the root causes of unresolved issues or hidden problems and suggest possible solutions. To achieve this goal, key decision-makers, including the Mayor, two deputy Mayors, the head of a borough, Members of Parliament, and city and local councillors, visited local sites where there were long-standing issues and met residents affected by those issues. The MMO employed multi-channel communication tools (the CCF, *Suk-Ui* and other online communication tools) during the course of its operation.

SMG ran two types of MMO: an MMO for boroughs in Seoul and an MMO for selected issues.[9] Borough-level MMOs took place regularly while MMOs for selected issues only took place when a certain issue became pressing.

Borough-level MMOs typically ran for two days. A preparation team, which usually consisted of officers from the Local Authority Team at SMG and from a borough office, selected ten major issues within the borough. The team also set out a visiting plan and arranged citizen meetings. The MMO started with a briefing for decision-makers on the issues, followed by visits to key places and meetings with local representatives. During the first day, key decision-makers and their working teams often came across new issues that they felt should be added to the list of critical issues to be discussed. In the evening of the same day, key decision-makers and their working teams had an internal meeting to review what they had experienced and heard during the day. Their discussion typically ended with some conclusions on immediate actions, mid to long-term plans and who should be assigned ownership of these actions and plans. On the second day, the Mayor presented the suggestions agreed from the previous night's meeting and followed this with an open town hall meeting with citizens. The whole process was broadcast through the 'Live Mobile Mayoral Office'[10] website and reported live on Twitter and Facebook. As a final step, a new governance committee was set up to monitor and discuss agreed actions after the completion of the MMO. The committee members included the directors of the Local Authority Team in SMG, managers of relevant SMG teams, directors of relevant borough divisions and citizen representatives.

The second type of MMO was run to solve specific high-profile issues. For instance, in 2013, SMG ran an MMO to invigorate traditional markets, which were rapidly losing their customer base to big supermarket chains. This MMO lasted for four days and included visiting four traditional markets and having various citizen meetings including a *Cheong-Chek* Forum. The committee continued to monitor whether the action items that came out of the process were implemented.

Between 2012 and 2014, Seoul City organised nineteen MMOs. SMG's Local Authority Team summarised four key outcomes: providing solutions to collective petitions or problems causing serious conflict among diverse stakeholders; setting out next steps and clear directions for projects under long-standing review; solving unexpected problems and providing additional resources and clear decisions for prolonged projects; and offering an opportunity for close collaboration between SMG and local boroughs. The more detailed outcomes of an MMO are discussed in the next section through a case study.

Case study: unsold apartments in EunPyeong Newtown

The unsold apartments in the EunPyeong New Town development had been a long-standing problem for Seoul City's administration that put a significant burden on city finances (SH Corporation, 2013). The SH Corporation, the public housing company owned by SMG, had 618 unsold apartments remaining at EunPyeong New Town three years after the completion of the apartment buildings (SMG, 2012). These unsold apartments were worth around 493 billion won (US$ 467 million), and it was crucial to sell them to address one of the biggest problems faced by SMG – a large amount of debt.[11] Local residents were also concerned about security, as a large number of apartments had been left empty for more than four years (Song, 2013). However, in January 2013, SMG announced that all 618 apartments were to be sold, within seventeen days of establishing a task force to address this problem (SH Corporation, 2013). This case study examines how SMG's various forms of communication made this possible.

SMG's overall communication strategy helped it to identify invisible and unexpected needs and to understand the nature of these needs. When the Mayor heard about the EunPyeong New Town problem, he wanted to understand the nature of this problem, analyse why these apartments had failed to attract buyers in Seoul and find a way to sell them. He asked his team to relocate his office to one of the unsold apartments and stayed there with SMG officers for ten days, listening to residents and identifying their needs (Song, 2013; J.E. Lee, 2013; Hwang, 2013). From this first MMO, SMG and SH Corporation started to discover hidden problems and get more insight into the severity of known problems. Residents' major complaints concerned infrastructure problems such as a shortage of nurseries, libraries and public transportation, and complaints about the existence of an army base near the complex. Through mechanisms such as the *Cheong-Chek* Forum and social media platforms, residents made a total of 146 suggestions to rectify these issues (MMO, 2012; SH Corporation, 2013). SMG and SH corporation made new attempts to attract homebuyers based on residents' suggestions. All key decision-makers visited the site to understand first-hand citizens' concerns.

SMG was then able to create innovative solutions through diverse types of collaboration. All of the people interviewed for this chapter repeatedly commented that the creation of new types of collaboration had been a key outcome of SMG's communication approach (J. Ryu, 2013; Hwang, 2013; J.E. Lee, 2013; K. Ryu, 2013). New forms of collaboration were made between SMG and other civic groups – including individual citizens – and between SMG and other public parties such as boroughs, councillors, MPs and other public organisations. This was because SMG's communication strategy aimed to strengthen citizen engagement; the end results of various communications were, therefore, the creation of policies or programmes that implemented citizens' proposals. To achieve this, SMG had to collaborate with actors that had close relationships with citizens.

In the case of EunPyeong, these new forms of collaboration were crucial in solving the problem of unsold apartments. By inviting a range of key decision-makers from a number of departments into the same space, silos that existed between departments and organisations were removed and a new way of thinking started. The power of the EunPyeong case lay in creating a space for key decision-makers to gather in one place to work together within a limited period of time. Furthermore, the limited time frame intensified the pressure on decision-makers and their working teams to compromise on difficult areas of dispute and find shared solutions. The fact that they were making a promise to the citizens face-to-face (rather than announcing it on a webpage) added weight to the commitment they were making (J.E. Lee, 2013; J.S. Lee, 2013; Hwang, 2013; K. Kim, 2013). Solutions suggested were reviewed within 24 hours by the public through a *Cheong-Chek* Forum and various social media platforms, including live Internet broadcasting.

The open and participatory nature of SMG's communication approach helped to provide legitimacy to its new policy decisions. The people interviewed for this chapter, mainly SMG officers, reported that Seoul citizens, especially those living in deprived and underserved areas, felt that their voices were being properly heard by the authorities for the first time (J. Ryu, 2013; K. Ryu, 2013; Hwang, 2013). According to SMG, citizens started to trust civil servants and this, in turn, led them to cooperate with SMG and accept its suggestions, even if they were unpopular. Interviewees also commented that opportunities to watch the Mayor's face-to-face promises at a CCF or live broadcast, and the Mayor's personal briefings via SNS, contributed to growing trust among citizens. One interviewee explained that:

> The ultimate goal of public administration is efficient and effective delivery of public services. In this sense, SMG's new communication exercising openness and citizen engagement has certainly contributed to the achievement of such a goal. Whereas communication with citizens might have delayed the whole process of SMG's administration, it offered the most valuable opportunity for SMG to gather very different, sometimes conflicting and contrasting, opinions among citizens and let citizens and SMG express their thoughts openly and come up with agreeable new solutions. By doing so, citizens could accept SMG's decisions and enjoyed the public services delivered by SMG. (J. Ryu, 2013)

Challenges

SMG's new communication strategy has faced several challenges. First, it became clear that new communication tools and programmes –

including online and offline channels – did not guarantee access to a wide range of people's voices. Given the high usage rate of the Internet and smart phones in Seoul,[12] SMG's online communication tools certainly increased its opportunities to listen to citizens' views. However, the main groups who actively used these tools to express their views were younger generations or certain outspoken groups. Offline communication activities mainly attracted citizens who were already active participants in public discourses or had close relationships with civic groups invited to a CCF or MMO.

Second, the new communication tools and programmes contributed to solving only a limited range of problems. Each communication channel had strong features that helped to solve certain issues. However, it was not clear that these new channels were good at handling all types of social issues.

Third, new communication tools and programmes required larger resources to operate and it was hard to provide sufficient resources under conditions of public sector austerity. This was particularly true for offline programmes, because most of these led to ongoing conversations within committees that lasted until ideas and solutions were realised. This follow-up procedure[13] demanded almost one full-time SMG officer to resource it (K. Ryu, 2013; K. Kim, 2013). However, this was a new type of role within SMG and the scale of SMG's debt made it hard to recruit new staff.

Fourth, trust between SMG, civic groups and individual citizens was required to obtain positive results from citizen engagement. Although distrust between SMG, civic groups and individual citizens had started to diminish, there had not previously been many opportunities for professionals in different sectors to co-create successful solutions together. The new communication channels brought a shift towards a collaborative culture based on stronger bonds of trust between different sectors. However, many interviewees felt that SMG needed to continue to strengthen trust and bonding relationships with civil society and individual citizens.

Finally, strong leadership was required to make new communication work. The core principles of SMG's new communication strategy were dialogue, openness and sharing. These principles required SMG to give up some of its power, focus more effort on citizen engagement and be monitored by over 10 million Seoul citizens at any time. On the surface, these requirements imposed extra burdens on SMG officers. Under these circumstances, the power of a strong leader who truly understood these principles and was able to communicate them cannot be underestimated. Such strong leadership was needed to positively influence not only SMG officers but also many different stakeholders outside SMG. This study has observed Mayor Park's strong leadership and its impact on the success of the EunPyung case using an MMO. However, this in itself became a challenging point since strong leadership meant that new communication models greatly depended on one individual. Interviewees felt that SMG needed to build a system and a culture to sustain and stabilise new communication tools and programmes fostering citizen engagement.

Conclusion

This chapter has examined the link between citizen engagement and social innovation in the context of Seoul City. SMG was going through a rapid change in the way it worked with citizens under the leadership of Mayor Wonsoon Park. The motto 'citizens are mayors' was embedded in the new models of communication and citizen engagement was seen as one of the core elements that could catalyse social innovation.

SMG was starting to understand that citizens were 'experts in their own lives' (The Young Foundation, 2012) and that citizen involvement in the policy-making process helped to draw out social needs and identify potential solutions (Bason, 2010). In particular, the EunPyeoung Mobile Mayoral Office showed that bringing together key decision-makers with residents brought about deeper insights into the problem at hand. Furthermore, this type of engagement forged new collaborations and interactions between citizens, civil servants and policy makers, going beyond usual working partners, 'creating new roles and relationships, developing assets and capabilities' and 'better using assets and resources' (The Young Foundation, 2012), thereby enhancing society's resilience and capacity to act.

There were challenges to SMG's citizen engagement and communication strategies. Due to the nature of the tools, there may have been limited representation of diverse voices. These tools may have been adequate for only a limited range of problems and were resource-intensive to administer. There was a need to ensure that long-term sustainability of these engagement approaches did not depend on one leader. Perhaps the biggest challenge lay in encouraging trust between citizens, public officers, civic groups and experts to work together and co-create new solutions. Past experiences led many South Koreans to think that citizen engagement processes were a waste of time and this created a sense of apathy towards citizen engagement activities.

Nevertheless, Seoul City was attempting to build the confidence of its citizens by providing them with new – positive – experiences of engagement. SMG's multi-channel communication approach offers valuable lessons to other cities that are ambitiously planning to initiate and drive social innovation.

Notes

Spreadi (www.spreadi.org), for further information, contact: jungwon@spreadi.org or sojung@spreadi.org.

1. Prior to the election in 2011, Mayor Park was a human rights lawyer and social justice activist and founder of the non-profit watchdog organisation People's Solidarity for Participatory Democracy; the Beautiful Foundation and the Beautiful Store, Oxfam-inspired models aimed at growing culture of giving; and the Hope Institute, a social innovation think and do tank.
2. For the 2014 election campaign for his second-term mayorship, Mayor Park carried a GPS tracker in his rucksack, so that citizens could track his whereabouts by using 'findwonsoon' webpage and find him to have a conversation with him. The campaign camp, which was called 'honeybee camp', had a non-hierarchical structure and was open to citizens who wanted to use the space (Chosun Biz, 2014).
3. In 2014, Wonsoon Park won 56.12% of the 4.9 million votes cast (National Election Commission, 2014).
4. South Korea's GNI per capita rose from to $110 in 1962 to $25,920 in 2013. GNI per capita (formerly GNP per capita) is the gross national income, converted to US dollars using the World Bank Atlas method, divided by the midyear population (World DataBank, 2014).
5. Another good example is the Citizen Hall. The basement areas of the Seoul City Hall covering two floors, named as the 'Citizen Hall', were provided for citizens' use. The Citizen Hall had an exhibition hall, gallery space, open lounge, event space available for hire, café and more. These efforts were made with the goal of enabling citizens to feel ownership of the City Hall.
6. Seoul-based social enterprises have used this media to advertise their products or programmes, supported by donations from major advertisement agencies. Around 60 enterprises benefited from this scheme between January and July 2013 (PCB, 2013).
7. MeToday (me2day.net) is a popular Korean social media platform, similar to Twitter, run by Korean company Naver.
8. SMG runs thirty-three Twitter accounts, six Facebook accounts, four MeToday accounts and two blogs. The Mayor uses his own Twitter account, @wonsoonpark, with 736,519 followers and Facebook account, www.facebook.com/wonsoonpark, with 170,894 followers.
9. Seoul has twenty-five boroughs. However, their budgets are quite small and many hope to get some financial support from SMG to solve daily issues of Seoul citizens together. In order to provide a programme directly beneficial to citizens, SMG runs the MMO with each local borough.
10. www.seoul.go.kr/runningmayor/

11. The city's debts stood at 20 trillion won (around US$ 19 billion) when Mr. Park was elected as Mayor. The debt decreased to 18.861 trillion won (around US$ 17.6 billion) at the end of May 2013 (SMG 2013b).
12. South Korean high-speed wireless Internet penetration rate reached 100.6% in 2012, according to the OECD (Moran, 2012).
13. These procedures include arranging committee meetings, providing feedback to committee members and citizens and coordinating them to agree on one finalised policy or programme (K. Ryu, 2013; Hwang, 2013; K. Kim, 2013).

References

Bason, C. (2010) *Leading Public Sector Innovation: Co-Creating for a Better Society.* Bristol: Policy Press.

Brodie, E., Cowling, E. and Nissen, N. (2009) *Understanding Participation: A Literature Review.* London: IVR, NCVO and Involve.

Chosun Biz (2014) 'There Were Wearable and Augmented Reality Apps Behind Won-soon Park's Reelection' *Chosun Biz.* Available from http://goo.gl/p1EgJc [Accessed 22 September 2014. In Korean].

Davies, A. and Simon, J. (2013) *The Value and Role of Citizen Engagement in Social Innovation.* A deliverable of the project: 'The theoretical, empirical and policy foundation for building social innovation in Europe' (TEPSIE). Brussels: European Commission, DG Research.

Davies, A., Simon, J., Patrick, R. and Norman, W. (2012) *Mapping Citizen Engagement in the Process of Social Innovation.* A deliverable of the project: 'The theoretical, empirical and policy foundation for building social innovation in Europe' (TEPSIE). Brussels: European Commission, DG Research.

Hwang, I. (2013) Interview with Hwang, InSik (Director of Local Autonomy Adimination Division, Seoul Metropolitan Government).

IAP2 (2014) *IAP2 Spectrum of Public Participation.* Available at http://goo.gl/dveiVR [Accessed 15 September 2014].

Kim, C. (2012) *Social Media Administration of the Seoul City.* Available at http://www.bloter.net/archives/133994 [Accessed 15 September 2014. In Korean].

Kim, D. (2013) Interview with Kim, DongKyung (Campaign Director, Public Communication Bureau).

Kim, H. (2013) Interview with Kim, HyunSung (Media Advisor of Seoul Metropolitan Government).

Kim, J. (2013) 'Listening to Citizen Opinions Using Social Media: The Case of Social Media Center at Seoul Metropolitan Government'. In *Seoul 2013 SNS Conference*, pp. 41–55 [In Korean].

Kim, K. (2013) Interview with Kim, KwonKi (Team Leader of Local Authority Administration Division, Seoul Metropolitan Government).

Kim, T. (2013) Interview with Kim, TaeGyun (Team Leader of Social Innovation Division, Seoul Innovation Bureau, Seoul Metropolitan Government).

Kim, Y. (2013) Interview with Kim, Y. (Social Innovation Advisor, Seoul Metropolitan Government).

Kim, J. and Han, S. (2011) 'A Guided Tour of Social Innovation in Korea'. Hope Institute. Available at http://goo.gl/OAMMn3 [Accessed 19 September 2014].

190   *Jungwon Kim, Sojung Rim, Sunkyung Han and Ahyoung Park*

Lee, J.E. (2013) Interview with Lee, JongEon (Chief of Marketing Division, SH Corporation).

Lee, J.S. (2013) Interview with Lee, JongSun (Manager of Public Relations, SH Corportation).

MMO (2012) 'There is an answer at the on-site'. Mobile Mayoral Office, S.M.G. (Presentation).

Moran, A. (2012) 'OECD: South Korea high-speed Internet penetration rate tops 100%'. *Digital Journal.* Available at: http://digitaljournal.com/article/329199 [Accessed 22 October 2014].

National Election Commission (2014) Available at http://goo.gl/jFkG4R [Accessed 17 September 2014. In Korean].

Noland, M. (2014) 'Six Markets to Watch: South Korea'. *Foreign Affairs.* Available at http://goo.gl/6S6qWN [Aceessed 21 September 2014].

OECD (2014) OECD Stat Extracts. Available at http://stats.oecd.org/ [Accessed 22 October 2014].

Oh, K. (2014) 'Inequality threatens Korea's growth: Report'. *The Korea Herald.* Available at http://goo.gl/iPYb1K [Accessed 17 September 2014].

Park, W. (2014) 'Unusual Suspects Special: Seoul's Mayor Park Talks About Collaboration'. SIX (Social Innovation eXchange). Available at http://goo.gl/ WiZfjg [Accessed 10 September 2014].

PCB (2012) *2012 Annual Report of Public Communication Bureau.* SMG: Public Communication Bureau [In Korean].

PCB (2013) *2013 Major Work Plan of the Public Communication Bureau.* SMG: Public Communication Bureau [In Korean].

Phillips, M. (2013) 'Korea is the world's top producer of unhappy school children'. *Quartz.* Available at http://goo.gl/oBiurd [Accessed 17 September 2014].

Ryu, J. (2013) Interview with Ryu, J. (Team Leader of New Media Divison, Public Communication Bureau, Seoul Metroplitan Government).

Ryu, K. (2013) Interview with Ryu, KyungHee (Coordinator of Smart Work Committee).

Ryu, H. and Kwon, W. (2014) 'I don't want to leave anything as the Seoul Mayor'. *Ohmynews.* Available at http://goo.gl/kaW5Lz [Accessed 15 September 2014].

Seok, J. (2011) 'Park Won-soon reaches fundraising goal in 52 hours'. *The Hankyoreh.* Available at http://goo.gl/AoX5Pa [Accessed 22 September 2014].

SH Corporation (2013) *EunPyung Newtown 3-RE Smart White Paper.*

SMG (2012) 'Eunpyeong's worth is Geumpyeong [golden]'. Seoul Metropolitan Government. Available at: http://goo.gl/rvhjmV [Accessed 15 September 2014].

SMG (2013a) *2012 Seoul Citizen Communication White Paper.* Seoul Metropolitan Government. [In Korean].

SMG (2013b) 'Seoul Metropolitan Government's debt on the decline since Mayor Park Won Soon's inauguration'. Seoul Metropolitan Government.

SMG (2013c) 'Communicate between citizens and the Seoul City through SNS'. Seoul Metropolitan Government. Available at http://goo.gl/tZMywb [Accessed 15 September 2014. In Korean].

SMG (2013d) *2012 Seoul City White Paper – 100 Policies.* Seoul Metropolitan Government. [In Korean.]

Song, S. (2013) Interview with Song, SoonKi (Team Leader, Sales Team, Marketing Division, SH Corporation).

The Young Foundation (2012) *Social Innovation Overview – Part 1: Defining Social Innovation*, A deliverable of the project: 'The theoretical, empirical and policy foundations for building social innovation in Europe' (TEPSIE). Brussels: European Commission, DG Research.

Westley, F. (2008) *The Social Innovation Dynamic*. Canada: Social Innovation Generation at the University of Waterloo. Available from http://goo.gl/CdyGb2 [Accessed 15 September 2014].

World DataBank (2014) Available at http://goo.gl/Gmi9gI [Accessed 17 September 2014].

Yoon, S. (2014) 'Until citizens open their hearts'. *Nocut news online*. Available at http://goo.gl/XG2hqT [Accessed 15 September 2014].

9

Can Collective Intelligence Produce Social Innovation?

Ola Tjornbo

Introduction

The development of modern information and communication technologies (ICTs) has led to a renewed interest in the phenomenon of 'collective intelligence' (also described as the 'wisdom of the crowds', Surowiecki, 2005). Collective intelligence refers to the capacity to mobilise and coordinate the expertise and creativity possessed by large groups of individuals in order to solve problems and create new knowledge. Although this can be done offline, ICTs make it far easier for large groups of individuals to work collectively on common tasks, for example by removing the need for physical proximity, allowing for asynchronous communication and making it possible for single individuals to transmit information to very large groups (Wellman, 1997). These advantages have allowed online networks to solve iconic mathematics problems (Polymath, 2009; Gowers and Nielsen, 2009), create the world's largest reference work, Wikipedia (Almeida, 2007), and even challenge grandmaster Garry Kasparov to a game of chess (Nielsen, 2011).

In the light of these developments, scholars have suggested that by harnessing collective intelligence, it may be possible dramatically to improve society's ability to tackle seemingly intractable social problems (e.g., Rushkoff, 2003; Howe, 2006; Tapscott and Williams, 2006; 2010). Theoretically, it is clear that there are certain types of tasks that groups perform better than individuals. For example, large groups are good at predicting the outcomes of elections or guessing the number of beans in a jar (Sunstein, 2006). However, these types of problems have concrete 'right' answers, whereas the answers to social problems are rarely so clear cut (Funtowicz, 1993; Head, 2008).

As Homer-Dixon (2001) and Westley *et al.* (2007) have argued, it may be possible to address some of the most pressing social problems by producing social innovations – new approaches to tackling familiar problems when established answers and responses have proven ineffective. But are collective intelligence tools valuable to the production of social innovation? On the one hand, there are some promising indicators. Online networks are typically made up of diverse nodes that are weakly tied, exactly the sort of networks that should be effective at mobilising knowledge and resources (Granovetter, 1973). Furthermore, they tend to have relatively flat hierarchies and high degrees of autonomy for individual nodes, which is characteristic of innovative organisations (Mintzberg, 1991). Finally, because online networks are potentially open to anyone who has access to the internet, they encourage a sharing of diverse knowledge sets that has been identified as critical to innovation, both technical (Arthur, 2009) and social (Mumford and Moertl, 2003; Mumford and Licuanan, 2004). On the other hand, it is becoming increasingly clear that online collective intelligence has serious limitations. For example, online groups tend to become polarised between opposing opinions when it comes to dealing with complex problems that are politically contested (Sunstein, 2006). Moreover, online groups struggle with tasks that require careful coordination (Nielsen, 2012; Kittur, Lee, and Kraut, 2009). These factors suggest limitations in terms of how far collective intelligence may be able to drive social innovation, which typically aims to address problems that are the consequence of complex systems and that require changes in the flow of resources, authority and beliefs if they are to be addressed (Westley *et al.*, 2007).

This chapter draws on the work of Arthur (2009) and a number of social innovation scholars (Mulgan *et al.*, 2007; Westley *et al.*, 2007; Mumford, 2002), to provide a framework for examining how collective intelligence can support social innovation. It divides social innovation into phases and mechanisms. It then explores how three existing collective intelligence platforms have promoted social innovation. These three cases illustrate the different models that exist for tapping into collective intelligence online, with each one having different strengths and weaknesses in terms of generating social innovation. This analysis suggests that using collective intelligence to produce social innovation is possible, but that no single collective intelligence platform is likely to be useful throughout the whole social innovation process.

The challenge of using collective intelligence to drive social innovation

Social innovation has been defined as 'an initiative, product, process or program that profoundly changes the basic routines, resource and authority flows or beliefs of any social system'.[1] Although this is just one definition, it shares much in common with those used by other authors working in this field (Mumford, 2002; Wheatley and Frieze, 2006). What is particular about this perspective on social innovation is that it is 'systemic', meaning that it is concerned with the impact an innovation has on a whole social system, not just in the context of a particular organisation or industry. This kind of systemic change inevitably involves conflicts of interests, different perspectives on the system and the nature of the social problem, and unanticipated consequences due to unpredictable relations of cause and effect. In short, and using the language of systems perspectives, social innovation is 'complex' (Westley *et al.*, 2007; Duit and Galaz, 2008; Pierre and Peters, 2005).

So, from this viewpoint, complexity is inevitable when dealing with social innovation. This is a problem for collective intelligence (Nielsen, 2011; Sunstein, 2006; Sunstein, 2007). In order to mobilise collective intelligence, participants must be able to share and communicate information in such a way that the specialised knowledge that each individual possesses can be combined into a coherent whole or 'answer'. There are two characteristics that a problem can have that make this easier.

Collective intelligence is easier to apply when the amount of coordination between participants required to solve a problem is minimal (Kittur, 2008; Kittur *et al.*, 2009). In some applications of collective intelligence, each individual only needs to supply their best answer to a problem, with the collective answer being determined by the average of all the responses. This is called a 'low coordination' problem. Collective intelligence is more difficult to apply when new contributions only make sense in relation to what has gone before. A famous example of such a 'high coordination' project was the publishing house Penguin's attempt to write a book using an online collaboration platform, which largely failed (Kittur *et al.*, 2009; Pulinger, 2007).

Collective intelligence is also easier to apply when a problem has a definite answer, one that is clearly recognisable when it is found, and where the method for finding it is known and agreed on by the group (Nielsen, 2011). This is also called an 'intellective', as opposed to a 'judgmental', task (see Laughlin and Adamopoulos, 1982). Typically, the former condition holds in fields like mathematics where it is possible to distinguish clearly between a correct and a wrong answer, and there is a common praxis shared by those working in the field for arriving at problem solutions. However, this may not be the case when dealing with social problems where the difference between right and wrong may be based on value judgements not shared by all involved, and where there is a lot of uncertainty surrounding what is known about a problem (Funtowicz, 1993). Collective intelligence becomes increasingly difficult to employ when incorporating knowledge from different academic disciplines or non-scientific knowledge based in traditional cultures (Berkes, 2008) or unarticulated lay practices. It is almost impossible when the knowledge that one party professes to possess is dismissed as worthless by other parties, such as is common in highly politicised or value-laden debates (Head, 2008).

Social innovation meets neither of these conditions. It is complex, with high coordination requirements, and requires judgmental evaluations. As such, it is tempting to say that social innovation is simply not a good arena to use collective intelligence. However, a deeper look at how social innovation happens makes this conclusion appear less certain.

The process of social innovation

Social innovation is still an emerging field of study and, thus, there are still relatively few papers dealing with how social innovation happens from a systemic perspective (Mumford and Moertl, 2003). However, there are other disciplines that look at innovation in complex systems – especially research into socio-technical systems – that can offer useful conceptual frameworks for understanding this phenomenon. This chapter describes the process of social innovation with reference to social innovation theory (Wheatley and Frieze, 2006; Westley *et al.*, 2007; Westley and Antadze, 2010; Mumford, 2002), as well as work on socio-technical systems (e.g., Geels and Schot, 2007; Geels, 2005; Smith, Stirling and Berkhout, 2005), and especially the work of Arthur (2009).

Scholars of innovation in complex systems tend to break the process into three (Mumford, 2002; Arthur, 2009) or four phases (Westley *et al.*, 2013). Table 9.1 presents three phases of social innovation. At each phase there are crucial mechanisms for making the innovation successful. These mechanisms are described in greater detail in the paragraphs below.

Table 9.1 Phases and mechanisms of social innovation

Phase of social innovation	Associated mechanisms
Invention	(Re-)combination; exchange of information and ideas between different domains
Development	Matching problems and solutions; clustering; niches; shadow networks
Implementation	Cross-scale networks; institutional entrepreneurship

Source: Author's compilation.

The 'invention' stage is when a new innovation is first born. Most theorists propose that innovations are born out of new combinations or recombinations of existing ideas, practices, technologies and other elements, to produce new and surprising outcomes. Mumford notes that social innovation seems to emerge most often when modes of reasoning that are common in one domain are applied to surprising effect in another domain (Mumford and Moertl, 2003). The invention phase can be encouraged by fostering the exchange of ideas and information between individuals working in different domains. Arthur (2009) argues that the greater the number of existing technologies, the more potential re-combinations there are – so the faster innovation happens.

Invention is followed by 'development', in which the initial idea is adapted to its purpose. In some cases this involves finding a previously unexplored application for an existing technology or idea (Cohen *et al.*, 1972; Arthur, 2009). Often this stage of development involves linking the invention to other ideas that help to refine it. As both Westley *et al.* (2007) and Arthur (2009) have noted, successful innovations often consist of clusters of products, programmes and processes that come together to allow the invention to fulfil its purpose.

Developing an innovation requires an investment of time and, usually, both human and financial capital. Finding resources for fledgling ideas is difficult. Innovation scholars have noted the importance of 'niches' in protecting innovations during this growth period (Schot and Geels, 2007; Smith, 2006; Kemp *et al.*, 1998). Such niches may be housed within larger organisations and institutions, as spaces reserved for radical innovation, or they can be small markets where the innovation has a limited application that does not reflect its systems changing potential. Related to the concept of a niche is the concept of a 'shadow network' (Olsson *et al.*, 2006). Shadow networks are groups of individuals who work together to develop an innovation, often without compensation, in order to create an alternative to the existing way of doing things. Sometimes shadow networks can exist for a long time, developing and utilising an idea before it ever enters the mainstream. For example, in Chile, artisanal fishers had to wait sixteen years before the collapse of the dictatorial regime allowed them to replace existing fisheries policy with their own ideas (Gelcich *et al.*, 2010). The third stage is institutionalisation and 'regime shift'. As Westley *et al.* noted (Westley *et al.*, 2007; Westley and Antadze, 2010), in order to establish themselves, innovations often need to access resources and opportunities that are located outside the system in which they are operating. While resistance to change within a system may be high, there may be opportunities at other levels to build support for the innovation. This means that an actor trying to achieve change within a local context may find it necessary to look outside the system they are trying to change in order to find support. Just as within the legal system a ruling may be appealed and overturned in a higher court, a social innovator may be able to approach national or international organisations for help. In the example of the Great Bear Rainforest in Western Canada, environmental organisations were able to put pressure on logging companies acting in the region by targeting the international buyers of their timber products (Tjornbo *et al.*, 2010). The ability to reach outside the system in this way is greatly facilitated by the creation of networks that span administrative and geographic boundaries. These can be created by both formal partnerships and informal connections (Moore and Westley, 2011; Slaughter, 2004).

An innovation may have to wait before it has an opportunity to establish itself, but agents can work actively to look for opportunities to find resources at other scales. Throughout the innovation process, but particularly at the institutionalisation phase, the success of the innovation is heavily dependent on the support and skills of agents, often called institutional entrepreneurs, who are skilled at finding these kinds of opportunities (Dorado, 2005; Levy and Scully, 2007; Child *et al.*, 2007). Institutional entrepreneurs help innovations to secure resources to grow and are adept at finding opportunities to establish them in systems (Westley *et al.*, 2013, Mumford, 2002).

According to the definition of social innovation provided above, a social innovation can only be described as such if it moves through all of these three stages (although not necessarily consecutively – since they can occur simultaneously or even out of order on occasion). Thus, all of the mechanisms described above are important to a social innovation's progress. However, no single organisation or institution has to carry out all of these activities. Westley *et al.* (2013) argued that agency in social innovation processes is best understood as a distributed quality, where many different actors are involved in making a social innovation happen, contributing different skills at different times. Collective intelligence platforms are not agents in themselves, rather they are mechanisms that can help to mobilise and coordinate agency. Moreover, different types of platform might provide support to social innovation at one phase, without being useful throughout the whole process.

The role of collective intelligence platforms in social innovation: Three case studies

Collective intelligence platforms are virtual spaces, usually websites – though they can also take the form of mobile applications – that are set up in order to allow people to come together to work on common problems in ways that require the mobilisation of knowledge and creativity. A recent study identified three main types of collective intelligence platform (Tjornbo, 2013): challenge grants, innovation communities and open innovation platforms. This chapter explores, qualitatively, what role each of these different kinds of platform might play in promoting social innovation and to what extent they have been successful in doing so. This chapter examines one leading example of each of these types of collective intelligence platform. Platforms were selected on the basis that they had large memberships, had attracted financial resources and had achieved recognition in the media (measured by the number of hits generated by a Google 'news' search). The aim of looking at these sites was to answer two questions:

1. To what extent are these innovation platforms already producing social innovations?
2. How well are these three different types of online innovation platforms adapted to the task of stimulating social innovation and to what extent do they represent mechanisms of social innovation in action?

Each case is now considered in turn.

Challenge grants: Innocentive

Challenge grants are perhaps the most established model for regularly accessing the innovative capacity of virtual social networks. A challenge grant allows those facing a problem to put out an open call for potential solutions. Anyone who thinks they have a solution to the challenge can submit a proposal and they typically compete with other 'solvers' to win a cash prize for the best solution, either determined by the 'challenger' or by an independent jury. Challenge grants require some coordination since 'solvers' have to meet the expectations of the 'challengers'. This becomes more difficult depending on the nature of the challenge issued. However, as the example of Innocentive illustrates, while the challenge grant approach is most easily applicable to simpler, technical challenges, it does still have some application for complex social challenges.

Operational since 2001, Innocentive is undoubtedly one of the largest open innovation platforms. Over 1,650 challenges, worth over $40,000,000 in total, have been posted on the site, and Innocentive can boast some notable successes. For example, it has produced breakthroughs in oil spill clean-up and in treating Amyotrophic Lateral Sclerosis (ALS).[2] Like most challenge grants, the principal aim of Innocentive is to connect people with a problem to those who think they might have an answer.

The majority of challenges posted on Innocentive are purely technical in nature. However, some of the challenges concern social problems and could potentially produce social innovation. To identify such challenges, three criteria were set out based on the definition of social innovation above: challenges could be defined as potentially producing social innovation if they concerned a social problem; took a holistic/systemic view of the problem; and invited solutions with a potentially radical impact on the way that problem was tackled, that is, they did not constrain problem solvers to work within an existing mode of practice. Challenges listed on Innocentive were then evaluated to identify those that met the criteria. As well as the author, a second researcher performed the same evaluation in order to reduce the subjectivity of the judgement. Based on these criteria, four Innocentive challenges out of the 138 challenges active at the time of the research were identified as supporting social innovation.

These 138 challenges only present a snapshot of the activities of Innocentive. However, using the same criteria to look at the most successful problem solvers involved in Innocentive over the last five years also gives an indication of the primary activities of the site. Between 2007 and 2011 not one 'top solver' was involved in challenges that could be described as socially innovative.[3]

While Innocentive indulges in some social innovation, the data does not tell us how successful the platform is in this arena. Innocentive's general measure of success is that 85% of challenges find winning solutions, but there is no such figure that focuses solely on social innovations. Nevertheless, two of Innocentive's high-profile success stories involve social innovation. The first was a challenge to find new ways of providing education to populations in poor and developing countries[4] and the second was a challenge to find a means of measuring 'human potential'.[5] Thus, although social innovation is just a small part of Innocentive's activities, it is possible to use the Innocentive model to stimulate social innovation.

Innocentive's success seems to hinge on its ability to leverage two of the core mechanisms of social innovation: matching problems and solutions and exchanging information across domains. The challenge grant structure is also suited to innovation in that it opens problems up to a wide audience of potential solvers. A typical way for an organisation or individual to attempt to find a solution to a problem might be to hire a consultant or other experts in the particular field it is operating in, but these people are often too committed to existing ways of operating or established best practices to generate truly innovative ideas (Nielsen, 2011). As the literature on social innovation suggests, innovation is usually the product of the novel combination of adjacent fields of knowledge (Arthur, 2009). This certainly holds true for Innocentive, where many winning solutions have come from experts in fields different from that of the challenger (Nielsen, 2011).

However, while Innocentive might be good at stimulating new inventions, it seems to be poor at supporting innovations through to implementation (Tjornbo and Westley, 2012). Once a solution has been matched to a problem, there is not much more support available from Innocentive in terms of developing the idea. The section of the site entitled 'Solver Resources' mostly contains a few brief articles on the basics of how to answer challenges. There are built-in supports for people hoping to partner with others in designing their solution and an online forum where members of Innocentive can chat about a broad range of topics, but these tools seem to have limited impact. The global forum, for example, sees a new topic opened at most once or twice a month and most of these receive two or fewer replies. At the time of writing, the first three posts in this forum were all observations about how difficult it is to form a team.[6] Based on a sample of twenty randomly selected challenges, the average number of public comments in the public project rooms is less than three. This suggests that Innocentive is not effective in building shadow networks.

In addition, Innocentive does not have built-in tools to help innovations establish themselves in broader systems. Once a solution is accepted by a challenger, then the role of the site, and possibly of the innovator, may be over. There is no systematic attempt to encourage the involvement of institutional entrepreneurs, to develop such skills, or to look for cross-scale opportunities. All of this is left up to the challenger or innovator. Thus innovations may fail because of a lack of resources or because the innovator is not able to help tailor the innovation to its particular application. The two successful social innovations profiled on the site were achieved in partnership with *The Economist* magazine, which may have helped to raise the profile of the competitions.

Innovation communities: Open Source Ecology

Innovation communities do not promote innovation generally; rather, they focus on a single problem and attempt to find solutions to it. The emphasis in these groups is not on generating ideas but on fine-tuning them and seeing them successfully implemented. Unlike the other types of innovation platform, therefore, innovation communities rely heavily on their ability to coordinate action. This can be accomplished in a number of different ways. For example, although it is not an innovation community *per se*, Wikipedia has been very successful at coordinating large numbers of individuals in accomplishing a shared project by developing an elaborate set of rules and guidelines for evaluating articles, with a dedicated group of volunteer moderators who do most of the work of editing articles (Butler *et al.*, 2008). In order to succeed, it needs to keep volunteers motivated and prevent fragmentation of the project (Hertel *et al.*, 2003; Mustonen, 2003).

Open Source Ecology (OSE) was born from the frustration experienced by one man: farmer, technologist and physicist Marcin Jakubowski. When he was unable to repair his brand tractor that broke down frequently, he designed a cheap, robust and easily repairable alternative that could be built entirely using locally available materials. He then made the blueprint for this new tractor available to the public. His work attracted outside attention and supporters and soon expanded into the vision of the Global Village Construction Set (GVCS), a set of blueprints for 50 machines that could be built and maintained locally on a small scale. Jakubowski's farm became the site of a community dedicated to producing blueprints and prototypes of these machines, and their work attracted the interest of others, like TED, who gave Jakubowski a platform to share his idea. Jakubowski's TED talk describing Open Source Ecology has had over a million views at the time of writing[7] and helped launch a community on the global stage.

The OSE project is a social innovation in itself as it is a radical reconceptualisation of manufacturing that turns its back on the centralisation and global supply chains of the mainstream economy and is a direct response to concerns about the social and environmental impacts of globalisation and the consumer economy. In order to make this possible it relies on many different types of community support. Some of this is financial, as provided by the hundreds of 'True Fans' who contribute ten dollars a month to the project,[8] but much of it relies on collective intelligence. The blueprints for the GVCS machines are open source and have been developed by a virtual network of contributors as well as those working on the farm. A few early adopters have also created these machines and provided feedback on how they need to be improved.[9] Although it is still in its infancy, OSE has been developing a coherent alternative to a society based on centralised industrial production and demonstrates that innovation communities can play a role in social innovation.

The idea for OSE was generated by Marcin Jakubowski and, as such, people who become involved in the OSE project are attracted by the idea of the Global Village Construction Set and share at least some of Jakubowski's values. This reduces a lot of the complexity inherent in using collective intelligence for social innovation and is, perhaps, what allows OSE to work as a social innovation platform.

Web platforms like OSE make use of collective intelligence during the 'development' phase of social innovation. The farm became a 'niche' that attracted resources, both financial and in the shape of talented volunteers, who came to work at the farm, as well as those who contributed to development online. These resources soon saw the production of a cluster of innovations (different prototypes of Global Village Construction Set machines). OSE became the focus of one of the early crowdfunding campaigns (online platforms that allow members of the public to support projects with small donations), with 500 supporters creating a small monthly revenue for Jakubowski (Thomson and Jakubowski, 2012). One of the volunteers at the farm won a Thiel '20 Under 20' Fellowship of $100,000 to allow him to continue his work on the farm. By using crowdfunding, OSE explored ideas that would not be supported by mainstream funding organisations, whether private or philanthropic (Thomson and Jakubowski, 2012). However, its success depended entirely upon its ability to build a committed 'shadow network' of supporters.

The lesson from other similar online projects is that these initiatives must attract both casual volunteers and a core group of very committed enthusiasts (Howe, 2006). In the case of Wikipedia, while casual volunteers create the bulk of new material, it is a small group of 'moderators' who ensure that articles abide by Wikipedia's standards and maintain a consistent style (Kittur *et al.*, 2007).

In the case of OSE, the project received a big boost after Jakubowski was invited to make a presentation at TED. This brought a significant amount of interest to the project and an infusion of extra investment and resources (Thomson and Jakubowski, 2012). The central premise of the OSE project caught on and led to an expansion of the idea into new locations, a process social innovation scholars sometimes refer to as 'scaling out' (Westley and Antadze, 2010). A shadow network grew up around the OSE project, through the OSE forums and wiki. Most significantly, this included a German OSE node with its own OSE Wiki and active forums.[10]

However, the core OSE community has not been consistently strong. Recently, the OSE fora have not been particularly active.[11] Even more significantly, the OSE farm has gone through periods of inactivity, with the last of the initial volunteers having departed in February 2013. The reasons for this collapse appear to be partly related to the leadership of Jakubowski.[12] The problems associated with a charismatic leader who is at first instrumental to the growth of a new initiative, but later comes to limit it, are well known and documented in the management literature (Westley *et al.*, 2007). Such leaders are often able to attract support because of the strength of their vision but may be reluctant to adapt their ideas to specific contexts, tend to stifle creativity in their followers and can ultimately strangle the innovation they championed. From other open source projects it is clear that a horizontal and non-hierarchical leadership style is essential to maintaining such communities.

Despite a lack of more recent activity, the OSE project is not a failure. The central idea has been considerably developed since Jakubowski first invented it, and a network has grown up around it so that work is now being continued in other locations. However, there may be a tension between maintaining the kind of intense community needed to sustain a project like the OSE and the activities associated with institutionalising an innovation, such as identifying opportunities for cross-scale interactions.

Open innovation platforms: TED

Open innovation platforms are platforms that publicise people's good ideas. At their simplest, they are open message boards where anyone is free to submit their proposals for public scrutiny. More typically however, they also encourage visitors to comment on ideas and to vote for those they like, thus giving the 'best' ideas greatest prominence. Open innovation platforms do not draw much use from collective intelligence directly, since most ideas are the product of a single mind or a small team rather than a large group. However, in allowing for comments on ideas, they create opportunities for collaboration. More importantly, by spreading ideas effectively, they may open people up to a greater diversity of ideas, invigorating recombination processes.

TED is the largest open innovation platform in terms of visitors. It started in 1984 as an organisation that put on conferences bringing together speakers from the worlds of technology, entertainment and design. Today, it is mostly famous for the videos of its talks available online through its website. It currently hosts over 19,000 talks, and some of the most popular have over 20 million views.[13] TED differs from standard open innovation platforms in that only specially selected invitees are able to share their ideas, which are carefully curated to fit the TED format. It also has an unusually sophisticated multimedia distribution platform.

TED works well as a social innovation platform. Several of the talks on the site promote ideas that are intended to tackle social problems, take a holistic, systemic approach and have potentially radical implications, such as Ken Robinson's[14] proposal to reform education systems in the West to put more emphasis on creativity or George Papandreou's proposal for a Europe without political borders.[15] This is not to say that TED is exclusively or even mainly a social innovation platform. The most common talk topics on TED are those related to its core areas – technology (558 talks), entertainment (272) and design (326), with the only exceptions being science (421) and business (278). Topics like politics (146), health (124) and poverty (44) lag far behind.[16]

The greatest strength of TED is its ability to communicate ideas. The most popular TED talks garner huge audiences, while talks with hundreds of thousands of viewers are fairly commonplace. At the most fundamental level, simply exposing people to a variety of ideas makes them more likely to come up with innovative recombinations (Arthur, 2009). Moreover, exposure often brings additional resources, as shown in the OSE example.

Although originally, TED's design was not directed at harnessing collective intelligence to spur social innovation, over time, it has evolved and added tools to develop ideas beyond the talks. One such tool is the forum, which allows for commentary on the talks. Of the three case studies here, TED has the most active forum, with the number of comments on a talk often numbering tens or hundreds (as opposed to OSE and Innocentive, which often only had a few comments). There is scope through these discussions to develop ideas further and to create clusters. However, so far, this activity has not been typically systematic, nor carried out with a particular end goal in mind.

Another development has been the TED Prize. The Prize is essentially a form of challenge grant where one individual is awarded $1 million for a plan that proposes a solution to a problem that will 'change the world' for the better. To date there have been nineteen TED Prize Winners, tackling topics such as nutrition in schools and marine protected areas.[17] Yet another innovation promoting development is the TED Fellows Programme, which is focused on supporting the work of young innovators.[18]

Largely, the impetus for these kinds of developments has come from the TED community. At the time of writing this online network had 149,441 members and its own forum. Moreover, TED receives feedback from the participants at its physical conferences. Much of this feedback concerns a desire to see the ideas at TED put into action with the support of the talented people in the room and the resources they have access to. A striking example of this potential came in the form of the *Mission Blue* project. This began with a TED talk from Sylvia Earle, who argued for the creation of a series of marine-protected areas to help build the resilience of ocean ecosystems around the globe. The speech garnered a huge amount of support, including a $1,000,000 pledge from philanthropist Addison Fischer. It also led to a voyage, with passengers made up of scientists, philanthropists and celebrities, which raised over $15 million.[19]

These examples show that TED has a potentially powerful ability to build cross-scale networks able to advocate strongly for social innovation. Another example of this came in the form of the TED Challenge (part of TED 2013), where small interdisciplinary groups worked together, with notable successes, to create action on a range of issues from vaccination to sex trafficking.

Thus far though, the kinds of deliberate activities described here are the exception rather than the rule. At its core, TED remains an idea promoter, not an advocacy organisation. Most of the attendees at TED conferences are scientists and business people rather than politicians, and TED remains committed to a politically neutral perspective. In fact, perhaps, there is a tension between TED's role as a promoter of ideas and as a place of community building and its potential role as an agent of institutional entrepreneurship and advocacy.

Conclusion

Despite the complex nature of social innovation processes and the limited theoretical literature exploring the phenomenon, it is clear from the case studies presented here that collective intelligence has a role to play in promoting social innovation, both directly and indirectly. All three of the web platforms examined here promoted social innovation to some extent. Innocentive – the challenge grant example – featured a small sample of social innovation challenges and at least two examples of successfully launched social innovations. OSE – the innovation community example – took a radically alternative model of production and self-sustainability and not only considerably developed the idea with several prototypes, but also created a global shadow network dedicated to taking it further. Finally, TED – the open innovation platform example – publicised several social innovations and helped them to gain greater prominence and resources. TED also created an online community dedicated to seeing some of these socially innovative ideas realised in practice. It has occasionally helped to build cross-scale networks to support the realisation process.

At the same time, no single platform seems to be able to support a social innovation from invention through to implementation. In fact, each of these different types of platform seems particularly strong in one particular phase: invention in the case of TED and Innocentive, and development in the case of OSE. Moreover, none of these platforms utilised all of the mechanisms associated with any one phase and none were particularly active in the implementation phase, although TED seems to have the greatest potential in this area.

In many ways this reflects the strengths and limitations suggested by the theoretical literature in the introduction to this chapter. Collective intelligence platforms are indeed good at mobilising resources and sharing knowledge and creativity (e.g., TED and OSE); they can help realise the benefits of applying diverse knowledge sets to a single problem (Innocentive); and they are places where truly radical innovation can thrive (OSE). However, they have yet to demonstrate a capacity to be effective in the implementation phase where the ability to navigate complex political environments and form cross-scale networks composed of diverse interest groups becomes crucial. It is interesting to note how successful OSE was at attracting a truly committed group of volunteers willing to invest a significant amount of time and resources into a shared vision. This is contrary to the expectation that online models are best at forming loose networks and this may be linked to the hybrid nature of this platform which includes both online and offline components. All of the networks have weaknesses that could be addressed to help them become more successful engines of social innovation. Innocentive could become better at building the kind of community observed in OSE, which might lead to a greater degree of collaboration in developing innovations past the initial idea. OSE might benefit from becoming less reliant on the leadership of Marcin Jakubowski and the relatively insular OSE community, perhaps by promoting its ability to share ideas as widely as TED has done (and indeed its success is in part due to TED) and by finding new ways to attract resources (as Innocentive did). Finally, TED could, perhaps, benefit from finding concrete applications for ideas and forming a community willing to help make ideas a reality (there are signs that this is happening). However, in each of these cases the platform in question risks losing something by expanding its remit. Innocentive might become less diverse by building a stronger and more committed community; OSE might become fragmented by turning away from the vision that drives it; and a more action-oriented TED might come to be seen as a political actor rather than a neutral repository of knowledge, reducing the breadth of its appeal.

Ultimately, perhaps it is very difficult for any single platform to be effective in all stages of the development of a social innovation. As might be expected, based on network theory, there are trade-offs involved in choosing to support either the formation of a strongly bonded community or shadow network or the formation of more loosely coupled cross-scale communities. Equally though, there are opportunities to draw on mechanisms that the platforms themselves were not doing enough to exploit, such as Innocentive's failure to promote greater use of its forums or TED's hesitation around mobilising its potential as a network organisation. Ultimately, this study suggests that those interested in promoting social innovation should make greater use of the full range of collective intelligence platforms in order best to use the strengths of each. However, it is acknowledged here that more work is needed to investigate further the patterns suggested by this exploratory study.

Notes

1. http://sig.uwaterloo.ca/about-the-waterloo-institute-for-social-innovation-and-resilience-wisir#About%20SI. Accessed 25 September 2014.
2. http://www.innocentive.com/about-innocentive/innovation-solutions-of-note and see also Nielsen (2011).

3. http://www.innocentive.com/for-solvers/top-solvers-2011. Accessed 26 November 2014.
4. http://www.innocentive.com/for-solvers/winning-solutions/21st-century-cyber-schools-challenge. Accessed 26 November 2014.
5. http://www.innocentive.com/for-solvers/winning-solutions/human-potential-index-challenge. Accessed 26 November 2014.
6. https://www.innocentive.com/ar/board/solver. Accessed 1 June 2013.
7. https://www.ted.com/talks/marcin_jakubowski. Accessed 26 November 2014.
8. http://opensourceecology.org/wiki/True_fans. Accessed 26 November 2014.
9. http://opensourceecology.org/wiki/FAQ. Accessed 26 November 2014.
10. http://opensourceecology.org/wiki/Germany. Accessed 26 November 2014.
11. http://forum.opensourceecology.org/discussion/1004/why-is-ose-so-quiet-lately. Accessed 26 November 2014.
12. http://opensourceecology.org/wiki/Yoonseo_Blog. Accessed 26 November 2014.
13. https://www.ted.com/talks. Accessed 24 November 2014.
14. http://www.ted.com/talks/ken_robinson_says_schools_kill_creativity.html. Accessed 25 September 2014.
15. http://www.ted.com/talks/george_papandreou_imagine_a_european_democracy_without_borders.html. Accessed 25 September 2014.
16. https://www.ted.com/topics. Accessed 24 November 2014.
17. http://www.ted.com/pages/prize_about. Accessed 26 November 2014.
18. http://www.ted.com/fellows. Accessed 26 November 2014.
19. http://blog.ted.com/2010/04/13/ocean_hope_at_m/. Accessed 26 November 2014.

References

Arthur, B. (2009) *The Nature of Technology: What It Is and How it Evolves*. New York: Free Press.

Almeida, R., Mozafari, B. and Cho, J. (2007) 'On the Evolution of Wikipedia', in *International Conference on Weblogs and Social Media*. Available at http://www.icwsm.org/papers/2--Almeida-Mozafari-Cho.pdf [Accessed 26 November 2014].

Butler, B., Joyce, E. and Pike, J. (2008) 'Don't look now, but we've created a bureaucracy: The nature and roles of policies and rules in Wikipedia', *Proceedings of the Twenty-Sixth Annual SIGCHI Conference on Human Factors in Computing Systems*: 1101–10.

Berkes, F. (2008) *Sacred Ecology*. New York: Taylor and Francis.

Child, J., Lu, Y. and Tsai, T. (2007) 'Institutional Entrepreneurship in Building an Environmental Protection System for the People's Republic of China'. *Organization Studies*, 28 (7): 1013–34.

Cohen, M., March, J. and Olsen, J. (1972) 'A Garbage Can Model of Organizational Choice'. *Administrative Science Quarterly*, 17 (1): 1–25.

Dorado, S. (2005) 'Institutional Entrepreneurship, Partaking, and Convening', *Organization Studies*, 26 (3): 385–414.

Duit, A. and Galaz, V. (2008) 'Governance and Complexity – Emerging Issues for Governance Theory', *Governance*, 21 (3): 311–35.

Funtowicz, S. (1993) 'Science for the Post-Normal Age', *Futures*, 25 (7): 739–55.

Geels, F. (2005) 'Processes and Patterns in Transitions and System Innovations: Refining the Co-evolutionary Multi-level Perspective', *Technological Forecasting and Social Change*, 72 (6): 681–96.

Geels, F. and Schot, J. (2007) 'Typology of Sociotechnical Transition Pathways', *Research Policy*, 36 (3): 399–417.

Gelcich, S., Hughes, T., Olsson, P., Folke, C., Defeo, O., Fernandez, M., Foale, S., Gunderson, L., Rodriguez-Sickert, C. and Scheffer, M. (2010) 'Navigating Transformations in Governance of Chilean Marine Coastal Resources', *Proceedings of the National Academy of Sciences*, 107 (39): 16794–99.

Gowers, T. and Nielsen, M. (2009) 'Massively Collaborative Mathematics', *Nature*, 461 (7266): 879–81.

Granovetter, M.S. (1973) 'The Strength of Weak Ties', *American Journal of Sociology*, 95 (3): 1360–80.

Head, B. (2008) 'Wicked Problems in Public Policy', *Public Policy*, 3 (2): 101–18.

Hertel, G., Niedner, S. and Herrmann, S. (2003) 'Motivation of Software Developers in Open Source Projects: An Internet-based Survey of Contributors to the Linux Kernel', *Research Policy*, 32 (7): 1159–77.

Homer-Dixon, T. (2001) *The Ingenuity Gap: Can We Solve the Problems of the Future?* London: Random House.

Howe, J. (2006) 'The Rise of Crowdsourcing', *Wired Magazine*, June (14): 1–5.

Kemp, R., Schot, J. and Hoogma, R. (1998) 'Regime Shifts to Sustainability through Processes of Niche Formation: The Approach of Strategic Niche Management', *Technology Analysis and Strategic Management*, 10 (2): 175–98.

Kittur, A. (2008) 'Harnessing the Wisdom of Crowds in Wikipedia: Quality through Coordination', *Proceedings of the 2008 ACM Conference on Computer Supported Cooperative Work*: 37–46.

Kittur, A., Lee, B. and Kraut, R.E. (2009) 'Coordination in Collective Intelligence: The Role of Team Structure and Task Interdependence', *Proceedings of the 27th International Conference on Human Factors in Computing Systems*: 1495–1504.

Kittur, A., Chi, E., Pendleton, B.A., Suh, B. and Mytkowicz, T. (2007) 'Power of the Few vs. Wisdom of the Crowd: Wikipedia and the rise of the bourgeoisie', Alt.CHI at CHI 2007; 2007 April 28–May 3; San Jose, CA.Laughlin, P. and Adamopoulos, J. (1982) 'Social Decision Schemes on Intellective Tasks', in Bradstatter, H., Darvis, J. and Stocker-Kreichgauers, G. (eds), *Group Decision Making*. London: Academic Press.

Levy, D. and Scully, M. (2007) 'The Institutional Entrepreneur as Modern Prince: The Strategic Face of Power in Contested Fields', *Organization Studies*, 28 (7): 971–91.

Mintzberg, H. (1991) 'The Effective Organization: Forces and Forms', *MIT Sloan Management Review*.

Moore, M.L. and Westley, F. (2011) 'Surmountable Chasms: Networks and Social Innovation for Resilient Systems', *Ecology and Society*, 16 (1): 5.

Mulgan, G., Tucker, S., Ali, R. and Sanders, B. (2007) *Social Innovation: What It Is, Why It Matters and How It Can Be Accelerated*. Oxford: Skoll Centre for Social Entrepreneurship.

Mumford, M. (2002) 'Social Innovation: Ten Cases from Benjamin Franklin', *Creativity Research Journal* (August 2013): 37–41.

Mumford, M. and Licuanan, B. (2004) 'Leading for Innovation: Conclusions, Issues, and Directions', *The Leadership Quarterly*, 15 (1): 163–71.

Mumford, M.D. and Moertl, P. (2003) 'Cases of Social Innovation: Lessons from Two Innovations in the 20th Century', *Creativity Research Journal*, 15 (2–3): 261–66.

Mustonen, M. (2003) 'Copyleft – The Economics of Linux and Other Open Source Software', *Information Economics and Policy*, 15 (1): 99–121.

Nielsen, M. (2011) *Reinventing Discovery: The New Era of Networked Science*. Princeton, NJ: Princeton University Press.

Nielsen, M. (2012) *Reinventing Discovery: The New Era of Networked Science*. Princeton, NJ: Princeton University Press.

Olsson, P., Gunderson, L.H., Carpenter, S.R., Ryan, P., Lebel, L., Folke, C. and Holling, C. S (2006) 'Shooting the Rapids: Navigating Transitions to Adaptive Governance of Social-Ecological Systems', *Ecology and Society*, 11 (1): 18.

Pierre, J. and Peters, B.G. (2005) *Governing Complex Societies: Trajectories and Scenarios*. Basingstoke: Palgrave Macmillan.

Polymath, D. (2009) 'A New Proof of the Density Hales-Jewett Theorem', *Arxiv preprint arXiv:0910.3926*: 1–34.

Pulinger, K. (2007) 'Living with A Million Penguins: Inside the Wiki-novel', theguardian.com. *The Guardian*. Available at: http://www.theguardian.com/books/booksblog/2007/mar/12/livingwithamillionpenguins [Accessed 30 September 2013].

Rushkoff, D. (2003) *Open Source Democracy*. London: Demos.

Schot, J. and Geels, F.W. (2007) 'Niches in Evolutionary Theories of Technical Change', *Journal of Evolutionary Economics*, 17 (5): 605–22.

Slaughter, A.-M. (2004) *A New World Order*. Princeton, NJ: Princeton University Press.

Smith, A. (2006) 'Green Niches in Sustainable Development: The Case of Organic Food in the United Kingdom', *Environment and Planning C: Government and Policy*, 24 (3): 439–58.

Smith, A., Stirling, A. and Berkhout, F. (2005) 'The Governance of Sustainable Socio-technical Transitions', *Research Policy*, 34 (10): 1491–510. Sunstein, C. (2006) *Infotopia*. Oxford: Oxford University Press.

Sunstein, C. (2007) *Republic.com 2.0*. Princeton, NJ: Princeton University Press.

Surowiecki, J. (2005) *The Wisdom of Crowds*. New York: Anchor, p. 336.

Tapscott, D. and Williams, A. (2010) *Macrowikinomics: Rebooting Business and the World*. London: Penguin Group.

Tapscott, D. and Williams, A. D. (2006) *Wikinomics: How Mass Collaboration Changes Everything*. Portfolio Hardcover.

Thomson, C. and Jakubowski, M. (2012) 'Toward an Open Source Civilization', *Innovations*, 7 (3): 53–70.

Tjornbo, O. (2013) *Complexity and Social Media: The Role of Virtual Social Networks in Supporting Democratic Responses to Complex Global Problems*. Phd Diss., Wilfrid Laurier University.

Tjornbo, O. and Westley, F.R. (2012) 'Game Changers: The Big Green Challenge and the Role of Challenge Grants in Social Innovation', *Journal of Social Entrepreneurship*, 3 (2): 37–41.

Tjornbo, O., Westley, F. and Riddell, D. (2010) *CASE STUDY The Great Bear Rainforest Story*. Social Innovation Generation Series (003). Available at: http://sig.uwaterloo.ca/highlight/case-study-the-great-bear-rainforest-story [Accessed 27 November 2014].Wellman, B. (1997) 'An Electronic Group Is Virtually a Social Network', in Kiesler, S. (ed.), *Culture of the Internet*. Hillsdale, NJ: Lawrence Erlbaum, pp. 179–205.

Westley, F. and Antadze, N. (2010) 'Making a Difference – Strategies for Scaling Social Innovation for Greater Impact', *The Innovation Journal: The Public Sector Innovation Journal*, 15 (2): 1–19.

Westley, F., Patton, M.Q. and Zimmerman, B. (2007) *Getting to Maybe: How the World Is Changed*. Toronto: Random House.

Westley, F., Tjornbo, O., Schultz, L., Olsson, P., Folke, C. and Crona., B. (2013) 'A Theory of Transformative Agency in Linked Social-Ecological Systems', *Ecology and Society* 18 (3): 27.Wheatley, M. and Frieze, D. (2006) 'Using Emergence to Take Social Innovation to Scale', *The Berkana Institute*: 1–7.

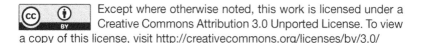

10
The Usefulness of Networks: A Study of Social Innovation in India

Lina Sonne

Introduction

India has seen a recent and rapid emergence of social enterprise as a potential alternative development channel. Social enterprises, defined in this chapter as organisations that combine a focus on financial sustainability with an explicit commitment to social impact through their products and/or employment and sourcing strategies, offer new and innovative ways of providing goods, services and livelihood opportunities for the poor. In other words, social enterprise is a hybrid – operating with the social impact objectives of an NGO and the market-driven financial aims of a for-profit firm. Social enterprise, therefore, involves the reconfiguring of social relations between the private sector market and civil society (Allen *et al.*, 2012; Koh *et al.*, 2012).

Innovation is central in social enterprises in emerging markets because many are creating new products and services, as well as accessing and, at times, creating new markets and value chains (Koh *et al.*, 2014; Rajan, 2013). However, to innovate and grow their social enterprises, entrepreneurs need to interact with other actors, including fellow entrepreneurs, suppliers, wholesalers, investors and incubators. They do so to access new information and knowledge, new sources of finance, new business connections along the value chain and new markets and customers.

Social enterprises in and around India's major cities (including Mumbai, Bangalore and Delhi) can increasingly rely on a range of support organisations to help them grow and flourish, including investors, incubators and networking platforms, as highlighted in a number of recent reports (Saltuk *et al.*, 2011; Allen *et al.*, 2012). However, accessing such financial and non-financial support can be difficult, especially outside of the large cities, as there are few formal mechanisms to connect with support or, even, information about the support that is actually available (Sonne, 2014).

Who the entrepreneur knows, therefore, becomes important for his or her ability to find suitable support to develop and grow a social enterprise. Networks, in other words, are central. In a country such as India, with multiple hierarchies, vast geographies and a large number of communities and religions, who you know and where you belong has historically been important. Today, while not as important as it has been, much of the activity in the economy still relies on trust, especially in the informal sector (Harris, 2002). Networks, and social ties, therefore, are particularly important not only to access new knowledge and financial and non-financial support but also because of the social capital that can be built.

This chapter[1] sets out to look at two interrelated areas: the role of networks for individual (social) entrepreneurs and the impact of these individual networks on social innovation at the system level. It does so by providing case studies of three social entrepreneurs and their organisations: Amit of Rose Computer Academy, Naveen of SMV Wheels and Vijaya of Under the Mango Tree. The case studies detail the kind of stakeholders on whom the three social entrepreneurs rely within their networks, as well as how those networks have evolved over time.

Social entrepreneurs and innovation

Social enterprises have attracted particular attention over the last decade or so (EU, 2013; OECD, 2011; Koh *et al.*, 2012; 2014). As agile, often self-sustaining non-state actors, they are particularly important as drivers of social innovation in the early stages when it often remains weakly institutionalised (OECD, 2011).

Social entrepreneurship and innovation are intricately intertwined since successful social entrepreneurs are continuously innovating when starting, growing and scaling their enterprises. Given the nascent stage of the social enterprise sector and the difficulty in balancing social needs with commercial requirements, many of the challenges social entrepreneurs face are innovation challenges (Sonne, 2014). These include the creation of a new product or service, building demand for a new product or service, reaching the market or accessing inputs.

Innovation – here defined as the continuous process of *upgrading* using new knowledge or a new combination of existing knowledge – can be seen to emerge from actors whose interactions, behaviour and patterns of learning are conditioned by institutions (Freeman, 1987;

Lundvall, 1992; Edquist, 1997). The institutions that facilitate the flow of information between various actors are, as a consequence, particularly important for the innovation ecosystem.

The importance of networks

Actors within the social enterprise ecosystem – the individuals or groups of individuals (or organisations) who are able to influence outcomes and cause change – are in many ways the repositories of knowledge and skills for social innovation in a fast-changing environment where there is limited codified information. Because knowledge is spread across actors, interaction is required for the different knowledge types to mix. It follows that collaborative knowledge accumulation and learning processes are essential bases for (socially) innovative activity (Arora, 2009). In other words, the performance of a social innovation process is a function of the structure of its knowledge-sharing network. Most information flows through informal channels, including word of mouth and an actor's social network (Cowan and Kamath, 2013).

An effective network structure – characterised as *wide* (a range of different sources of knowledge types, including geographical, sectoral and professional) and *open* (ensuring access to knowledge both within the network and outside it) – helps knowledge and information flow between different actors (Sonne, 2011; Castilla *et al.*, 2001). The size, positioning[2] and relationship structures of a network matter in its efficiency to generate new knowledge and support innovation.

The relationship between network characteristics and innovation outcomes is often complex. Dense network ties, for example, are likely to result in trust among actors since they sanction against opportunism (Coleman, 1988). Such trust is important because actors are likely to cooperate with those whom they trust and with whom they share stronger ties (Dakhli and Clerq, 2004).

Dense ties have their limits, however: social embeddedness helps build trust, but after a point it constrains actors in a network because the expected reciprocal behaviour may stop actors from seeking new knowledge, information and collaboration outside their network (Cowan and Kamath, 2012). Since dense networks can hinder innovation, Burt (1992) argued that, for innovation, the spaces between separate unconnected networks – 'structural holes' – are particularly useful since they allow actors to connect different knowledge networks. While strong ties build trust and coherence, weak ties are likely to provide the most opportunities for new knowledge to emerge (Cowan and Jonard, 2004). An ideal ecosystem would have both.

Furthermore, networks provide actors with social capital or 'the ability of actors to secure benefits by virtue of membership in social networks or other social structures' (Cowan and Kamath, 2012). The quality of an actor's contacts and his or her network as a whole indirectly affects his or her standing and, in turn, the ability to access resources.

For social entrepreneurs, networks are important in order to access new business opportunities and contacts, finance, suppliers, markets and customers, technology, knowledge and credibility (Partanen *et al.*, 2011; Semrau and Wernes, 2013). Credibility, through social capital, is especially important in the early stages of a venture to attract good senior management, employees and government support, for instance (Partanen *et al.*, 2011).

Entrepreneurs may rely on a number of different sources of connections. Gebreyeeus and Mohnen (2013) found that, in the Ethiopian footwear cluster, small entrepreneurs relied mostly on family and business contacts, such as suppliers and fellow entrepreneurs, for new information and knowledge. However, they also found that family, while trusted, was not primarily used for innovative activities. Rather, business and knowledge interactions occurred with the same contacts, so business networks doubled up as knowledge networks.

According to Gebreyeeus and Mohnen (2013), the most common reasons for entrepreneurs to collaborate were to exchange information and experiences. Ebbers (2013) noted that entrepreneurs emphasising networking were more likely to know of business or collaboration opportunities. Strong ties such as friends and family and former business associates are especially important in the early stages of a social enterprise, because they are low-cost and critical resources (Ebbers, 2013; Partanen *et al.*, 2011). Family ties also help to test the business in the early stages (Greve and Salaff, 2003). Further, according to Allinson *et al.* (2011), most networks are geographically close, especially for smaller and newer enterprises. Larger social enterprises may have a more international network.

When networks do not emerge spontaneously, agents acting as catalysts can facilitate their emergence (Ceglie and Dini, 1999). A study on social enterprise in the United Kingdom noted that network brokers, regional catalysts and entrepreneurship support organisations (Kimmel and Hull, 2012) helped galvanise networks within the sector. In the Indian social enterprise ecosystem, there are several such agents and recent years have seen the emergence of network platforms (Unconvention, Sankalp

Forum, Artha Platform), facilitators (Dasra, Idobro) and incubators (Villgro, UnLtd India). However, a separate study on entrepreneurs and incubators noted that, on the whole, incubators, while expected to act as facilitators or brokers, often did not do so and, even when they did link entrepreneurs to external partners, the success rate was very small (Ebbers, 2013). In fact, Allinson *et al.* (2011) noted that the social entrepreneurs found interaction with fellow social entrepreneurs to be more helpful than that with incubators.

Research methodology

In order to explore the role of networks for social entrepreneurs in India, primary and secondary data were collected and analysed. To study networks, an ego-centred method for data collection and analysis was employed (Greve and Salaff, 2003; Knoke and Kuklinski, 1982). This method looks at an individual's network of actors rather than the total system-level network. Respondents provided information on actors in their networks and on the nature of those relations. Ego-centred network methods are appropriate when data on the whole population is not available or only a small sample of the population is available (Greve and Salaff, 2003; Knoke and Kuklinski, 1982).

Interviews and visits to three social enterprises were undertaken to:

• Learn about each social entrepreneur's individual network in detail (such as the strong and the weak ties) and the roles that different actors play during the innovation process and the process of starting and growing a social enterprise;
• Learn how their networks evolved over time and how the use of networks had changed over time; and
• Understand the role of social enterprise support organisations.

The unit of analysis used was the social enterprise itself, and to select the three case studies, purposeful sampling was used. By using multiple cases, it is possible to study patterns, similarities and differences across cases while reducing the chance of coincidental occurrences (Eisenhardt, 1991; Yin, 2003). The criteria to select the three case studies were based on finding social entrepreneurs from a range of backgrounds (which means a different set of personal networks when starting out as social entrepreneurs), operating in different sectors and working in rural, peri-urban and urban areas across India. Since the aim was to understand the trajectory of relatively experienced social entrepreneurs from

Table 10.1 Case study selection

Enterprise	Sector	Rural/Urban	Entrepreneur's background
SMV Wheels	Cycle Rickshaw	Urban: Varanasi	Ran rickshaw organisation
Under the Mango Tree	Honey/ farming	Rural to Urban	Formerly World Bank
Rose Computer Academy	Education	Village/ peri-urban	Graduate/local IT teacher

Source: Author's compilation.

different backgrounds, this study focussed on entrepreneurs that had each received incubation support from UnLtd India.

Interviews were semi-structured and followed 'a conversation with a purpose' (Burgess, 1991) approach, which allowed interviewees to vary the detail of their answers and the order of the questions. The analysis followed a grounded and iterative process (Ritchie and Lewis, 2003). Each case is now considered in turn.

SMV Wheels

SMV Wheels, started by Naveen Krishna in Varanasi in 2010, offers rickshaw pullers the opportunity to become members of the SMV Wheels Cooperative and to apply for a loan to buy a cycle rickshaw. There are four different types of rickshaws: regular rickshaw (Rs 15,500; £155), rickshaw with double seating (Rs 15,500; £155), trolley (Rs 11,500; £112) and push cart (Rs 9,000; £90). Following the loan application and due diligence, SMV provides the rickshaw upfront and it is subsequently paid off in fifty-two instalments over one year, at Rs 200–300 (£2–£3) per week. The weekly payments are registered against the rickshaw puller's ID, providing him with a proven credit and payment record that can be used to access other loans or government schemes later. At the time of writing, there were 1,300 rickshaw pullers in the cooperative.

Naveen spent several years working for a government agency, setting up local rickshaw organisations through a government-funded programme and relied on this experience when setting up SMV Wheels:

I knew everything about this business, I had learnt about this business – I spent four to five years working with different models, so SMV Wheels was the outcome of all the interactions I had.

For example, a common issue with the government programme was that once project grant funding ended, the rickshaw organisation had to close. Naveen, therefore, chose to set up SMV Wheels as a for-profit entity. While Naveen had the knowledge and experience to set up an organisation supporting rickshaw pullers, he believed that the social enterprise idea came not from him but from rickshaw pullers: five rickshaw pullers he met when moving back to Varanasi co-funded his first rickshaw purchase so that he could start SMV Wheels.

Naveen's network

Naveen made a distinction between local networks that he needed to run his business day-to-day – including insurance and hospital partners, local government and customers – and the pan-Indian network that he used to attract funding and to learn how to grow and scale the enterprise.

Naveen relied on his social network a lot, especially when he started SMV Wheels. The most important person in this respect was a friend of his who was also his chartered accountant (CA) and one of his original investors. The CA helped register the company and took care of the legal formalities, turning it into a private limited company.

Naveen applied to business plan competitions through which he received initial funding as well as exposure and key contacts. The first competition he won was Village Capital with First Light Ventures. He then caught the attention of the founders of the KL Felicitas Foundation and First Light Ventures. This early interest led to a syndicate of five investors coming on board in 2012.

Naveen went on to participate in Dasra's accelerator programme through which he formed a good network of fellow social entrepreneurs. In addition, UnLtd India helped with capacity building, and a friend and mentor from UnLtd India was a central figure when it came to business strategy and advice. SMV Wheels also used networking platforms TiE Delhi and Action for India.

To gather information about the most useful rickshaw technology, Naveen and his team tapped into two sources: first, the rickshaw pullers themselves; and second, volunteer designers through a Dutch exchange programme and a collaboration with an Indian university, IIT-Guwahati. The SMV Rickshaw was a collaboration between the America-India Foundation and students at IIT-Guwahati.

Once Naveen knew which rickshaws and carts he wanted to offer to the rickshaw pullers, he set about searching for the best local manufacturers:

> We did market research for that, and we identified three market vendors in the beginning who were giving us good quality and

good price and then we started working with them. Finally we ended up working with only two vendors because of the quality. ... And that is how we arrived at the price and quality of the rickshaws.

To ensure their supply of rickshaws and materials was of a high standard, SMV Wheels closely interacted with suppliers and assemblers, even training manufacturers in how best to carry out their work, using engineering experts within their network.

Local stakeholders such as insurance companies and hospitals were important parts of the business network, as were local authorities. Naveen first approached the Municipal Corporation 'because you need the legal licenses first if you want to drive a rickshaw'.

Simultaneously, Naveen established partnerships with local hospitals and the insurance companies that reimburse hospital bills. SMV Wheels worked with a couple of other social enterprises to provide health-related services:

We have collaborated with Dove Foundation which works with HIV/ AIDS. They train our rickshaw pullers twice a month in HIV and other health and hygiene issues. We have also tied up with SEWA Mob in Lucknow to give them regular health insurance.

Banks were another local partner:

We send the rickshaw pullers' credit history to the banks and other microfinance organisations in Varanasi and recommend them for the different social government schemes.

Most of SMV Wheels' members who have become owners have got no-frills saving accounts in nationalised banks. Additionally, SMV Wheels introduced rickshaw pullers to government schemes, including housing, livelihood training and schooling for family members.

The customer network that SMV Wheels built up was used in several ways: to gather management information on rickshaw pullers; to mobilise new customers; as part of the due diligence process that the team carried out prior to giving a loan; and for monitoring post-loan to reduce the risk of default:

We don't go with the [loan application] to the family. We first go to the local tea stall and the paan stall and we come to learn about them [the applicant], then we talk to the neighbours and then finally we talk to the women members [of the family], tell them that this is the scheme your partner or husband is going to enter into. Just so that if the rickshaw pullers start drinking too much or gambling too much they can call us. The women help us in that, they say 'see, he is gambling too much'.

Under the Mango Tree

Under the Mango Tree (UTMT), started by Vijaya Pastala in 2007, links beekeeping farmers with markets for honey in cities through local partner organisations in rural areas and builds connections with supermarkets and high-end retailers in urban areas. UTMT operates a hybrid for-profit and NGO model, with a for-profit business purchasing and marketing honey as one arm, and an NGO training and supporting farmers to take up beekeeping as the other arm.

UTMT started as a proprietorship[3] in 2007, had its first sale in 2008, became a not-for-profit society in 2009 and registered as a private limited company in 2010. It is headquartered in Mumbai and operates across Western and Northern India. UTMT won the Village Capital business plan competition in 2009, became an incubatee with UnLtd India in 2009, received incubation support and funding from Villgro in 2012 and, at the time of writing, had recently been awarded the World Bank's Development Marketplace award.

Vijaya grew up and studied in Mumbai before moving to the United States for undergraduate and postgraduate studies. When she returned to India, she took on roles specialising in creating sustainable livelihoods for international foundations such as the Aga Khan Foundation, the KfW Bankengruppe and the World Bank. She based the business model of UTMT on this experience in working with livelihoods.

Vijaya's network

At UTMT, the wide range of networks and their central importance was striking, as Vijaya was a very active networker. The networks could be broadly and loosely divided between networks for access to marketing and retail based on Vijaya's social network, networks based on contacts from the social enterprise ecosystem for funding and scaling the enterprise, and value chain networks mostly drawn from a decade's worth of professional experience. Vijaya and UTMT spoke regularly to their contacts and continuously reenergised their most important networks.

In the early days while starting up, Vijaya relied heavily on her existing social network:

> The first network I called on would have been friends ... two people who were critical in my thinking were two friends I went to school with and then they followed me to Mount Holyoke College, US, and today they are on the board of the Society. One is a lawyer and one is a business woman.

Vijaya began contacting people who were doing similar work and she was, in turn, also contacted online by people interested in her work:

> One of the people I reach out to a lot is a guy who Googled me in 2010 because he was interested in beekeeping and thought it would be a great thing to do in India. He reached out to us and since 2010 he has been one of our patrons.

For fundraising Vijaya actively used her Board:

> There are a number of people on my board that are there for a reason. So I go to my board quite a lot now because they are people who have known me, who've seen the business, who understand.

The social enterprise ecosystem also connected her to mentors:

> When I got access to UnLtd India, I got access to a number of potential mentors and I reached out to all of them.

Vijaya found that as UTMT grew, private sector organisations came on board to provide support through their CSR programmes:

> Eidelweiss was one of our funders and now they provide us a lot of input – free staff time, employee engagements and so on. So my entire HR manual and job descriptions were developed by them. If we are struggling with HR we know we can talk to Eidelweiss because their HR team is available to us.

In rural areas, Vijaya primarily worked with local partners with whom she had already collaborated or who had helped her set up in her previous professional roles. The choice to work with large partners in rural areas was deliberate:

> We were very clear – we want to impact policy and for that objective it was important to work with partners that were well established. So we work with BIAF, BASIX, ATC, the Aga Khan Rural Support Program, Development Support Centre, the Taj Group of Hotels and so on.

While her local rural business partners were people that Vijaya had worked with in previous roles, her retail partners in urban centres in India were sourced from her wide Mumbai social network. When she wanted to make links with a premier retailer, she contacted a member of the owner family with whom she had gone to school. She received business advice early on from the founder of a retail brand whom she knew from school. She gained access to a large supermarket chain through one of her board members who knew the CEO. She was clear on using her social network: 'It is South Bombay, Cathedral School,[4] that network. It is very much there and I milk it. I went to MIT and I go to all the MIT alumni events'.

Rose Computer Academy

Amit Kataria's Rose Computer Academy in Haryana provides short computer courses, such as basic computing, accounting and graphic design, for villagers with little formal education. It was set up in a village outside the National Capital Region in 2006, with a little funding from a cousin and a friend, and became operational in 2007. In the first year the school had 119 students and, by 2013, a total of 5,000 students had completed a course there. There was at this stage a head office and three branches within a 12km radius. The organisation started out as a sole proprietorship, registered as a partnership firm in 2008 and as a private limited company in 2012. In 2013, Rose Computer Academy received funding from UnLtd India as an incubatee.

While in his final year at Delhi University, Amit returned to his village to teach basic computing with Literacy India in the mornings. Within a year he had started an entrepreneurship course with Dhriiti, an NGO that supports the formation of micro enterprises. While at Dhriiti, Amit created a plan to start a computer-training organisation.

Amit's network

Amit used his networks for general queries and did not divide it between access to finance or access to non-financial support, such as business advice and new information. Instead he distinguished between networks that he used to answer business, strategy and finance questions, for which his links were pan-Indian, and networks for customers (students) and suppliers (of IT infrastructure or teachers), which were local.

Amit's sister had taken computer training with Literacy India when the NGO first opened a branch in their village and told Amit about it when he returned to look for work. Literacy India, in turn, was a partner of Dhriiti, and Amit was convinced by his Literacy India colleagues to apply for its entrepreneurship course. Dhriiti was the first entrepreneurship organisation that helped Amit write a basic business plan and provide training on business skills: 'I didn't have any expertise but with Dhriiti I learned how you can start your business, how to create a budget and how you can create relationships with customers'. A key person at Dhriiti was one of the trainers who became a mentor: 'she was the first person to give me confidence and told me "Amit you can do it"'.

His mentor at Dhriiti brought Jagriti Yatra to Amit's attention, and he joined the eighteen-day train journey visiting social enterprises across India (on sponsorship), in 2009. This was a real turning point:

It was a great experience for me because I had lots of restrictions from my parents [because of a disability making walking difficult]. It was the first time I went by train, by bus, by cab. And today I am at a point where I can go anywhere.

The Jagriti Yatra built Amit's confidence and provided him with his first major network platform, connecting him to key people who have since been vital in providing access to social enterprise support:

In our group we had 20 Yatris and they belonged to all parts of India and we shared our expertise. Even now we have about 1,000 people networking on Jagriti's online [alumni] group. If I need anything, I can now get any kind of help from any part of India – I just write a message.

Amit used the online forum when he went to Bangalore, asking fellow alumni to put him in touch with Infosys. He was connected to Infosys, Yahoo and Dell.

Another person he met at the Yatra was from Intellecap, and persuaded him to apply for the Sankalp Forum Award.[5] A second person from the Yatra was vital in helping him to capitalise on the doors that opened through Sankalp:

> One of the biggest changes in my life came when I met [my mentor]. We met on the train and he has spent the last one year [working] with me. That is why we are here now – I have learnt lots of things from him.

Amit's mentor was a chartered accountant and he helped Amit to write application forms, undertake initial communication with the social enterprise support network, and fundraise:

> From Sankalp I got connected with UnLtd India and he helped me present our case to them and talked to them. One of the biggest problems is the language barrier as my English wasn't good, so he handled everything.

UnLtd India subsequently invested in Rose Computer Academy in 2012.

Two additional organisations that became part of Amit's network through Sankalp were TiE Delhi and Dasra. Dasra's accelerator programme provided Amit with the opportunity to write, and present, a more detailed business plan. The other entrepreneurs who made up the Dasra cohort were a source of cheerleading, information and future collaborations.

To find qualified teachers to work in the Academy, Amit relied on three sets of networks: he picked bright graduates from his courses who were interested in teaching; he hired local people through word-of-mouth or advertisement; and he hired students from nearby Amity College. Lastly, the infrastructure upon which Rose Computer Academy relied – its computers – was supported locally:

> I take help from two persons: one of the guys has a hardware store so he looks after hardware things. The other provides sales support on devices ensuring efficient electricity usage.

Discussion: Networks of social enterprises

The three social enterprises relied on networks to access new knowledge, information and business strategy, access business partners along the value chain and access markets and customers, as summarised in Table 10.2.

Table 10.2   Summary of case studies' networks

	SMV Wheels	UTMT	Rose Computer Academy
Information, business strategy	UnLtd India supported in developing strategy and building the business. Alumni from Dasra Impact Programme provided advice. New rickshaw technology was developed with a Dutch CSR skills exchange programme and students at IIT-Guwahati.	UnLtd India gave Vijaya access to mentors. Former colleagues and friends acted as a sounding board. Her board was important for strategy. She received support through CSR initiatives like finance firm Eidelweiss.	Dhriiti taught Amit business strategy and business planning. UnLtd India helped with management. A key advisor wrote funding applications. A network of social entrepreneurs provided information and contacts.
Finance	Naveen first received finance via a Village Capital business plan competition. A syndicate later invested in SMV Wheels.	A business plan competition provided early funding, followed by incubator Villgro in 2012 and in 2013, World Bank's Development Marketplace.	Early on friends and family invested. UnLtd India provided finance to stabilise operations and expand.
Business partners along value chain	Naveen used local manufacturers and assemblers of rickshaws and partnered with local insurance firms and hospitals to offer medical cover.	Local partners supplied honey. These were large local NGOs Vijaya worked with or set up in her previous jobs.	A local foundation (NIT) provided certificates on completion of computer courses. A local dealer provided computer infrastructure.
Customers	Naveen built a network of rickshaw pullers through personal interaction. Five rickshaw pullers supported him financially and helped build the network. When signing new pullers, SMV visited family and friends to reduce risk.	Vijaya's customer network included large supermarket chains in India's main cities, accessed through Vijaya's personal network as well as networks of board members.	Rose Computer Academy's students were all based in local villages. He later found students through word-of-mouth, and employed a campaign manager to increase student numbers.
Confidence and day-to-day support	UnLtd India helped Naveen increase his business confidence, and the fellow entrepreneurs he met through the Dasra programme were also helpful.	Through Dasra and UnLtd India, Vijaya met social entrepreneurs and mentors that she relied on for day-to-day queries.	Dhriiti boosted Amit's confidence through mentoring. At Jagriti Yatra he met people who later supported him.

Source: Author's compilation.

The case studies showed that there was often no clear distinction between different kinds of networks. For example, often, key people were the same in networks for accessing new knowledge, advice and finance. Vijaya from UTMT, for instance, relied heavily on her board for advice on fundraising, but also for more general advice related to her expansion plans. Naveen of SMV Wheels relied on his friend and mentor at UnLtd India for both fundraising and knowledge connections.

However, networks used for fundraising, business strategy and new information were distinct from those used for business inputs along the value chain and for reaching customers. The value chain and market networks tended to be considerably more local, while the advice, information and finance networks were usually pan-Indian and often based in India's largest cities. Rose Computer Academy, for instance, had a highly localised business and customer network. SMV Wheels' business network of stakeholders providing value-added services, or government officials, was also local, based in Varanasi. However, UTMT's customer and business partner networks were not as localised as those of Rose Computer Academy or SMV Wheels, as UTMT generally relied on Vijaya's personal network, rather than contacts provided by the wider social enterprise support ecosystem. Having a personal network of contacts appeared, therefore, to be very important for the way in which social entrepreneurs were able to develop their businesses.

A less tangible area highlighted as important by all social entrepreneurs in the study was personal support and confidence boosting – being able to talk to somebody who understands what the social entrepreneur is going through. Here, all case study entrepreneurs emphasised the vital role played by networks of fellow social entrepreneurs.

Change: The evolutionary nature of networks

While each social entrepreneur's networks varied, all relied on social networks (including professional networks built in previous jobs) when starting up their social enterprise. This meant that the social entrepreneur's background mattered a great deal when it came to how useful his or her existing network was (see Table 10.3). For example, Vijaya was able to rely extensively on her social network from school, as well as on her professional network from previous roles, in building both the urban and rural parts of her business. Amit, on the other hand, relied considerably on the contacts that he made during various business plan competitions and social enterprise programmes.

Table 10.3   Change in networks over time

	SMV Wheels	UTMT	Rose Computer Academy
Starting out	Friends were important, especially the chartered accountant who helped register the company and process all legal formalities.	Vijaya relied heavily on friends from college and former colleagues. She also searched online and contacted people working on similar issues.	Amit relied on friends and key people, including his brother who co-funded, a friend and a cousin who invested, and a trainer from Dhriiti, who gave him confidence.
Now	Incubators and investors became important advisors. Naveen still relied on his personal network (including old and new friends and fellow entrepreneurs). SMV's network revolved around Naveen.	UTMT expanded its network around growth, with the board playing an important role. Other social entrepreneurs provided peer support and advice. Networks became less centred around Vijaya, as senior staff had their own networks.	Amit's brother was still important, as was the friend who invested. Other important people were his advisor and mentor, and peers from Jagriti, UnLtd India and Dasra. Rose's networks still centred around Amit.
Change	Personal networks and friends became less important compared with professional contacts, but for local hires, Naveen still relied on personal contacts. The contacts and advice he looked for became increasingly specific.	Vijaya estimated UTMT's network had changed from 70% social network when starting out to 40% at the time of writing. As the business grew, she sought more specialised or nuanced advice.	Amit's network was family and friend-focussed at the start and he was not part of the social enterprise or start-up ecosystem. Through forums and programmes he made a lot of contacts that were now important for his business.

Source: Author's compilation.

In terms of progress in the network, Amit from Rose Computer Academy initially relied almost exclusively on his local social network, with his friend, brother and cousin helping him to launch the enterprise. However, as he progressed through different social enterprise support programmes, he made contacts who then became cornerstones of his networks. For example, while at the Jagriti Yatra, he met somebody who invited him to the Sankalp Awards; at Sankalp, he met UnLtd

India, which subsequently invested in him and Dasra, which took him on as a fellow and improved his business plan. He was able to take advantage of these opportunities because of meeting his partner and mentor at the Jagriti Yatra.

Vijaya of UTMT had a very strong professional and social network prior to starting her enterprise, built during her studies in the United States, work experience with international foundations and the World Bank, and growing up in South Mumbai. Taken together, these put her in a unique position to use her network to further her enterprise from the start. Naveen of SMV Wheels also used his professional background extensively when starting his social enterprise, since he had previously worked with a government agency setting up rickshaw organisations.

All the social entrepreneurs noted that their networks had become more heavily based on professional sources, reducing reliance on friends and family. Vijaya of UTMT pointed out that this was partly because the more her enterprise evolved, the more she needed specialist advice. Naveen of SMV Wheels also emphasised that targeted, specific and concrete help and advice was most useful now, while when starting out, he had found more general advice helpful.

Lastly, it is noteworthy that in many cases there were specific key people or organisations acting as triggers for the social enterprises. For Naveen from SMV Wheels, meeting a member of UnLtd helped him create a viable business model, while taking part in the business plan competition led to him meeting the founders of the KL Felicitas Foundation and First Light Ventures, who later provided access to finance. Meanwhile, Amit of Rose Computer Academy found an advisor and mentor through the Jagriti Yatra. This individual was able to help Amit apply for Sankalp and UnLtd India's incubation programme, since Amit did not speak English well at that point.

Individual networks and system impact

The case studies show that support organisations have a clear role to play in creating networks, as seen by the example above of UnLtd India, the accelerator programme Dasra and the social enterprise tour Jagriti Yatra. Once created, these networks become powerful tools in their own right and appear to be managed more by the social entrepreneurs themselves, further strengthening the network. They have an impact on the social enterprise ecosystem as a whole in three ways: social entrepreneurs support each other and provide advice; they collaborate; and they expand their networks further across the country.

The importance of the support that social entrepreneurs provide to each other has been documented in the literature (Allinson *et al.*, 2011), and this study found that social entrepreneurs often find the advice of fellow entrepreneurs the most useful. For instance, Vijaya from UTMT noted that she spoke to fellow social entrepreneurs on a very regular basis because they were the only ones that understood the journey she was taking.

Lastly, all three entrepreneurs found the use of social enterprise networks very helpful for day-to-day advice and support. Amit in particular pointed out that the large alumni network of Jagriti Yatra was a very good source for contacts across India. In that sense, the network expanded individual networks to provide a much greater reach across India. This is especially important for social entrepreneurs working out of smaller cities and towns across India, who often miss out on the important networking, both formal and informal, that happens in the major Indian cities.

Conclusion

This chapter set out to improve the understanding of how innovative social enterprises use networks. In spite of coming from very different backgrounds, all the social entrepreneurs found that their networks changed substantially over time. In the beginning they generally relied more heavily on family and friends, while later they had more professional contacts on board, whether as mentors, investors and/or Board members. It was striking how important the social entrepreneurs found the connection to other social entrepreneurs as a source of day-to-day support and best practice advice. The impact of individual networks went beyond the individual social entrepreneurs to affect the wider social enterprise ecosystem by multiplying through network platforms and creating large networks of actors within the social enterprise ecosystem, such as the Jagriti Yatra network or the Dasra cohort network.

The case studies highlighted that entrepreneurs starting from very different backgrounds can gain access to support that enables them to become financially sustainable social enterprises. Nevertheless, the case studies also showed that it can be difficult to access support for those not based in one of India's major cities, where the social enterprise support ecosystem is concentrated. Further, there is a bias towards the use of English among the organisations providing financial and non-financial support for social entrepreneurs (such as incubators and impact investors). Increasingly, programmes and application forms are provided in Hindi and regional languages, but the fact that English remains the primary language is likely to make it difficult for some social entrepreneurs to access support, since the vast majority of people in India do not speak fluent English.

Lastly, the case study organisations showed that innovation and innovating social enterprises do not grow in isolation but are dependent on many different connections, knowledge flows and collaborative efforts. All three social enterprises collaborated extensively with not-for-profit and for-profit organisations in order to execute their activities, as well as during the innovation process.

Notes

1. This chapter is based on a project and longer chapter on networks of social enterprises for Villgro Innovation Foundations, financed by IDRC.
2. Actors include, for example, entrepreneurs, suppliers, traders, wholesalers, end users, investors, incubators, banks, self-help groups, cooperatives, competitors, NGOs and government.
3. A sole trader for tax and legal purposes.
4. Cathedral School is a well-known private school in Mumbai, and South Mumbai is a well-to-do part of the city.
5. Sankalp is an annual social enterprise award and forum organised by Intellecap.

References

Allen, S., Bhatt, A, Ganesh, U. and Kulkarni, N.K. (2012) *On the Path to Sustainability and Scale: A Study of India's Social Enterprise Landscape*. Mumbai: Intellecap.

Allinson, G., Braidford, P., Houston, M., Robinson, F. and Stone, I. (2011) *Business Support for Social Enterprises: Findings from a Longitudinal Study*. London: Department for Business, Innovation and Skills.

Arora, S. (2009) *Knowledge Flows and Social Capital: A Network Perspective on Rural Innovation*. PhD Thesis. Maastricht: University of Maastricht and UNU-MERIT.

Burgess, R. (1991) *In the Field: An introduction to Field Research*. New York: Taylor & Francis.

Burt, R.S. (1992) *Structural Holes: The Social Structure of Competition*. Cambridge, MA: Harvard University Press.

Castilla, E., Hwang, H., Granovetter, E. and Granovetter, M. (2001) 'Social Networks in Silicon Valley', in Lee, C.H. (ed.), *The Silicon Valley Edge*. Stanford, CA: Stanford University Press.

Ceglie, G. and Dini, M. (1999) SME Cluster and Network Development in Developing Countries: The Experience of UNIDO. UNIDO Research Report. Vienna: UNIDO.

Coleman, J.S. (1988) 'Social Capital in the Creation of Human Capital', *The American Journal of Sociology*, 94: S95–S120.

Cowan, R. and Jonard, N. (2004) 'Network Structure and the Diffusion of Knowledge', *Journal of Economic Dynamics and Control*, 28: 1557–75.

Cowan, R. and Kamath, A. (2012) Informal Knowledge Exchanges under Complex Social Relations: A Network Study of Handloom Clusters in Kerala, India. UNU-MERIT Working Paper No. 2012–031.

Cowan, R. and Kamath, A. (2013) Interactive Knowledge Exchanges under Complex Social Relations: A Simulation Model. UNU-MERIT Working Paper No. 04-2013.

Dakhli, M. and de Clerq, D. (2004) 'Human Capital and Innovation: A Multi-Country Study', *Entrepreneurship and Regional Development*, 16: 107–28.

Ebbers, J. (2013) 'Networking Behavior and Contracting Relationships Among Entrepreneurs in Business Incubators', *Entrepreneurship Theory & Practice*, 38 (5): 1159–81.

Edquist, C. (1997) *Systems of Innovation: Technologies, Institutions and Organizations*. London: Pinter.

Eisenhardt, K.M. (1991) 'Better Stories and Better Constructs: The Case for Rigor and Comparative Logic', *Academy of Management Review*, 16: 620–27.

EU (2013) *European Commission Guide to Social Innovation*. Brussels: European Commission.

Freeman, C. (1987) *Technology Policy and Economic Performance: Lessons from Japan*. London; New York: Pinter.

Gebreyeesus, M. and Mohnen, P. (2013) 'Innovation Performance and Embeddedness in Networks: Evidence from the Ethiopian Footwear Cluster', *World Development*, 41: 302–16.

Greve, A. and Salaff, J.W. (2003) 'Social networks and entrepreneurship', *Entrepreneurship Theory and Practice*, 28: 1–22.

Harris, J. (2002) *On Trust and Trust in Indian Businesses: Ethnographic Explorations*. LSE Working Paper Series, 02–35. London: LSE.

Kimmel, C and Hull, B. (2012) 'Ecological Entrepreneurship Support Networks: Roles and Functions for Conservation Organizations', *Geoforum*, 43 (2012): 58–67.

Knoke, D. and Kuklinski, J.H. (1982) *Network Analysis*. Newbury Park, CA: Sage University Papers 28. Series: Quantitative Applications in the Social Sciences.

Koh, H., Karamchandani, A. and Katz, R. (2012) *From Blueprint to Scale: The Case for Philanthropy in Impact Investing*. Monitor Group & Acumen Fund.

Koh, H., Hegde, N. and Karamchandani, A. (2014) *Beyond the Pioneer: Getting Inclusive Industries to Scale*. Monitor Group and Deloitte Touche Tohmatsu India.

Lundvall, B-A. (1992) *National Systems of Innovation: Towards a Theory of Innovation and Interactive Learning*. London: Pinter.

OECD (2011) *Fostering Innovation to Address Social Challenges: Workshop Proceedings*. Paris: OECD.

Partanen, J., Chetty, S. and Rajala, A. (2011) 'Innovation Types and Network Relationships', *Entrepreneurship Theory and Practice*, 38 (5): 1027–55.

Rajan, T.A. (ed.) (2013) *India Venture Capital and Private Equity Report 2013: Convergence of Patience, Purpose and Profit*. Madras: Indian Institute of Management.

Ritchie, J. and Lewis. J. (2003) *Qualitative Research Practice: A Guide for Social Science Students and Researchers*. London: Sage.

Saltuk, Y., Bouri, A. and Leung, G. (2011) *Insight into the Impact Investment Market*. JP Morgan and GIIN.

Semrau, T. and Wernes, A. (2013) 'How Exactly Do Network Relationships Pay Off? The Effects of Network Size and Relationship Quality on Access to Start-Up Resources', *Entrepreneurship Theory and Practice*, 38 (3): 501–25.

Sonne, L. (2011) *Innovation in Finance to Finance Innovation*. PhD Thesis. Maastricht: University of Maastricht and UNU-MERIT.

Sonne, L. (2014) *Regional Social Enterprise Ecosystems in India: A Conceptual Framework*. Mumbai: Villgro and Okapi.

Yin, R. (2003) *Case Study Research: Design and Methods*. California: Sage.

OPEN

Conclusion: The Task of the Social Innovation Movement*

Roberto Mangabeira Unger†

The social innovation movement: its defining impulse

Social innovation is a practice that is becoming a worldwide movement. I address it in its better nature and take it at its most ambitious. In this spirit I consider in turn the circumstance, the work, the direction and the methods of the movement.

The shared impulse of all versions and understandings of social innovation is the effort to design initiatives in a particular part of society – an organisation, a practice or an area of activity – that signal a promising path of wider social change even as they meet a pressing need. The innovations that the movement seeks to advance convert experiments designed to solve social problems into transformative ambition: the effort to change some part of the established arrangements and assumptions of society. The focus of the movement falls on problems that have not been solved by either the state or the market.

The hopeful truth, from which all versions of this practice begin, is that the established ways in which society provides for its own revision never exhaust the ways in which it can be changed. This truth, in turn, rests on two facts: one about society; the other about us.

The fact about society is that our social life contains more than the market and the state. Social experience is never just the sum of our economic and political activities. Our conceptions of a market economy or of a political democracy are always wedded to flawed, relatively accidental institutional arrangements. We must occasionally resist and redesign

---

*This chapter is the revised transcript of a talk given on November 15, 2013 at the Social Frontiers Conference in London.
† © Roberto Mangabeira Unger

these arrangements for the sake of interests and ideals that they fail to satisfy. Meanwhile, we retain an inexhaustible reservoir of vision and of contrariness. Once this power of resistance enlists practical ingenuity and living social forces in its service, it can do more than may seem feasible. The fact about us is that we are the beings who never entirely fit into the social and conceptual worlds that we build and inhabit. There is always more in us than in them. Although we can improve them, we can never improve them enough to lose reasons to resist them. We can – indeed we must – deny them the last word, and keep it for ourselves. We can – indeed we should – see, do and create more than they countenance.

Social innovation is the creation of a new way of acting and cooperating in some part of society. As society is divided into distinct domains that are arranged according to different rules and conceptions – the worlds of business, of politics, of social services, of the 'third sector', of the academy or of the media – the practice of social innovation must always begin in one of these areas. It must identify a problem that has not been solved in that corner of society and that cannot be solved by its conventional practices and established institutions. It must exemplify, through a practical initiative, a way of understanding the problem and of dealing with it.

It must do its work in such a way that the initiative does more than address the immediate problem. It must also suggest a path for the reform of the part of social life in which it began, with implications for the larger society. For example, if it begins as business it must be successful as business and yet effective as well in the advancement of a concern that business, as now organised, commonly fails to share. Its innovations must point beyond themselves.

Today the opportunity for such a practice is likely to be greatest in departments of social life that are orphaned by both the state and the market, or that lie in a netherworld between economic and political action, or that require initiatives that neither business firms nor political parties seem capable of conceiving and promoting.

Such an activity cannot take place unless it has an agent. Social regimes are organised to reproduce themselves. If they allowed no room for their own reshaping, social innovation would be impossible – except through individual and collective rebellion, in the favouring circumstance of crisis. If they had done much more to open themselves to challenge and change than they have, social innovation might be unnecessary. It is in the real, intermediate situation that social innovation becomes both needed and possible as a practice bidding to become a movement. It takes its cue from the failure of political parties and of business firms, and more generally of all established organisations in society, to do what needs to be done to address the unresolved problems of society.

Thus arises the figure of the social innovator or social entrepreneur, the civic activist – the missing and self-created agent of the social innovation movement. He seizes on a role already established in business, politics or any other part of social life. However, in seizing on it, he uses this role incongruously. He bends and stretches it. He must be both an insider and an outsider, a practical visionary. He offers tangible down payments on another future. He envelops his tangible initiatives in a discourse promising more and anchors his promises of more in something that people can see and touch now.

It is a remarkable feature of a wide range of contemporary societies that they produce an unlimited stock of candidates for this role: men and women who are unresigned to 'the long littleness of life' and determined to place their practical powers at the disposal of a larger aspiration. These people are the lifeblood of the social innovation movement. They exist as who they are before they have a programme or know what to do. Most of them come from a faction of the professional-business class in both richer and poorer countries. Their outlook combines unwillingness to spend their lives rising through the ranks of established business and political organisations with disbelief in the dogmas that have served progressives and leftists in the past. Their public quarrel is with society. Their private quarrel is with the passage of time and the waste of life – of their own lives as well as of the lives of others.

As they struggle and search, they face two initial and connected problems. The first problem is that the empire will strike back. Their endeavours will be either suppressed or accommodated, and, if accommodated, reconciled with the established regime, unless the small changes result over time in bigger changes and the many focused actions converge and cumulate. The second problem is that they require if not a programme, at least a direction. Ingenuity is indispensable. There is, however, no substitute for vision.

Minimalist and maximalist understandings of the social innovation movement

The minimalist view of the movement is that it is headquartered in civil society and deals with civil society. According to this view, society has three large spheres: business, politics, and the residual realm of civil society, influenced and supported, but also orphaned or victimised, by both politics and business. We should think of the social innovation movement as encased within this third world – sometimes called 'the third sector' – from which it emerges and to which it is addressed.

A corollary of this minimalist conception of the setting and of the object of the movement is that it need have no comprehensive project for society. Its properly piecemeal changes are then best seen as a complement to the limitations of both business and politics.

The label 'third sector' has a reference: it refers to the world of associations and foundations, of philanthropy and do-gooding, of pro-bono activity, under secular or religious auspices, and of public and social services, insofar as they are organised from the bottom-up by society as well as provided top-down by the state. Its ideological affinity is with the traditions that are hostile to both statism and economism, to state socialism and to the established varieties of the market economy that we call capitalism. Its resonance is with solidarity and communitarianism or, more generally, with a discourse critical of classical liberalism. It nevertheless has affinities with the tradition within classical liberalism that prizes voluntary associations as well as with the strand within socialist thinking that proposes a non-statist socialism.

The minimalist view of the social innovation movement has the attraction of modesty. It is easy to mistake modesty for realism.

There is a fundamental objection to the minimalist view. Taken on its own terms, it represents both a failure of insight and a loss of opportunity.

It is a failure of insight because the truth that the powers of self-reconstruction of society are not exhausted by the present practices of the market economy and party politics fails to tell the whole story. What those practices exclude is not some potential action narrowly cabined within a third sector of life that is neither market nor state. It is rather a penumbra of accessible insight and action surrounding every aspect of present social experience. To remain blind to that penumbra, and to accept the present political and economic arrangements as the unsurpassable horizon within which the social innovation movement must act, is to reduce the movement to the job of putting a human face on an unreconstructed world. Such is already the perspective of conventional social democracy, of the fossilised forms of the confessional religions and of a secular humanism devoted to the political pieties of the day. For such work, we need no movement.

It is a loss of opportunity because there is now throughout much of the world a chance to do something more than to humanise a reality that we feel powerless to reimagine and remake: to develop institutions, practices and activities increasing our powers of agency, of individual and collective self-construction. Solidarity and community on such a basis mean something different from solidarity and community as compensations for the lack of those goods.

There is nevertheless a legitimate point to the minimalist view that we must salvage from the illusions surrounding it. It is that although the present arrangements of business and of politics help shape all social life, they do not shape all of it equally. There are aspects of our experience, including our political and economic experience, that bear this influence more lightly. Such is the netherworld between politics and business in which we are doing something other than seeking and wielding governmental power or making and spending money. It is in this netherworld that the movement has the best chance to advance.

I here defend a maximalist view of the work to be done. According to this view, in whatever sectors the movement may take its infant steps and whatever issues it may begin by addressing, its concern should be the whole of society, of its institutional arrangements and of its dominant forms of consciousness.

Taken at its maximalist best, the social innovation movement must undertake the small initiatives that have the greatest potential to foreshadow, by persuasive example, the transformation of those arrangements and of that consciousness. It must launch such initiatives even as it seeks to redress recognised and immediate problems in a particular piece of society. Unless the horizon of transformative ambition expands to include the economic and political institutions, as well as the beliefs informing and sustaining them, the effort cannot succeed. It will be reduced to a minimalist role even if it began with maximalist aspirations. The movement had better heed the perennial maxim of those who would change the world: break or be broken.

The circumstance

We live under a dictatorship of no alternatives: only a small and inadequate set of ways of organising different fields of social life is on offer in the world. The goal of the social innovation movement, under its maximalist understanding, is to help overthrow that dictatorship.

In this situation progressives come to believe that the preservation of the essentials of the social-democratic settlement of the mid-20th century is the best for which they can hope. They retreat to what they take to be their last line of defence: the preservation of a high level of social entitlements, paradoxically funded by the regressive and indirect taxation of consumption. The problem, however, is not the retreat from that settlement so much as it is the settlement itself. The historical achievement of European social democracy – the most widely admired model of social and economic organisation in the world – was massive investment in people by the state. From the outset, the paramount limitation of social democracy has been that it abandoned any effort to reshape production and power: the institutional arrangements of the market and of democracy.

Today, none of the major failings of contemporary societies, richer or poorer, can be redressed within the limits of the social-democratic compromise. Its institutional conservatism and its passive acceptance of the dominant forms of consciousness condemn that compromise to near impotence. The best to which it can aspire is to soften the realities that it is unable to change or even to defy.

Among the problems that cannot be solved within the bounds of contemporary social democracy or social liberalism are all those besetting contemporary societies, including the advanced democracies of Western Europe and North America. Consider the following open list. First is the new form of the hierarchical segmentation of economies: the exclusion of the major part of the labour force from the new vanguards of production – production as permanent innovation, as experimentalism incarnate – that increasingly take the place of traditional mass production. The majority of workers are relegated to make-work. Second is the reorganisation of labour on a global scale on the basis of networks of decentralised contractual arrangements and the consequent consignment of increasing parts of the labour force to a precarious status, for which trade unionism and collective bargaining serve as inadequate antidotes. Third is the disengagement of finance from service to the real economy, accompanied by its usurpation of the lion's share of profit and talent. Rather than being a good servant, it becomes a bad master. Fourth is the ineffectiveness of using easy money and easy credit as a substitute for arrangements and policies that democratise the economy on the supply side, rather than just on the demand side. Such policies and arrangements would require an institutional redesign of the market economy, not simply its regulation by the state or the attenuation of its inequalities through retrospective, compensatory redistribution. Fifth is the failure of the present way of providing public services – the provision of low-quality, standardised services by a governmental bureaucracy – to distribute the public goods that the most advanced forms of production and culture require. Sixth is the lack of any form of universal public education that would equip more than a meritocratic elite to thrive in the midst of permanent destabilisation and to reshape received knowledge. Seventh is the insufficiency of money transfers organised by the state as social entitlements to provide an adequate basis for social cohesion, especially in societies that can no longer lean on the crutch of ethnic and cultural homogeneity. Eighth is the continuing dependence of the flawed, low-energy democracies of the present day on crisis as the condition of change and the consequent perpetuation of the rule of the dead over the living.

What these problems have in common is that they depend for their resolution on change – piecemeal and gradual in method but never-theless radical in ambition – in the institutional structure of society. In particular, they depend on change in the way of organising produc-tion and power. The relinquishment of any hope of changing both those arrangements and the ways of thinking with which they are associated was part of what defined the social-democratic settlement in the first place.

The reform programme embraced with either confident alacrity or sullen resignation by the governing elites of the advanced societies is no such attempt to overcome the limits of historical or chastened social democracy. It is simply the effort to make it more 'flexible' by enhanc-ing the prerogatives of capital in the name of economic necessity.

To rebel against this circumstance and against this response is one of the starting points of the social innovation movement.

In its search for an alternative approach the movement confronts, however, a characteristic contemporary conundrum. Like the socialists and liberals of the 19th century, we contemporaries may recognise the need for structural solutions. Unlike them, however, we can no longer believe in structural dogmas: in definitive blueprints for the organisa-tion of society. Our arrangements must, therefore, be corrigible in the light of experience; such corrigibility must become their most impor-tant attribute. Our initiatives must be informed by structural vision without succumbing to structural dogmatism.

The work and its enabling conditions

The most important resource that the activists of the social innova-tion movement have at their disposal is the multitude of small-scale experiments – the countless rebellions, discoveries and inventions – that abound throughout the world. Their task is to identify the most promising of these experiments as points of departure for the develop-ment of more consequential alternatives: the kinds of alternatives that the servants of the dictatorship of no alternatives would rather not brook and seek preemptively to discredit.

The movement cannot perform this role without marking a direction for itself and for society. How it can reconcile the demarcation of a direction with the repudiation of dogmatic institutional blueprints is a conundrum that I next address.

The first criterion of choice can be readily recognised because it has the closest affinity with the practices of the movement and with the motivations of its activists: the enhancement of agency – of the ability of ordinary men and women to reshape their world. Only one word can do justice to this ideal: freedom. Those innovations must have priority that contribute most to freedom – not the theoretical freedom of the philosophers but rather freedom in practice, expressed in the ability to turn the tables on one's social and cultural setting.

The vast Brownian motion of the innovations already present in the world provides material for this pursuit. Three connected facts about society ensure that there is prospect of success.

A first enabling condition for the execution of the task of the social innovation movement is that all functional imperatives of social life – such as the use of new technologies to accelerate the pace of economic growth – can always be realised through alternative institutional pathways. There is never a one-to-one relation between a functional constraint or opportunity and a way of organising the economy and the polity. Look around you and you see in the contradictions of the established social order vestiges that may also be prophecies and small breakthroughs that may be turned into larger ones.

The existing variations suggest different ways to deal with the constraints and take advantage of the opportunities. We can rarely know beforehand which will prove most beneficial. Some may be easier to implement in the short term; often, however, they will prove less fertile in the long term. Once you appreciate the range of possible response, and act on this recognition, the established regime of social life begins to lose its aura of naturalness.

A second enabling condition is that in dealing with the functional imperatives, in seizing the opportunities, in facing the constraints and in reckoning with what the economists call exogenous shocks, there always exists, in every historical circumstance, an alternative to the path of least resistance. The path of least resistance is the one minimising disturbance to the dominant interests and to the ruling preconceptions. The path of least resistance will, by definition, be the easiest one to travel. To create alternatives to the path of least resistance is the point of transformative thought and practice. It is, thus, also the concern of the social innovation movement. Those who would create such alternatives must use existing variation – the crowd of little epiphanies – as their chief resource.

Any view of society and of its present that disregards the existence of alternatives to the path of least resistance puts mystification in the place of insight. It is retrospective rationalisation, a right-wing Hegelianism, rationalising the real, and cannot serve as a guide to action. To understand a state of affairs is to grasp what it can become under different provocations and interventions. By this criterion, it is mystification rather than insight that now prevails across the social sciences.

A third enabling condition is that there are always two main sets of ways of defining and defending group interests, including the interests of social classes or of segments of the labour force. It would do us no good for there to be alternatives in principle to the path of least resistance if real people in real groups and classes lacked grounds to identify these alternatives with their interests.

Some ways of defining and defending a group or class interest are institutionally conservative and socially exclusive. They take existing arrangements – including both the social and the technical division of labour – for granted. They cling to the niche that a given group now occupies. They see other groups, neighbouring in social and economic space, as rivals.

Other ways of defining and defending a group or class interest are institutionally transformative and socially solidaristic. They see the interest advanced through a change of arrangements that may ultimately result in its reinterpretation. They define as allies groups formerly seen as rivals. It is because group interests can be defined and defended in this way that alternatives to the path of least resistance have a fighting chance and that the social innovation movement can hope to find friends in the real forces of society.

The direction

A consequence of the maximalist understanding of the movement is that its initiatives and experiments should exemplify and foreshadow a direction for society. The movement need not and should not commit itself to a single programme for any of the societies in which the innovators act, much less to a shared worldwide programme. The innovators must nevertheless have a direction. Their direction can result only from the path that they propose for society.

Each group of participants in the movement must therefore struggle to see the social experiments that it tries to develop as the foreshadowing of such a direction. And each such direction must be defined, tentatively, by a dialectic between the innovations in practical arrangements and in consciousness for which it fights and the vision animating those initiatives. Music, not architecture, and sequences, not blueprints, are the handiwork of the programmatic imagination.

The two most important attributes of the ideas from which it seeks guidance are that they mark a direction and that they select, in the circumstance of action, first steps by which to begin to move in that direction. Such steps are moves in the penumbra of the 'adjacent possible' surrounding every state of affairs: the 'theres' to which we can get from here, from where we are now, with the materials at hand. These materials include existing arrangements and practices, the established stock of institutional ideas, the active social forces and the received understanding of interests and ideals, subject to the duality on which I earlier remarked.

The target of transformative ambition is always some piece of the formative institutional and ideological structure of social life: the framework of arrangements and assumptions shaping the routine contests and exchanges of a society, especially those over the control and use of the economic, political and cultural resources with which we create the future within the present. According to a prejudice resulting from the influence of necessitarian social theories, especially the theories of Karl Marx, the structures that we seek to change are indivisible systems. We must consequently choose between the revolutionary substitution of one such system by another and its reformist management. Fundamental change is wholesale; gradualism is reformist tinkering.

The truth is just the opposite: the formative institutional and ideological regimes of a society are recalcitrant to challenge and change, although we may design them to diminish this recalcitrance and to invite their own revision. However, they are not indivisible systems; they are contingent, ramshackle constructions. Change can be, and almost always is, fragmentary in scope and gradual, albeit discontinuous, in pace. Fragmentary and gradual but discontinuous change can nevertheless have radical effects if pursued, cumulatively, in a particular direction. Only because the piecemeal can be the structural can the social innovation movement do its work.

Approached in the maximalist spirit that I advocate, the social innovation movement offers a space for the experimental pursuit of a family of programmatic endeavours. The common theme – or the unifying thread – is the enhancement of agency. Such an enhancement is manifest in our power to master and to change the institutional and ideological regimes in which we move. It is expressed, as well, in the design of regimes facilitating the development and the exercise of that power.

Within this space, different orientations may coexist, clash and converge. I outline one such orientation, describing it as a series of overlapping and reciprocally reinforcing projects in the change of both institutions and sensibilities. A vision of who we are and can become animates them. The vision acquires clarity and authority only through its expression in projects such as those that I next outline.

The first project is the advancement of what one might call 'vanguardism outside the vanguard'. In every economy, or every moment in economic history, a sector of production will be the most advanced. In that sector production most closely resembles imagination: the aspect of the mind that is neither modular nor formulaic; that enjoys the power of recursive infinity – freely to recombine everything with everything else – and that exhibits the faculty that the poet named 'negative capability', achieving insight and effect by transgressing its own methods and presuppositions.

Today the most advanced practice of production is the one that has emerged in the aftermath of mass production and its decline. It is often mistakenly equated with the high-technology industry, the terrain in which it has become best established. Its most important features go beyond the accumulation of capital, technology and knowledge. They are those that bind it to our imaginative experience: the attenuation of the contrast between conception and execution, the relativising of specialised work roles, the cultivation of common purpose and higher trust, and the development of methods of permanent innovation. When combined with their characteristic technologies, these arrangements and practices make it possible to reconcile decentralised initiative with coordination and the variation (or 'destandardisation') of products with economies of scale.

Such traits should be applicable, with suitable adjustments, to almost any sector of the economy. They should be easier to disseminate than the attributes of the productive vanguard of an earlier age: the mechanised manufacturing of the period following the Industrial Revolution. Just the opposite has happened. In the aftermath of the Industrial Revolution, every part of the economy, including agriculture, was reshaped on the model of mechanised manufacturing. The new 'post-Fordist' vanguards tend, on the contrary, to remain only weakly linked to other sectors of each national economy: although the technologies that they produce are widely used, the advanced practices around which they are organised remain largely foreign to major parts of even the richest economies in the world. Most of the labour force remains locked out of these vanguards.

There are two conventional ways to counteract inequalities in the rich North Atlantic societies, as well as in the many countries that have come under the spell of their established institutions and predominant beliefs: compensatory redistribution through tax-and-transfer and the defence of small business against big business. Neither of these approaches is adequate to the task of dealing with the consequences of the new hierarchical segmentation of the economy. Any effective response must begin in innovations that result in a sustained broadening of economic and educational opportunity and that, therefore, influence the primary distribution of advantage and capability. Among such responses will be those that take the new vanguardism out of the islands to which it remains confined, and propagate its practices widely.

Today an increasing part of humanity finds itself in circumstances of precarious labour. Work is once again organised, as it was before the rise of mass production, in the form of decentralised networks of contractual arrangements: now on a worldwide basis. Countless millions of people, whether thrown into radical economic insecurity or lifted above it, aspire to a modest prosperity and independence: the petty-bourgeois perspective demonised traditionally by the Left. By default, they often fix their sights on isolated family business.

Here is a world in which the social innovation movement has a mission of immense importance: to show, by exemplary initiatives, how precarious labour and retrograde small business can be lifted up and transformed by the mastery of the new advanced practices of production. Part of the task needs to be carried out from above, in the form of arrangements associating governments with small and medium-sized firms in the advancement of vanguardism beyond the vanguard. Neither the American model of arm's-length regulation of business by government nor the Northeast Asian model of imposition of unitary trade and industrial policy by the state can do this job. We require a form of coordination between governments and firms that is decentralised, participatory and experimental. Its complement is cooperative competition – combining competition with pooling of resources – among advanced small and medium-sized firms. Such innovations can serve as the points of departure for alternative regimes of private and social property – different ways of arranging the decentralised allocation of access to productive resources – that would come to coexist experimentally within the same market economy.

The cause of vanguardism outside the vanguard requires movement from the bottom up as well as well from the top down: directed to the circumstances of small business and of precarious labour and to the dealings of such work and such firms with local governments and communities. It is here that the social innovation movement may find some of its most rewarding endeavours.

Such initiatives in reimagining and in remaking the market economy have a horizon. They move towards an economic future in which decentralised economic activity will bear the marks of a greater freedom. Our economic arrangements will no longer radically restrict the ways in which we can cooperate across the lines of division and hierarchy in society. The market economy will cease to be fastened to a single version of itself, as alternative regimes for the access to productive resources – our systems of contract and property – come to share the same market order.

The individual worker and citizen must be and feel secure in a haven of protected immunities and capabilities – universal endowments assured by the state and unattached to particular jobs – so that the society around him can be open to perpetual innovation. Work throughout the economy, as well as in the most advanced sectors, must come to exhibit the traits of the imagination; the technical division of labour becomes then a mirror of the imaginative side of the mind.

No human being should be condemned to do the work that a machine could execute. In Adam Smith's pin factory or Henry Ford's assembly line, the worker worked as if he were a machine. We have machines, however, so that they may do for us whatever we have learned to repeat and so that our time may be saved for the not yet repeatable. Then, the combination of worker and machine will achieve its greater potential.

It is unlikely to achieve it so long as economically dependent wage labour remains the principal form of free labour. It must, as both the liberals and the socialists of the 19th century hoped, give way to the higher forms of free labour: self-employment and cooperation, combined with each other. This transition cannot take place unless we develop regimes of conditional and temporary property rights organising the coexistence of different kinds of stakeholders in the same productive resources, and thus enabling us to reconcile, to a greater extent than we now can, decentralisation and scale.

These are distant goals. In the exercise of its prophetic task, the social innovation movement must nevertheless find or invent the initiatives that might prefigure them – the first steps in the penumbra of the nearby possibles. It cannot hope to invent or find them unless it has a view of what, farther ahead, it seeks.

A second project is the reform of education and, through education, of consciousness. For the social innovation movement, the role of the school under democracy is to serve as the voice of the future rather than as the tool of either the state or the family. It is not enough to make the student capable of moving within the present order; it is necessary to equip him to distance himself from that order, to resist it, and to reshape it bit-by-bit and step-by-step. The school must allow him to be both an insider and an outsider, an agent who participates without surrendering.

Such an education gives pride of place to the cultivation of powers of analysis and of recombination. It prefers selective depth in the marshalling of information to encyclopaedic superficiality. It puts cooperation in teaching and learning in the place of the combination of individualism and authoritarianism. It approaches every subject dialectically, from contrasting points of view. It combines such a form of general education with practical or vocational training that accords priority to generic conceptual and practical capabilities, to the meta-capabilities suitable to an age of flexible meta-machines, rather than to job-specific and machine-specific skills. For such an education to become prevalent, especially in countries that are large, very unequal, and federal in structure, we must forge the instruments needed to reconcile local management of the schools with national standards of investment and quality.

Exemplary initiatives in education can begin at any point in this ambitious programme. They can start with the method and content, in schools providing models for the others or with the institutional setting. Or they can focus first on the requirements for reconciling local management and national standards. The innovators outside government lack the resources and powers of a state. They have, however, the advantage of their disadvantages: licence to experiment episodically, undeterred by the constraints of universal rules and vast scale.

A third project is innovation in the provision of public goods and public services beyond education. Public goods make people strong; public squalour, even when in the face of private affluence, weakens them. It inhibits the strengthening of agency that must represent the core concern of the social innovation movement.

We should not have to settle for what now exists by way of providing public services: an administrative Fordism – the provision of low-quality standardised services by a governmental bureaucracy. Nor should we need to accept the privatisation of public services in favour of profit-driven firms as the sole alternative. There is another way, with promise for the central aims of the social innovation movement.

The state should ensure universal minimums. It should also take the lead in the development of the most complicated and expensive services. In the broad middle range between the floor and the ceiling, government should engage civil society in the competitive and experimental provision of public services not-for-profit – for example, through cooperatives. It should finance, train, prepare and coordinate civil society outside the state to take part in the work of building people: people with an enhanced power of initiative and creation, people equipped to change both their world and themselves. It is both the most reliable means to improve the quality of public services and the most effective inducement to the self-organisation of civil society.

A fourth project is to energise and deepen democracy. A high-energy, deepened democracy meets a triple test, probing three aspects of the same advance. It increases our ability collectively to master the structure of society: its formative arrangements and assumptions. It overthrows the government of the living by the dead. It weakens the dependence of change on crisis.

Such a project requires a series of convergent institutional innovations. Some would raise the temperature of politics: the level of organised popular engagement in political life. Others would hasten the pace of politics, resolving impasse among parts of the state quickly. Others would reconcile a capacity for decisive action at the centre of government with radical, experimentalist devolution in both federal and non-federal states, so that different parts of the country or even different sectors of the economy and society can offer counter-models of the national future. Others would establish in the state a power, or even a distinct branch of government, designed and equipped to come to the rescue of groups that cannot escape exclusion or subjugation by the means of collective action available to them. And others yet would enrich representative democracy with elements of direct and participatory self-government.

The social innovation movement cannot change constitutional arrangements. It can, however, launch experiments and ideas in each of the areas covered by these needed institutional changes, experiments prefiguring the direction that it proposes. Or it can commit itself to initiatives that, by compensating for the omission or paralysis of government, evoke the missing agenda. True to character, it can show how not to wait for salvation from on high.

Both a practice and a purpose should inform and unify the pursuit of these four projects. The practice is democratic experimentalism: structural ambition cleansed of structural dogmatism and advanced through fragmentary initiatives that both mark a path and take initial steps in travelling it. The purpose is not simply an attenuation of inequalities. It is the enactment of experiments that show how we can move towards giving the ordinary man and woman a better opportunity to live a larger life, with greater intensity, broader scope, and stronger capabilities.

No one conception of humanity and of the self can claim uniquely to guide such an endeavour. The social innovation movement can only gain by being a field hospitable to such clashing prophecies. There they will be received, developed and tested less as abstract doctrines than as messages that we read into actions the better to find directions.

For one such conception – the one that I take as my touchstone here – we are the beings who – formed in social and conceptual contexts – can nevertheless immeasurably transcend the regimes of society and of thought that we inhabit. Because there is always more in us than there is, or ever can be, in them, we can exceed them and remake them. We can reduce the extent to which they imprison us and deny or suppress our powers of defiance and reinvention.

The methods

There are two chief methods by which the social innovation movement can advance projects such as those that I have just sketched. These practices are not just means to the larger end of enhancing agency; they are also concentrated instances of that enhancement.

The first such practice is the method of foreshadowing – foreshadowing a larger life for the ordinary man and woman. The localised and small-scale initiatives that are the province of the movement can be represented as anticipations of a trajectory under the light of a vision. Innovators can represent and develop their tangible, practical experiments as down payments on the execution of a more distant promise. It is the method of the prophets, who must join visionary insight to exemplary action: action that is exemplary because it consists in deeds that point towards a form of experience in which we can increase our purchase on the traits that most make us human.

Schopenhauer wrote that a talented man is a marksman who hits a target that others cannot hit, whereas a genius is a marksman who hits a target that others cannot see. The prophet is not the one who thinks more cleverly. He is the one who sees more. What he sees is a greater life, a higher humanity, an increase of our share in some of the attributes – especially the attribute of transcendence – that we regard as divine and rightly or wrongly may attribute to God. That vision must be translated into exemplary deeds, giving palpable signs – signs that we can experience now – of such an existence.

The inherited image of the prophet is that of an inspired individual conveying a message that is vouchsafed to him by virtue of his special proximity to the divine. He then gathers around himself a band of followers who may reduce his teaching to writing. He and they have an ambivalent relation to the temporal authorities of the societies in which they emerge.

The core creed of democracy is faith in the constructive genius of ordinary men and women and therefore as well in the dissemination of prophetic powers among them. The democratic answer to the question 'Who is the prophet?' must be: everyone. Everyone can and should act, according to his circumstance, in a prophetic spirit. Society and culture may be so organised that they either nurture or discourage the widespread development and exercise of such powers.

The social innovation movement must be, in this sense, prophetic. It must both act in a prophetic spirit and use the instruments characteristic of prophecy under democracy. Therein lies the larger meaning of the method of foreshadowing.

The second practice distinguishing the movement is the method of incursion – innovation in our economic and political arrangements, proposed and launched from a base outside both the economy and politics. The innovators have a seat in civil society outside both the state and the market. The powers of society are never reduced to the activities of market exchange or of governmental politics alone.

It is in society, insofar as it is not wholly shaped by our economic and political arrangements, that the social innovation movement finds the cradle in which it is nurtured. The category of the 'third sector' is inadequate to describe this reality; a set of 'third-sector' or non-governmental organisations is no more than a fragment of this vast part of social experience, which towers, as if it were a horizon, over both the market and the state.

It is from some place in those trans-political and trans-economic parts of society that the social innovators most often begin their work. (Social innovators may also take their point of departure from some place within either market action or governmental activity. Then they often have to face, at the outset, obstacles that the innovators who start outside the economy and the state would have to confront only when they later began to challenge economic or political arrangements.)

Regardless of where the social innovators take their initial steps, they do not end where they began. Having started in one part of social life, they push the chain of analogous experiments to another part. The divisions of social life, and the distinct criteria of success that are supposed to apply to each – profits for corporations, votes for politicians – fail to impress and intimidate them. They see the deeper unity and discount the finality of the divisions. They reinvent a social initiative as an economic or a political one. To this transgression of boundaries and logics within society, I give the name 'the method of incursion'.

There is no part of society that the social innovation movement cannot engage, including corporate enterprise, the media and popular culture, the provision of public services, and the activities of charitable organisations. What matters is that in engaging each of them it remain faithful to its prophetic vocation.

Constraint and opportunity

The barriers faced by the social innovation movement, pursued under its maximalist understanding, are many and formidable. Mankind remains almost everywhere bent under the yoke of the dictatorship of no alternatives. The hegemonic project in the rich North Atlantic region – the reconciliation of European-style social protection within American-style economic flexibility, undertaken as an accommodation of the mid-20th century institutional and ideological settlement to present economic realities – excludes more ambitious innovations even if advanced by fragmentary and gradualist means. Outside the North Atlantic region, the major emerging powers have little to show by way of alternatives other than state capitalism, combined with pieces of neoliberalism and compensatory social democracy. Their potential for spiritual rebellion and institutional invention continues to be suppressed under the burdens of a mental colonialism that their increasing power makes all the more surprising.

The most insidious opposition, however, comes from the high academic culture, in which the social innovators might have expected to find friends. There, across the whole range of social and historical studies, tendencies of thought prevail that would, if they were to be believed, deny authority to what the innovators seek to accomplish.

In the hard, positive social sciences – beginning with the most influential, economics – rationalisation predominates: a way of explaining present arrangements that justifies their superiority or inevitability by suggesting that they are the outcome of a cumulative convergence to best practice. In the normative disciplines of political philosophy and legal theory, humanisation takes over: an appeal to pseudo-philosophical justifications of the ameliorative practices of compensatory and retrospective redistribution and of the systematic idealisation of law in the vocabulary of impersonal policy and principle. In the humanities, consciousness embarks on an adventurism of subjectivity detached from any disposition to reimagine and to remake the present regime of society.

The representatives of these three tendencies are practical allies in the disarmament of the transformative imagination and of the transformative will. The convergent and cumulative effect of their ways of thinking is to cut the connection – on which all insight depends – between the understanding of the present settlement and the imagination of its accessible transformations. The consequence for the social innovation movement is that it must develop its own social theory along the way, raiding the counter currents within the academy for whatever help they can provide.

No matter. The opportunity is enormous. The message has been carried throughout the world that ordinary men and women are not as ordinary as they appear to be and that every human being has a vocation for a higher life and contains infinities within him- or herself. Contemporary societies cannot solve, or even address, their fundamental problems within the restraints of the very limited stock of institutional options for the organisation of different parts of society that are now available. Meanwhile, most people remain condemned to live small and demeaning lives, even when they have escaped the extremes of poverty and oppression.

Humanity, however, seethes, churns and searches, everywhere generating a multitude of small-scale experiments from which larger changes might begin. The world chafes, restless, under the dictatorship of no alternatives. Let this restless world find an unexpected ally in the social innovation movement.

Index

This page intentionally left blank

This page intentionally left blank

This page intentionally left blank

Made in the USA
Coppell, TX
22 August 2022

81872512R00167